ARMS AND LETTERS: MILITARY LIFE WRITING IN EARLY MODERN SPAIN

FAITH S. HARDEN

Arms and Letters: Military Life Writing in Early Modern Spain

UNIVERSITY OF TORONTO PRESS
Toronto Buffalo London

Toronto Buffalo London
utorontopress.com

ISBN 978-1-4875-0704-6 (cloth)
ISBN 978-1-4875-3545-2 (ePUB)
ISBN 978-1-4875-3544-5 (PDF)

Library and Archives Canada Cataloguing in Publication

Title: Arms and letters : military life writing in early modern Spain / Faith S. Harden.
Names: Harden, Faith S., 1980– author.
Series: Toronto Iberic ; 53.
Description: Series statement: Toronto Iberic series ; 53 | Includes bibliographical references and index. | Text in English; includes some text in Spanish.
Identifiers: Canadiana (print) 20200212117 | Canadiana (ebook) 20200212125 | ISBN 9781487507046 (cloth) | ISBN 9781487535452 (ePUB) | ISBN 9781487535445 (PDF)
Subjects: LCSH: Spain – Armed Forces – Biography – History and criticism. | LCSH: Soldiers – Spain – Biography – History and criticism. | LCSH: Spain – Armed Forces Military life. | LCSH: Honor – Spain – History. | LCSH: Soldiers' writings, Spanish – History and criticism. | LCSH: Honor in literature. | LCSH: Military biography. | LCSH: Autobiography.
Classification: LCC U54.S7 H37 2020 | DDC 355.0092/246–dc23

This work has received a publication subvention from the Spanish Ministry of Education, Culture, and Sport.

Publication of this book is made possible in part by a grant from the Provost's Author Support Fund of the University of Arizona.

University of Toronto Press acknowledges the financial assistance to its publishing program of the Canada Council for the Arts and the Ontario Arts Council, an agency of the Government of Ontario.

Canada Council for the Arts
Conseil des Arts du Canada

Funded by the Government of Canada
Financé par le gouvernement du Canada

Contents

Acknowledgments

It gives me great pleasure to recognize and thank all of the people who have supported me in the writing of this book. First, I must thank some of my earliest and most inspiring teachers, Linda Bernick, Alison Ridley, and Daniel Murphy. I am indebted to my advisors and mentors at the University of Virginia, and especially to the brilliant Alison Weber, a truly exemplary scholar and teacher. With deepest admiration and gratitude I thank Michael Gerli, Ricardo Padrón, David Gies, and Ruth Hill, all of whom provided expert guidance during my graduate studies and beyond. At UVA I was fortunate to find a group of intelligent, inspiring, and wonderful friends, including members of my graduate cohort in the Department of Spanish, Italian, and Portuguese. I would like to thank especially Emmy Smith Ready, Sarah Bogard, Jennifer Barlow, and Stephen Silverstein for rich conversation, laughter, and advice throughout and beyond the various stages of this project.

I am grateful to have been surrounded by excellent colleagues in all the academic departments in which I have worked. Thanks are due for the warm welcome I received from the faculty in the Department of Modern and Classical Languages at the University of St. Thomas, particularly Dan Tight and Michael Scham, and from the faculty, staff, and students of the Department of Latin American and Iberian Cultures at the University of Southern California, especially Roberto Ignacio Díaz, Erin Graff Zivin, Jaclyn Cohen-Steinberg, Lori Mesrobian, and Alfredo García-Pardo. My most heartfelt thanks to outstanding colleagues, students, and staff in the Department of Spanish and Portuguese at the University of Arizona. I am grateful for the material support facilitated by Malcolm Compitello, the skilful administration provided by Mary Portillo, and the generous mentorship of my senior colleagues Judith Nantell, Richard Kinkade, Kátia da Costa Bezerra, and Mónica Morales. Many thanks to Bram Acosta, Anita Huizar Hernández, Anne Garland

Mahler, and Kaitlin M. Murphy, both for their sharp insights on earlier versions of this manuscript as well as for their friendship. A very special thanks to Antxon Olarrea and Beatriz Urrea for their mentorship, solidarity, and inexhaustible kindness. Deepest gratitude to my friend Aileen A. Feng on the other side of the hall in the Department of French and Italian, both for sustaining spirited intellectual exchange as well as for her brilliant comments on several chapters of this manuscript. For their deep critical engagement with many of the texts and contexts that appear in this book, I also thank the graduate students in my Spring 2019 and Fall 2015 seminars on the literature of war.

I am incredibly fortunate that this book found a home with the University of Toronto Press. Many thanks to Suzanne Rancourt for her interest in and support of the project from the beginning. Thanks, too, to Charles Stuart, Barbara Porter, and Amyrose McCue Gill and Lisa Regan of TextFormations for their professionalism and skill in the production of this volume. I am deeply grateful to two anonymous readers from the Press for their astute comments and suggestions on the manuscript. I am also thankful for helpful feedback from conference panelists and audiences at the Renaissance Society of America, the Sixteenth Century Society & Conference, and the Modern Language Association.

Finally, I would like to acknowledge my local support system and thank my family. Thanks to the 2017 Academic Mamas group and to Patti Podgornik for moral support, advice, and – in Patti's case – skilled and sensitive assistance without which I would have been unable to complete this book. I am forever grateful to my wonderful parents, Mark and Suzanne Harden, and to my parents-in-law, Mark and Rachel Selisker, for their unwavering love and support. Lastly, my deepest debt of gratitude, in writing this book as in so many other things, is to Scott Selisker. Words cannot express the depth of my appreciation, admiration, and love. This book is for him and for our daughter, Vera.

ARMS AND LETTERS

Introduction: Arms and Letters

Yo por bien tengo que cosas tan señaladas, y por ventura nunca oídas ni vistas, vengan a noticia de muchos y no se entierren en la sepultura del olvido, pues podría ser que alguno que las lea halle algo que le agrade, y a los que no ahondaren tanto los deleite. [...] Porque, si así no fuese, muy pocos escribirían para uno solo, pues no se hace sin trabajo, y quieren, ya que lo pasan, ser recompensados, no con dineros, mas con que vean y lean sus obras y, si hay de qué, se las alaben. Y a este propósito dice Tulio: "la honra cría las artes."

(*Lazarillo de Tormes*, Prologue: 3–6)

(It is only right, to my mind, that things so remarkable, which happen to have remained unheard and unseen until now, should be brought to the attention of many and not lie buried in the sepulcher of oblivion. The reader may find matter here to entertain him, and even he who does no more than dip into this book will have his reward in pleasure. [...] If it were otherwise, there are very few who would write just for one reader, because it is hard work, and those who undertake it hope to be rewarded, not in money, but in having the efforts seen and read and, when possible, praised. That is why Cicero says: "Honor is the nurse of the arts.")

(*The Life of Lazarillo de Tormes: His Fortunes and Adversities*, Prologue: 3–4)[1]

Lazarillo de Tormes (Burgos, 1554) is simultaneously a satire of sixteenth-century Spanish mores, a trove of sayings, fabliaux, and entertaining vignettes, and an ironic guide on how (not to) succeed in the world. The prologue, cited above, also offers a wry meditation on life writing, highlighting the conflicting motives and strategies for creating a textual image of the self. In this latter capacity, the novel provides an apt introduction to the life writing of sixteenth- and seventeenth-century soldiers, men whose occupations were frequently as physically perilous and financially precarious as those of the eponymous anti-hero.

In the prologue Lázaro delineates two economies of honour engaged in autobiographical writing: one symbolic and the other material. On the one hand, he declares along with Cicero that "la honra cría las artes" (honour is the nurse of the arts), thereby claiming that his work is a response to a desire for recognition. Like other accomplishments, the cultivation of the (literary) arts brings renown, a positive projection of the self that transcends physical and temporal limits. According to this formulation, honour is a kind of capital in that its value is instantiated in the act of circulation. Lázaro goes on to claim that he, like all writers, desires not financial compensation but the recompense of readerly attention and delight: "quieren … ser recompensados, no con dineros, mas con que vean y lean sus obras y, si hay de qué, se las alaben" (6) ([writers] hope to be rewarded, not in money, but in having the efforts seen and read and, when possible, praised) (4). In connecting the artifice of writing to the rendering of a life story, even in a sardonic mode, *Lazarillo* articulates perhaps for the first time in Spanish letters the link between a "literary" retelling of a life and the honour that should follow such an exercise. Lázaro even goes so far as to compare the audacious autobiographer to the soldier who throws himself into battle ahead of his comrades: "¿Quién piensa que el soldado que es primero del escala tiene más aborrescido el vivir? No, por cierto; mas el deseo de alabanza le hace ponerse al peligro; y, así, en las artes y letras es lo mesmo" (6) (Does anyone suppose that the soldier who is first on the scaling ladder is there because his life is abhorrent to him? Certainly not. It is the desire for praise which leads him to run such risks. And it is the same with the arts and the art of letters [4]). Here Lázaro makes reference to the binary opposition between arms and letters, understood traditionally as two paths to honour, in order to underline, to ironic effect, their parallels with life writing; both entail a kind of self-exposure, whether to enemy hordes or ruthless critics. The risks and possible rewards inherent in each practice, Lázaro suggests, are doubled in the autobiographical act, as the author submits not only a literary text but also a record of his life to public praise or condemnation.

The larger context of Lázaro's life story eventually reveals the tragicomic dimensions of his stated desire for honour and recognition. Traditional masculine honour – understood as social status and sexual propriety – is precisely what Lázaro lacks, and it soon becomes apparent that the autobiographer narrates his life not out of an ambitious wish for self-aggrandizement, but in response to a judicial injunction to explain why he appears to be profiting from his wife's infidelity.

Ultimately, Lázaro does in fact see his name and his story circulate widely, but as gossip rather than laudable literature, to his detriment rather than his praise. While in the prologue Lázaro poses as primarily interested in the fame that his entertaining and edifying tale might elicit, the rest of the novel exposes his original, occluded motive for writing as one of self-defence. Far from the elevated company of exemplary authors, Lázaro trafficks in a second economy of honour whose risks and rewards are quite tangible; he writes in order to justify the exchange of favours and sex from which he has allegedly benefited, in an effort to save his own skin. By the novel's end, the aspiration to participate in a symbolic economy of honour, referenced in the prologue, has been substituted by the imperative to repair a criminally defamed reputation.[2]

The perils and possibilities of life writing that are articulated in *Lazarillo* – the autobiographer's desire for recognition, his intuition of virtuosity, the awareness of the dangers, pleasures, and possible rewards of self-exposure, the need to make known the hidden and justify the suspicious – all connect the picaresque pseudo-autobiographer to the writing soldiers whose autobiographies are the focus of this book. Like Lázaro, soldier-autobiographers communicate a variety of concerns and desires through the flexible framework of honour, even as the resulting texts disclose a deficit of honour at their core. Indeed, the economic, social, and sexual dishonour in which Lázaro finds himself, and which he attempts to remedy by textual means, is analogous in some respects to the ways in which soldiers were portrayed both individually and collectively across an array of sixteenth- and seventeenth-century cultural production. By the end of the sixteenth century, the perceived decline of the nobility's participation in warfare, in addition to the recruitment of mercenaries and conscripts drawn from the urban poor, meant that one of the most visible faces of Spanish imperial power was that of the common soldier. Armed with weapons like the pike or harquebus, and affiliated with an institution that lacked the logistical sophistication to provide fully for the needs of food and shelter, much less completely enforce discipline, soldiers inspired fear and hatred in the civilians who were often their victims. Humanists such as Erasmus denounced the destructive acts and mercenary motivations of such men, condemning war itself as "human butchery" that makes a mockery of the Christian religion (33). Within the context of the wars that racked Europe, pacifists and reformers alike decried the devastation visited upon innocent civilians, from the fields and villages destroyed by locust-like armies, to the violent offences and sex crimes perpetrated against local non-combatants (G. Parker, *Army* 82). Likewise, the cruelties of the conquistadors were publicized in graphic, widely circulated texts such as Bartolomé de las Casas's *Brevísima relación de la destrucción de las Indias* (Seville, 1552) and in images like those found in Theodor de Bry's multivolume collection of copper engravings *America* (Frankfurt, 1593). In his preface to the latter work, de Bry cautions that although Spaniards "have often behaved in a cruel, greedy and unjust fashion ... we must not impute such a behaviour to their nation but to the license of soldiers" (qtd. in Gravatt 242), echoing the sentiment, widespread in lettered circles, that the work of warfare had become morally reprehensible.[3] Meanwhile, in the fiction of the period the figure of the rank-and-file soldier was most often identified with vagrancy and extra-legal violence. In Francisco de Quevedo's *El Buscón* (Zaragoza, 1626), for example, the shifty soldier that Pablos encounters on the road is a blustering braggart who claims his blistered feet as war wounds and almost burns down the inn, mad with rage, when his (stolen) service papers are misplaced. For his part, Vicente de la Rosa or Roca, the recently returned soldier whose story is recounted in *Don Quixote*, regales his former neighbours with tales of his unbelievable feats before swindling a wealthy young woman out of her father's money. In writing of their own lives, soldiers alternately embrace such negative portrayals and dispute them. As in *Lazarillo*, some soldiers' life writing situates individual actions of dubious morality in a broader context of economic hardship, social precarity, and existential danger. In contrast, other soldiers' autobiographies roundly reject any association with dissipation and depravity, opting instead for a sober self-presentation grounded in religious and historiographical discourse. The resulting autobiographical texts offer less a space of introspection than a stage whose quasi-public parameters transform even the most banal events into significant, or at least entertaining, deeds. In this way, both noble and non-elite soldiers leverage their experience and narrative skill to seek recognition on their own terms, performatively embodying the honourable status that formerly had been the exclusive domain of the aristocratic warrior class.

From the middle of the sixteenth century through the end of the seventeenth century, Spanish soldiers produced, circulated, and in some cases published an unprecedented number of autobiographical texts. Defined here as first-person, retrospective prose narratives that emphasize the author's military service in the course of accounting for a broad life trajectory, the corpus of military autobiography includes works by Diego García de Paredes (1468–1533), Alonso Enríquez de Guzmán (1499–c. 1547), Diego Suárez Corvín (1552–post-1623), Jerónimo de Pasamonte (1553–post-1604), Pedro Ordóñez de Ceballos

(1547/50?–1634/5), Alonso de Contreras (1582–post-1645), Diego Duque de Estrada (1589–1649), Miguel de Castro (1590–post-1617), Catalina de Erauso (1592–1650), Domingo de Toral y Valdés (1598–post-1635), and Félix Nieto de Silva (1635–91).[4] In their works these soldiers recount a range of experiences throughout the sprawling domain of the Hispanic Monarchy, from the disease and disorder of the Spanish Road to the terrors of traversing the contested waterways of the Mediterranean, Atlantic, and Pacific. While some of these works couch a plea for remuneration within the context of the soldier's life story, others stage amorous or bellicose dramas with the sole stated aim of entertaining the reader. At the same time, several of these works appeal to the authority of eyewitness experience to critique everything from contemporary religious and social practices to aspects of imperial policy and warfare. As forays into textual territory that was relatively uncharted, military life writing makes use of the themes and formal elements of several coevolving genres, including military treatises, martyrs' tales, travel narratives, juridical testimony, the *comedia*, chivalric fiction, and the picaresque novel. This discursive heterogeneity reflects the early modern soldier's diverse social origins and varying degrees of education. The men – and one woman – whose autobiographies are studied here include members of the urban artisan classes, impoverished rural *hidalgos*, and second sons of the titled nobility. Although each soldier's tale is unique, a shared military culture is evident in their writing, particularly in their emphasis on two related concepts: honour and the value of military labour.

This book traces how constructions of honour animate early modern military life writing, considering the intersections among military professionalism, gender, social mobility, political and religious affiliations, and the divergent discursive means through which each life is rendered. As a concept that condensed many kinds of social relations, from everyday interactions among friends and family members to the more abstract bonds between superiors and subordinates, or subjects and the monarchy, the principle of honour was both highly visible and controversial throughout the period. It was also a concept continually under revision as the medieval society of orders – with its understanding of honour as a hereditary property, acquired at birth and linked to aristocratic status and the practice of arms – slowly transformed with the advent of a monetary economy and the appearance of new avenues for social mobility. Part of this sea change was due to a concurrent evolution in military technology and structure that simultaneously democratized military service while preserving the aristocratic language of honour to connote both skill and command, regardless of the circumstances of a soldier's birth. Thus soldiers' autobiographies attest to a variety of idiosyncratic approaches to the question of what it might mean to be an honourable soldier, subject of the Spanish Crown, and man. *Arms and Letters* investigates the mutual constitution of the autobiographical form and the fashioning of various modes of honour in the archive of military life writing,[5] relating the material conditions of writing with the prevailing cultural narratives surrounding honour. Through an analysis of the cultural narratives, literary conventions, and institutional configurations converging upon these texts, this book explores military autobiography as a form of self-fashioning that takes on a variety of purposes – critique, self-exoneration, exhibitionism – that both reflect and create new understandings of honour. In what follows, I lay the groundwork for this analysis by addressing, in a preliminary fashion, the following questions: What did the concepts of the nearly synonymous *honour/honra* signify in the early modern Spanish world? How was the concept of honour shaped within the many textual paradigms within which it appeared? What was the role of honour in writing within or about early modern military culture? And, finally, how might we conceptualize the links between life writing and early modern ideas about honour in ways that are mutually illuminating? I begin with one of the key contexts in which soldiers' autobiographies developed and to which they respond: the military revolution of the sixteenth century.

The Early Modern Military Revolution

In 1495, three years after the fall of Granada and the conclusion of the campaign to "reconquer" Iberian territories under Muslim political authority, the Catholic Monarchs promulgated one of the first military reforms in the peninsula. The Ordenanza of 5 October 1495 required all Christian men – except the clergy and the indigent – to be armed (Quatrefages 63). Implicit in this decree was a claim of authority over all present and future military formations in the united kingdoms of Castile and Aragon; in contrast to the seigneurial or municipal armies of the medieval period, henceforth every company – and every soldier – would answer ultimately, at least in theory, to the Crown. Later decrees would establish a system of recruitment, instructions for payment and billeting, the arms and equipment associated with each formation, and the expected comportment of soldiers. The Ordenanza of 26 September 1503 compiled and expanded upon these directives in a single document sixty-two chapters long (Quatrefages 66–7). In reality many of these and subsequent regulations proved impossible to enforce consistently as they outstripped the logistical capabilities of Spain's far-flung military enterprise. Throughout the sixteenth and seventeenth centuries the disbursement of soldiers' salaries posed a significant and recurring problem due the state's depleted funds. The irregular payment of soldiers was a frequent source of complaint and even a cause for mutiny. In the face of insufficient financial resources, commanders like Fernando d'Avalos, marchese di Pescara, appealed to a concept of military honour, drawn partly from classical sources like the newly rediscovered Vegetius and partly from feudal aristocratic culture, in order to quell a burgeoning rebellion. According to Paolo Giovio's account, d'Avalos managed to rally his demoralized and mutinous troops by proclaiming that "Spaniards do not fight as labourers for money, like the custom of mercenary soldiers, but are accustomed to fight for glory, for empire, for victories, for honor" (*La vita* 98r; qtd. in Sherer, *Warriors* 39). Despite the counterforces of financial deficit, distance, and entrenched local loyalties that impeded the rapid consolidation and centralization of royal authority, the political reforms emanating from the Crown and the strategic and tactical innovations arising from the experience of battle would rewrite the terms of military labour, framing it as a potentially ennobling contract between the monarchy and its servants, regardless of their social extraction.

In attempting to account for the radical changes that define the early modern period, including the beginnings of absolutism, the expansion of bureaucracy, the rise of a monetary economy, and the reorganization of increasingly permeable social strata, the military historian Michael Roberts has pointed to developments in the military-technological field. Noting the tactical reforms instituted by Northern European armies between 1560 and 1660, Roberts linked the widespread use of firearms to the deployment of smaller infantry units, larger standing armies, and the development of increasingly complex bureaucratic and financial structures to underwrite them. Geoffrey Parker subsequently elaborated on Roberts's thesis, pointing to the concomitant development of distance weapons and more robust siege fortifications as the primary elements that worked to assure protracted wars. Parker placed the "heartland of the military revolution" in the Hapsburg states and their immediate neighbours (Parker, *Military* 25). As Roberts put it, these developments had wide-ranging consequences, becoming "agents and auxiliaries of constitutional and social change" (Roberts 13). Eventually, for those with luck, strategic skill, technical prowess, and a gift for self-promotion, such developments would provide unprecedented opportunities for individual social and economic advancement. Like any expansive idea, the military revolution thesis has been somewhat controversial. Many of the revisions to the thesis have been chronological, with some scholars placing the key developments as early as the fourteenth century while others have extended the period of change either through the beginning of the eighteenth century, with the high point of the increase in the size of standing armies, or even through the beginning of the nineteenth century, a period marking European global military supremacy (Parker, *Military* 157–9).[6] Most recently scholars have questioned the Eurocentrism implicit in the military revolution narrative (Jacob and Visoni-Alonzo 15). Regardless of the exact nature of the relationship, causal or corollary, among these developments, it is clear that the sixteenth and seventeenth centuries witnessed a dramatic expansion in the scale and impact of war on European soil, which was accompanied by new possibilities for social and economic mobility. As Roberts has argued, "The social consequences of the military revolution were scarcely less important than the constitutional. In the Middle Ages war had been almost the privilege of a class; by the seventeenth century it had become almost the livelihood of the masses … The new armies, in fact, served as the social escalators of the age" (23). Although certainly not the case for all or even most soldiers, compelling examples of meteoric social ascents were commemorated and celebrated in both historical writing and the *comedia*, from the published letters in which Hernán Cortés narrated his account of the conquest of Mexico, to plays like Lope de Vega's *La contienda de García de Paredes y el capitán Juan de Urbina* (1600) and *Julián Romero* (c. 1597–1604).[7] In form and content, the life writing of early modern soldiers registers these transformations.

As Miguel Martínez has demonstrated, the technological innovations associated with the military revolution would collapse the ancient binary of arms and letters as the conditions of fighting and writing altered the practice and representation of warfare. Martínez highlights the key role played by paper and other writing technologies: "Paper and other basic tools of writing were as important for the military revolution as other enabling technologies readily associated with it, such as gunpowder and military engineering" (22). Paper could be found everywhere, along supply routes, in garrisons, and even on the battleground, in forms as diverse as coded orders, recruiting logbooks, drilling manuals, mass-produced poetry and reportage, and the service papers that were a soldier's primary source of identification. Soldiers had relatively higher literacy rates than other professional groups, owing in part to the ubiquity of the written word in the military institution's complex and far-flung operations (18–19, 35). With the advent of the military revolution travelling camps of armies became spaces for the circulation and production of texts – laboratories for the generation of a vibrant textual culture that included classical sources as well as popular imaginative literature. War and soldiering became objects of knowledge, and technical manuals on everything from horseback riding to marching in formation proliferated. In addition to food and other necessities, other commodities travelled along the supply lines, including print material. Soldiers were eager to consume and produce this new material. Likewise, their technical expertise as well as their varied experiences, including travel and eyewitness testimony to momentous events and unusual scenarios, invested them with the authority to write, while the chaotic nature of warfare compelled them to preserve traces of these experiences through textual creation. The result, as Martínez has compellingly argued, was the rise of a "soldierly republic of letters" (4), a space in which a collective military identity was shaped by literary sociability.

This military-literary scene accommodated a variety of genres, beginning with a new version of the epic. Michael Murrin connects what he calls the migration of martial themes – from the medieval romance to the early modern epic – with the development of weapons and artillery using gunpowder, which had been introduced into Europe by way of China in the fourteenth century. While, broadly speaking, medieval warfare was distinguished by its reliance on knightly combat, usually on horseback, the development of the gun led to the creation of new divisions of men fighting primarily on foot. This technological and strategic shift is registered in the period's poetic descriptions of battle. According to Murrin, "The two genres present two different kinds of war ... Romance ... fits the old cavalry battles of the Middle Ages, while classical epic better accommodates the new styles of infantry fighting adopted by the English, Swiss, and Spanish" (13). Accompanying these changes in poetic form as well as content is the stance of the poet with regard to imperial historiography. In contrast to poets of an earlier generation, who tended to employ history in a self-consciously fictional frame, Murrin maintains that "The Iberian poets of the later sixteenth century ... wrote something more like actual history. The poets of Lepanto and Luíz Vaz de Camões chose the recent past, but Alonso de Ercilla and others like Gaspar Pérez de Villagrá who imitated him, went further and composed eyewitness history" (13). Ercilla's epic poem *La Araucana*, which narrates the battles between Spanish forces and the Mapuche in present-day Chile, is explicitly autobiographical, as the poet describes conflicts in which he participated, weaving the long-standing topos of arms and letters into the epic in lines echoing Garcilaso: "la pluma ora en la mano, ora la lanza" (now the pen in hand, now the lance) (Canto XX).

The transformation in the tactics, strategies, and to some extent the tenor of warfare in the early modern period was refracted through various literary genres, leading to this revitalization of the epic and also contributing to the creation of new genres such as the picaresque novel. As Stephen Rupp has pointed out, military themes are omnipresent in the literature of the period:

> Representation and scrutiny of warfare ... are not limited to epic and chivalric romance. Renaissance lyric explores the internal conflict between the claims of service in arms and courtly devotion to the beloved. Pastoral retirement offers space for celebration of martial achievements and for reflection on the rewards of commitment to an active life. Picaresque narrative presents the lives of common soldiers in the lower ranks of Spain's armies and the lower tiers of the contemporary social order. (14)

Similarly, life writing provided an expansive frame in which to portray the distinctive contours of a soldier's life, a space in which both evolving and more established literary forms could be repurposed and appropriated in order to explicitly intervene in the arenas of public reputation and personal identity.

Life Writing in Early Modern Spain

Early modern Spain witnessed a marked increase in life writing of all kinds, including autobiographical texts drafted by members of the privileged classes as well as people traditionally excluded from authorship, including cloistered religious adepts, craftsmen, and low- and mid-ranking soldiers (Amelang 11). This explosion in life writing was the result of a multitude of factors, including increased literacy, expanded access to books and other narrative models, including models of self-representation originating in the bureaucratic apparatus, more material resources and leisure time, and a new emphasis on individual perspectives and personal experience. In Spain as elsewhere in Europe, literate soldiers, who had many material and cultural precedents for storytelling, were among the most prolific practitioners of the genre. In the context of sixteenth-century France, dozens of noble commanders wrote self-justifying memoirs in the wake of civil and religious strife (Knecht 9–10). Likewise, building on a tradition of aristocratic authorship on military matters, Swiss, Austrian, Swabian, and Franconian commanders produced apologetic memoirs marked by the assertion of noble prerogative (Cohn 23–4). By the beginning of the seventeenth century, the social and geographic mobility afforded by the military revolution was reflected in an increasing number of autobiographies written by soldiers drawn from outside the ranks of the elite (Amelang 191). This seems to be particularly true in the case of Spain where, as Peter Burke has ventured, "the autobiographies of soldiers were almost common enough to form a sub-genre of their own" (27).[8]

Autobiography has been defined in a variety of ways: from a simple identity between author, narrator, and principal subject to a more circumscribed set of characteristics including voice, kind of prose, publication, and guarantee of authorship.[9] In light of the evolving nature of the genre during the early modern period, it is more useful to consider life writing not as a fixed textual form but rather, as James Amelang puts it, "as a social and cultural practice" (3). Taking a cue from the multifaceted approach to writing the self adopted in the primary texts studied here, I use the terms *autobiography*, *memoir*, and *life writing* interchangeably to refer to these first-person, retrospective prose narratives in which the author and subject coincide. As attested by the titles of these military-autobiographical works, an ample vocabulary for referring to such writing was available in the period, including *vida* (life), *memorias* (memoirs), *memorial* (account), *relación* (report), and even *suma* (summary), although these terms do not always point to clearly defined genres.[10] Military life writing in particular must be seen as part of a wider textual ecology that includes other kinds of self-promoting records (including service papers, petitions, and letters) that arose as a feature of what Alexandra Shepard has described as early modernity's "pervasive culture of appraisal" (27), which Alexandra Walsham has linked to the rise of the "fiscal-military state" (V). While an invocation of interiority is often taken as the defining characteristic of autobiography, the practice of (secular) life writing in the period was oriented less towards introspection than towards self-projection. Nevertheless, a sense of subjectivity – what Stephen Greenblatt has defined as "a sense of personal order, a characteristic mode of address to the world, a structure of bounded desires" (24) – is manifested in these texts through their sometimes contestatory content, as well as their evocation of contrary desires and frustrated agency.

The politics of imperial expansion implied a vigilant, outward-looking stance in its continuous confrontations with people of varying religions, cultures, national affiliations, and ethnicities; in contrast, the autobiographical genre of the *relación de méritos y servicios* (account of merits and services) encouraged servants of the Crown to look inward in order to fashion a credible and persuasive self-narrative whose chief purpose was professional advancement. Robert Folger traces the development of the *relación de méritos* to the Isabelline epoch, when the consolidation of monarchical power and the expansion of Spain's territories and influence abroad began to necessitate a new form of administration, one based primarily on written communications (21–5). Among these communications was the *relación de méritos*, a discursive curriculum vitae that argued for the subject's award or advancement. As Folger argues, the *relación de méritos* can be considered a significant source in the development of autobiographical discourse in that it provided both an incentive and a ready template for public servants – particularly soldiers – to narrate "a life in the service of the Crown that evokes the image of a deserving (and needy) subject of the King" (35). Much like the written confession, driven by the dynamics of "pastoral power" noted by Foucault, the self constructed in and by the *relación de méritos* exists in a dialogic relationship with a powerful interlocutor: a multilayered bureaucratic apparatus condensed in the figure of the king (28). Both soldiers' autobiographies and the *relación de méritos* are part of what Folger has termed an "economy of *mercedes* (gifts or grants)" (14), wherein privileges were granted to those able to create efficacious self-presentations. Soldiers' autobiographies, although their discursive heterogeneity exceeds the conventions of the bureaucratic *relación de méritos*, can nevertheless be understood as analogous to that genre, as they are structured by some of the same material and ideological necessities. By examining a select group of autobiographical documents, which participate to different extents and with different purposes in a generalized economy of honour, this book aims to shed more light on the intricate interactions between the soldier as autobiographical subject and the material concerns and textual precedents that shape each text.

Straddling documentary writing and fiction, the works of military autobiography studied here are structured according to the development of the author's career, even as they frequently trespass the boundaries of the purely professional. Alongside accounts of historical importance – the conditions and conduct of battle, or the results of intrigue or negotiation – soldiers' life writing also recounts episodes of personal reflection and individual action, including humorous interludes, sexual conquests, and conflicts among friends and acquaintances. While military experience often is named explicitly as an impetus for writing, the principal focus of these texts centres on the totality of the author's experiences. Likewise, soldiers' life writing often includes explicit commentary on the formal differences between the text and other, more properly "literary" works belonging to the established genres of history and epic poetry. For a soldier like Diego Suárez Corvín, the admission of a certain lack of polish is a defect that must be humbly admitted (*Discurso* 152). In contrast, for Captain Alonso de Contreras the lack of "rhetorical flourishes and clever turns of phrase" is a point of pride, and only serves to bolster the text's credibility (207).[11] In both cases, there is a clearly marked difference between the autobiographical text and imaginative writing associated with the representation of war. If, as Philippe Lejeune has suggested, autobiography is best understood as a strategy of both production and reception (30), then the life writing of Spanish soldiers demonstrates the existence of a mode of textuality defined in opposition to historical or heroic genres, one facilitated by certain aspects of the military institution but also exceeding it to encompass the entirety of the author's life.

The Concept of Honour

The practices associated with the military revolution in early modern Spain created a gulf between soldiers and non-combatants, even in a society that had long been "organized for war."[12] As J.R. Hale has noted, along with the professionalization of warfare there arose "a mental frontier between man of peace and man of war different in kind from the observation that had watched the peasant become temporary bowman" (129). The material conditions constituting this breach were reflected and amplified in the explosion of "military memoirs, books devoted to the art of war, [and] biographical compilations devoted to notable soldiers" (129). In other words, as the social identity of the soldier coalesced, a parallel textual figure emerged, often created by the soldier's own hand. Across the linked social and textual field, the concept of honour played a key role in the soldier's discursive fashioning. For some, the professionalization of armies, along with ever increasing theatres of war, could provide new horizons for self-fashioning and expanded opportunities for gaining material rewards and symbolic honour – the desire for *alabanza* (praise) that Lázaro mentions in the prologue as the soldier's spur to action. In the process the concept of honour itself, inextricably linked to warfare from its inception, was placed under revision.

As the definition given in the first monolingual Spanish dictionary indicates, honour was a concept inseparable from power. Sebastián de Covarrubias's *Tesoro de lengua española* (1611) identifies honour (*honra*) as the deference accorded to moral, political, and financial authority: "responde al nombre latino *honor*, vale reverencia, cortesía, que se haze a la virtud, a la potestad; algunas vezes se haze al dinero" (corresponds to the Latin word honour, it means reverence and courtesy that is rendered to virtue, to power, and sometimes to money) (1068). The three principles that accrue honour are sequenced in this definition on a continuum from more to less abstract: from intrinsic virtue to legal, customary, and material instantiations of authority, and finally to currency. The *Diccionario de Autoridades* (1734) likewise registers the polysemy of the term, as it defines *honra* in five entries. The first entry establishes the external locus of honour as the quality of respect accruing to a subject's virtue or authority: "Reveréncia, acatamiento y veneración que se hace a la virtúd, autoridad, o mayoría de alguna persona" (reverence, consideration, and veneration that is made to virtue, authority, or age) (173–4). In this formulation, honour is synonymous with an attitude of deference, a social relation materialized through the gestures and language of courtesy, and through the granting of titles conveying economic benefits and privileges ("vale tambien merced o gracia que se hace o se recibe"). Yet honour is also found within the subject: "pundonor, estimación y buena fama, que se halla en el sugeto y debe conservar" (point of honour, esteem, and good reputation, which is found in the subject and should be preserved). Thus, honour is located within the subject, when it is described as something to be preserved, while also being external to it, when it is used as a synonym for esteem or for material benefits and privileges. Taken together, these definitions illustrate the extent to which, at least in elite culture, the concept of honour was understood as a structuring principle of social relations, covering everything from everyday interactions to the disbursement of favours and the regimentation of sexuality – this latter manifestation embodied in the usage of *honra* that locates female honour in the intact hymen ("la integridad virginal en las mugeres" [the virginal integrity of women]) (173) – a key incarnation of honour addressed in chapter 4, in relation to the autobiography attributed to Catalina de Erauso, the virginal novice and military lieutenant.

The concept of honour permeated all registers of culture in early modern Spanish society, from politics and statecraft to literary production and the record of oral insults and self-defence found in legal documents. Juridical, theological, and moral texts rendered their precepts in the language of honour, codifying relatively recent relations of power in the old vocabulary of custom. For example, James Farr notes that the legal appropriation of honour was such that, under early modern statutes, disobedience was newly defined as "to rob king, commune, or God of honour" (128); in this formulation, punishment for dishonouring the representatives of political, social, and religious authority was not arbitrary, but rather rooted in centuries-old practices. Both external and internal political affairs were discussed within the framework of honour. Wars were initiated and prolonged in its name, including the disastrous Thirty Years War, a conflict sometimes pointed to as the first modern war in the vast scope of its destruction and the absolutist political configurations that arose in its wake. Within Spain the statutes of *limpieza de sangre* (blood purity) made issues of religious and ethnic ancestry into matters of honour, such that access to important or lucrative positions was restricted to those who could prove their "old Christian" pedigree. Thus, the gravest verbal insults were those that attacked the racial lineage or sexual "purity" of the victim or his or her family. In the literary realm, particularly in the theatre, the honour code was sometimes portrayed as an unyielding barrier between duty and desire, and sometimes depicted as a cruel source of injustice. In both cases, the theme of honour served a dramatic function in that it was multivalent and widely legible, while allowing for a convincing representation of interiority on the stage.[13] As Renato Barahona has noted, "In the lives of historical protagonists – socially, economically and legally – honor takes on vastly different meanings than, for instance, in the highly idealized works of literature and political and religious commentary" (120). Recent research has demonstrated that honour was not a concept limited to the elite. Court records from all over early modern Spain indicate that common people used the language of honour to justify their actions. As Scott Taylor has observed, based on his research with Castilian court documents, what has been called the honour code is better thought of as an archive of responses to offence, a "rhetoric of honor" (9). According to Taylor, "honor was not so important because it was an alternative ethical system. Instead it gained its importance because it was so useful as a way to prevent, or to mask, a lack of virtue" (155). As such, even for lower-class men the concept of honour covered practically every aspect of sociability, from sexual reputation to economic rectitude and creditworthiness.[14] In much the same way that the tangibility of fiat currency – which appeared in Spain around the end of the sixteenth century with the issue of token and restamped coinage – strained to close the gap between intrinsic and market value, the ubiquity of the early modern discourse on honour seems to point to uncertainties about the shifting ground of the social order.[15]

Among the earliest articulations of the link between honour and the practice of arms in the Iberian peninsula is found in the *Siete partidas*, the tenth-century juridical text compiled by Alfonso X, in which honour is defined as one of the three pillars of the nobility: "en defender yacen tres cosas, esfuerzo, e honra e poderío" (defence consists of strength, honour, and power) (Partida segunda, Título 21). Later, harking back to the military function of the feudal nobility, the language of honour appears in the texts that accompanied the early modern military's evolution as an object of knowledge and a permanent arm of the state. While the excesses of war are derided as dishonourable, within the Spanish military honour itself is taken up as a distinctive brand and disciplinary mechanism. Jerónimo de Urrea's *Diálogo de la verdadera honra militar* (Dialogue on true military honour) (Venice, 1566), for example, attempts to provide an alternate definition of honour rooted in rational self-mastery, rather than the easily outraged sense of self culminating in the duel. In a similar fashion, in an echo of Lázaro's example of the glory-seeking soldier, Sancho de Londoño declares in his *Discurso sobre la forma de reducir la disciplina a mejor y antiguo estado* (Discourse on how to return the military discipline to its ancient and better status) (Brussels, 1589) that Spanish forces are the best in the world precisely because of their fierce attachment to their own good reputations: "Son españoles que aman más la honra que la vida, y temen menos la muerte que la infamia" (They are Spaniards that love honour more than life, and fear death less than infamy) (43). As these brief examples indicate, honour was understood to be performative and relational, while serving as a powerful set of internalized behavioural norms.

Whether understood in its military, economic, social, sexual, or existential manifestations, honour – both because of its protean possibilities and the ways in which it was implicated in discourses around the military – is a principal preoccupation of the otherwise heterogeneous corpus of soldiers' life writing. As the armies of the period were populated by men from all walks of life, an ideological shift took place within and outside of the military. Within the military establishment, service itself began to be considered intrinsically, if not always materially, ennobling, recalling the medieval conception of honour that stressed "the equality and autonomy of all honorable deeds" (Harari 162). Outside of the military establishment, critics such as Erasmus and Juan Luis Vives held that contemporary combat had been stripped of religious and moral significance, both in its tactics and underlying motivations. These conditions gave rise to what we might call "honour anxiety": how to reconcile the poor pay of soldiers with the notion that their service was indeed valuable? How to reconcile the idea that military honour might not be accompanied by riches, or eternal fame, but in fact by abject poverty, physical mutilation, and an unmarked grave? If honour requires company – an "honor world," in Kwame Appiah's term, or a system in which actors and actions are recognizable as honourable – and if the changing conditions of military service had begun to create fissures in that "honor world," how to go about repairing it? Military life writing is propelled by these larger questions; inhering in the lists, the quantitative details, the minutely detailed sexual exploits, gambling, and unsanctioned skirmishes – and the rejection of such manifestations of soldierly habitus – is an attempt to recreate an honour world, calling forth the comprehension of an ideal reader.[16] Amidst this welter of ideas and differences of opinion, individual soldiers used the space of autobiography to create and inhabit new models of honour inflected by their individual experiences, circumstances of writing, and need.

Arms and Letters in Early Modern Spain

Arms and Letters builds on recent and valuable scholarship on the genealogy of autobiographical practice in the early modern period, including the related questions of subjectivity and self-fashioning: work on Inquisitional examination, bureaucratic documents associated with the colonization and exploitation of the Americas, and the imaginative literature that circulated ever more widely thanks to a burgeoning commercial book market, as well as on the relationship between the military institution and discourses of identity formation and textuality. This book argues that the archive of military life writing is central to understanding processes of identity formation and subjectivation in early modern Spain, due to the social heterogeneity of the authors, the discursive diversity of the texts, and the varied ways in which the concept of honour is wielded for the purposes of self-fashioning.[17] Stephen Greenblatt's seminal work on self-fashioning defines a process of identity formation through literary production, as practised by socially and economically mobile middle-class and aristocratic men (7). As *Arms and Letters* demonstrates, the early modern military granted at least an illusion of social and economic mobility, and provided even (or perhaps especially) non-elite subjects with the impetus to create legible identities.

While each soldier's trajectory is unique, *Arms and Letters* highlights the textualization of honour as one of the unifying principles of the corpus. Through an analysis of the cultural narratives, literary conventions, and institutional configurations that converge upon these texts, *Arms and Letters* demonstrates how a capacious and flexible concept of honour – the overarching metric of value that early modern men and women applied to themselves and others – animates this archive. As the early modern army evolved into a permanent institution, it was the subject of both praise and polemic in debates on the ethics of warfare and the role of the military within the body politic. *Arms and Letters* demonstrates that soldiers' autobiographies engage with these debates in highly personal ways, rendering in the language of honour a textual subjectivity that is informed by, yet distinct from, the mode of martial honour generated by the military as a distinctive brand and disciplinary mechanism.[18] By the middle of the sixteenth century, the practice of arms delineated a diverse social group whose conduct was alternately glorified and condemned. In response to the dangers of military labour, and against the ambivalent status accorded to soldiers, whose excesses were simultaneously despised and yet considered necessary to the Spanish imperial project, these texts articulate modes of honour drawn from custom, the law, and literature.

Arms and Letters argues that Spanish military life writing took two broad forms in the period, which in turn correspond to two distinct concepts of honour. On the one hand, some of these autobiographical texts are structured as implicit petitions, wherein the soldier's service is presented as a debt of honour requiring reward. Modelled partly on the official accounts of service required for career advancement, and conceived as compendia of historical and geographical knowledge, these autobiographical documents exceed those generic parameters in order to impress upon potential patrons the value of the author's experience and skills. The second group of military life writing corresponds not to a material economy of grants and privileges, but rather to a symbolic economy of fame. These texts describe military service as a series of (mis)adventures, staging honour as a spectacle that captivates the reader's attention. Incorporating the conventions of the epic and the picaresque novel, these autobiographical works do not explicitly request promotion or preferment; instead, they present their desired compensation in the form of the projection and preservation of memory. *Arms and Letters* traces these dynamics across a range of representative texts, beginning with one of the inaugural works of early modern Spanish military autobiography, the *Breve suma de la vida de Diego García de Paredes* (c. 1533) and concluding with the possibly apocryphal *Vida* attributed to the celebrated cross-dressing Lieutenant Nun, Catalina de Erauso (c. 1625).

The book's first chapter provides an overview of linked developments in the military, economic, and social realms that resulted in the professionalization and precariousness of military work, even as aristocratic values associated with a medieval model of chivalry persisted. The *Breve suma*, a brusque account of a quasi-legendary infantry colonel popularly known as "el Sansón de Extremadura," exemplifies the impact of these developments. The dubious exemplarity of this work has long baffled scholars, who have been perplexed to find celebrations of what appears to be excessive interpersonal violence, rather than evocations of historically significant events, in a text explicitly intended for moral instruction. This chapter argues that the critical dilemma posed by García de Paredes' *Breve suma* is, in fact, a defining feature of much early modern military life writing: elements of exemplarity and edification intersect with professional pride, and a tenacious sense of aristocratic prerogative, as the practice of arms is understood to be inherently ennobling and worthy of a kind of self-novelization.

The second chapter examines the petitionary mode of military life writing in two texts that draw on the discourses of military treatises and historiography. It begins with Diego Suárez Corvín's autobiographical sketches (c. 1592–1624), which precede his monumental history of North Africa. Rejecting prevailing stereotypes of the soldier as indolent and sexually depraved, Suárez mobilizes images of intellectual productivity and sexual purity in order to demonstrate his worthiness to take up the subject of history. The chapter then moves on to Domingo de Toral y Valdés, whose *Relación de la vida* (c. 1635) likewise unfolds in a "historical" register emphasizing eyewitness testimony and impartial observation. Through an analysis of these texts, the chapter shows how soldiers reformulated martial honour as a professional, lettered attribute, able to be acquired through study and experience. As such, professional honour could provide a stable ground – outside of the accident of wealth or social position – from which to issue wide-ranging critiques, including the critique of certain aspects of the military organization. Both texts mark a distinctive strategy for textual self-fashioning, as both the fact of military service and the expert perspective that accrues to such service are presented as the evidence of obligations that require recompense.

Chapter 3 investigates how the petitionary framework of military life writing, organized around a claim to specialized knowledge, might also be used to fashion an early modern Catholic religious identity. The chapter examines the intersection of corporeal discourse and experiential epistemology to show how physical mutilation and illness acquired in military service might be rendered both as a debt of honour and a sign of spiritual insight. Following Jerónimo de Pasamonte as he recounts in successive drafts of his *Vida y trabajos* (c. 1603) his childhood, capture, and enslavement by Ottoman Turks, and the persecutions he suffered upon his release, the chapter analyses Pasamonte's elaboration of a textual identity based on the figure of the *miles cristianus*, in light of the author's desire to gain recognition from his religious superiors and inscribe himself in a community of religious men.

While chapters 2 and 3 focus on the dynamics of the petition, wherein specialized knowledge is presented as evidence of the author's worthiness for reward and which unfolds in an intersubjective space defined by subjection and suppliance, chapter 4 returns to the autobiographical strategy of self-novelization, in which the wide range of experience associated with military service is presented as entertainment. This chapter examines Miguel de Castro's *Vida* (c. 1617) alongside the autobiography attributed to Catalina de Erauso (c. 1625), in light of the Spanish military's growing reputation for creating a culture of lawlessness. Through an analysis of scenes of sex, violence, gluttony, and gambling, this chapter shows how both texts appear to embrace an alternative rhetoric of honour characterized by delinquency and insubordination. The chapter argues that these texts create a simulacrum of defiance that, while it may appear to uncouple honour from hierarchy, works to reify such stratification. Almost a century after Diego García de Paredes wrote his *Breve suma de la vida* (c. 1533) in a laconic rendition of a disenchanted chivalric romance, Castro and Erauso adopt some of the key tropes of the picaresque novel to render their experiences legible and memorable.

This exploration, structured around six representative texts, unfolds in rough chronological order. While the case study model necessarily limits the number of works under consideration, it also has the benefit of preserving the narrative arc of each life story – such as it is – while leaving room for mutually illuminating juxtapositions: Suárez and Toral, although they move in geographically and temporally different spheres, share an interest in the discourses of objectivity, and their work bears the traces of personal failures that echo the geopolitical failures to which their writing bears witness. Likewise, reading Castro and Erauso side by side foregrounds their respective autobiographies' parody of the picaresque, with their emphasis on youthful aggression and gender instability, while highlighting the similarities among the portrayals of different imperial spaces. Although an exhaustive account of early modern military life writing is beyond the scope of this book, my aim is to shed light on the literary, cultural, and intellectual content and contexts of these particular works, with the hope that my conclusions will prove useful for the study of a variety of related textual production.

Building on historical and literary studies of honour, *Arms and Letters* analyses the modes of subjectivity arising in these texts through the interlocking frameworks of military identity, masculinity, and the projection of the self through writing, all of which intersect in the discourses surrounding honour. By charting the language and tropes of honour in these texts against the backdrop of changing conceptualizations of military labour and martial identities, the book endeavours to add to a critical genealogy of honour that includes its textual and performative aspects, and its role in self-fashioning, particularly among non-elite subjects. Finally, by uncovering the institutional practices and literary narratives that inform soldiers' life writing, *Arms and Letters* contributes to both a broader and more nuanced understanding of the interrelationship among legal discourses, historiography, imaginative literature, and autobiography, as well as the broader context of imperial expansion in which it developed. In this way, the project traces the dynamics of reception and appropriation that animate this significant subset of life writing in the period.

Chapter One

Virtue, Honour, and Exemplarity

One of the earliest examples of military life writing in early modern Spain is the subject of a brief but illuminating exchange in the first book of *Don Quixote*. At the inn where the would-be knight errant and his squire are lodging, the conversation turns once again to books when the priest asks the innkeeper to bring out the contents of his small library, which are held in a travelling case left behind by a previous visitor. Along with some manuscript papers, the priest finds three printed volumes: two chivalric novels and a work of history. The latter, the *Historia del Gran Capitán Gonzalo Hernández de Córdoba, con la vida de Diego García de Paredes*, is a chronicle of one of the heroes of the Reconquest and the Italian Wars, bound together with the *Breve suma de la vida* or autobiography of Paredes, a mercenary soldier who began his career in the personal guard of Pope Alexander VI and eventually rose through the ranks to become one of the Great Captain's most distinguished officers. This bipartite text, which circulated widely following its publication in 1580 in Seville, sparks a heated debate between the priest and innkeeper, each of whom reads the work within a different generic frame.

In a comical echo of Don Quixote's ingenuous mode of reading, the innkeeper judges all three of the printed books according to the same criteria; he accepts with credulity their claims to veracity and values them primarily for their escapist pleasures. Because his main interest is entertainment, he finds that even the most momentous battles and duels recounted in the *Historia* are inferior to the fantastical adventures of the two romances. The priest, for his part, attempts to persuade the innkeeper of the moral, and therefore aesthetic, superiority of the chronicle and accompanying autobiography by emphasizing their proximity to historical truth. He argues that Diego García de Paredes is a particularly impressive figure due both to his extraordinary strength and to the supposed humbleness of his self-presentation: "Diego García de Paredes fue un principal caballero, natural de la ciudad de Trujillo, en Extremadura, valentísimo soldado" (Diego Garcia de Paredes was a distinguished knight of the city of Trujillo in Estremadura, a most gallant soldier) (I.32, 395; 269).[1] He goes on to give two examples of Paredes's legendary feats that illustrate his status as an authentic chivalric hero, one who nevertheless writes of his own experience with dignified reticence: "detenía con un dedo una rueda de molino en la mitad de su furia; y, puesto con un montante, en la entrada de una puente, detuvo a todo un innumerable ejército, que no pasase por ella" (with one finger he stopped a mill wheel in full motion; and posted with a two-handed sword at the foot of a bridge he kept the whole of an immense army from passing over it) (I.32, 395; 269). Defining the difference between history and life writing as a matter of authorial perspective made explicit at the level of style, the priest suggests that if Paredes had not written the text himself – that is, if the *Breve suma* had taken the form of biography rather than autobiography – the resulting work would have been even more thrilling: "y hizo otras tales cosas, que como si él las cuenta, y las escribe él asimismo, con la modestia de caballero y de coronista propio las escribiera otro libre y desapasionado, pusieran en su olvido las de los Hétores, Aquiles y Roldanes" ([he] achieved such other exploits that if, instead of his relating them himself with the modesty of a knight and of one writing his own history, some free and unbiased writer had recorded them, they would have thrown into the shade all the deeds of the Hectors, Achilleses, and Rolands) (I.32, 395; 269). For the priest, Paredes's memoirs are preferable to the pseudohistorical biographies characteristic of chivalric romance, precisely because they recount a real life of epic proportions within the constraints of a gentleman's decorous reserve. While the innkeeper disdainfully dismisses the text as boring, the priest finds the content and form of the *Breve suma* to be exemplary.

Few of Cervantes's commentators have noted that the image that emerges of Paredes in his *Breve suma* differs considerably from the portrait sketched here by the priest and later by the canon, who urges Don Quixote to trade his novels of chivalry for histories of proper heroes like Paredes (I.49).[2] Paredes's autobiography begins with horse robbery and homicide, then goes on to recount his career as a mercenary, first in the employment of Pope Alexander VI, then in the opposing band under Guidobaldo di Montefeltro, and later Prospero Colonna, before eventually entering the service of the Catholic Monarchs in the army of the Great Captain. The text does not include the fabled episode with the mill wheel, nor does it mention some of Paredes's more noteworthy accomplishments, such as his decisive role in the Battle of Cerignola (1503), which secured Spanish hegemony in Europe for more than a century, or his naming as a Knight of the Golden Spur by Charles V, a spectacular achievement for this *hidalgo* of modest origins. The greatest detail is reserved for grisly encounters that underline the soldier's physical strength and ruthlessness, including a duel in which he refused to spare a defeated opponent, and an altercation with civilians in his native Extremadura that left one woman dead. At the end of the brief autobiography, Paredes retrospectively casts his deeds in a laudable light as he characterizes the story of his life as a model of comportment for his adolescent son: "Dejo esta memoria a Sancho de Paredes, mi hijo, para que en las cosas que se ofrecieren en defensa de su persona y honra, haga lo que debe como caballero, poniendo a Dios siempre delante de sus ojos y procurando tener razón para que le ayude" (I leave these memoirs to Sancho de Paredes, my son, so that he may do what he should as a gentleman, in defense of his person and honor, always putting God first and making sure to be in the right so that God may help him) (259).[3] While the autobiography is almost entirely comprised of episodic scenes of violence, such that a reader like the innkeeper might be excused for interpreting it as a somewhat prosaic tale of adventure, the *Breve suma*'s final lines inscribe the text within the tradition of exemplary biography and place Paredes within the pantheon of virtuous men worthy of imitation.

Diego García de Paredes's account of himself was widely disseminated, in both manuscript and print, in the years following his death in 1533. In addition to two known manuscript variants, each copied in a sixteenth-century hand, as early as 1580 the text was bound together with the chronicles of Gonzalo Fernández de Córdoba, under the title *Breve suma de la vida de Diego García de Paredes, la cual él mismo escribió y la dejó firmada de su nombre como al fin de ella aparece*.[4] The portrait that emerged of Paredes, based on a synthesis of historical sources like the *Historia* and the autobiographical presentation of the *Breve suma*, fascinated later historians and writers, including Tomás Tamayo de Vargas, the royal chronicler who published the first biography of Paredes in 1621, as well as Lope de Vega, who included Paredes as a character in several plays.[5] Throughout the late sixteenth and seventeenth centuries, Paredes appeared in historical and fictional works, including fantastical tales, collected from the oral tradition, which emphasized his military prowess, superhuman strength, and bravery bordering on recklessness. In his biography of Paredes, Tamayo de Vargas burnishes the soldier's rough edges and casts him as a new national hero, calling him "el exemplo del más verdaderamente Español que temieron los tiempos passados, ni obediecieron los nuestros" (the example of the most true Spaniard that ever past ages feared and that present ages obeyed) (2r). Less than a century after his death, due in part to the autobiographical account bearing his name, the "Samson and Hercules of Extremadura" – as he came to be known – had attained a reputation of mythic proportions, as a figure embodying both military-religious virtue and swashbuckling spectacle.

Chronologically and thematically, Paredes's *Breve suma* provides a productive point of departure for the study of early modern military life writing as it developed in Spain throughout the sixteenth and seventeenth centuries. Given the broad circulation of the text and the ubiquity of Paredes as a figure who would become identified with specifically martial and particularly Spanish virtues – and defects – it is likely that the *Breve suma* served, to different degrees, as inspiration for the memoirs written by soldiers like Jerónimo de Pasamonte, Diego Suárez Corvín, Domingo de Toral y Valdés, Diego Duque de Estrada, Alonso de Contreras, Miguel de Castro, Catalina de Erauso, and others. Moreover, the critical debates around other soldiers' autobiographies, regarding intentionality, historical authenticity, and their relationship to other genres of writing, are crystallized in the polemics surrounding Paredes's *Breve suma*, a work that has been characterized by Antonio Sánchez Jiménez as one of the most controversial texts of the Spanish Golden Age (*Sánson* 33).

Indeed, Paredes's terse, morally ambiguous narrative does seem at odds with the encomium pronounced by the priest in *Don Quixote*. Paredes's earliest biographer, Tamayo de Vargas, who draws on the *Breve suma* as a key source, admits in the biography's preface: "Confiesso que esta materia no es para prudencia" (I confess that this material does not exemplify the virtue of prudence) (n.p.). Writing more than two centuries later, Marcelino Menéndez Pelayo concluded that the *Breve suma* conveyed a life so incompatible with heroic virtue that it could not have been written by Paredes himself (cxxxii–cxxxiii). Not long after, Manuel Serrano y Sanz was tempted to concur, characterizing the soldier depicted in the *Breve suma* as an improbably fictional figure, "hombre malvado con ribetes de fanfarrón" (a wicked man and a braggart) (lx). More recent scholarship has acknowledged Paredes's authorship, while rightly describing elements of Paredes's memoir as "brutal" (Martínez 197) and "grotesco, violento y casi novelesco" (grotesque, violent, and almost novelistic) (Gastañaga 53). As suggested in the dialogue between the innkeeper and the priest in *Don Quixote*, one of the key elements of the controversy stems from the autobiography's failure to fully conform to the conventions of either chivalric romance or exemplary biography, although it contains elements of both – and both, in fact, are related genres. As it turns out, despite the innkeeper's lack of sophistication, his reading of the *Breve suma* is not entirely incorrect; the autobiography does employ a shared set of tropes and structural elements reminiscent of medieval aristocratic culture and its idealization in novels of chivalry, as Randolph Pope aptly notes (28–30). Yet the priest is also right to recognize the exemplarity implicit in the use of the (auto)biographical form, a claim to commendable comportment that is rendered more explicit in the final words of the text. The generic indeterminacy and apparent moral ambiguity associated with the work raise several related questions: What sort of virtue does Paredes claim to embody in the *Breve suma*? What mode of honour does he project throughout his self-portrayal? And how might these inform our understanding of the soldier's purported exemplarity?

In this chapter I read Paredes's *Breve suma* in light of the military, economic, social, and literary changes attendant upon the professionalization of military work. I argue that Paredes's life and career illustrate the wide-ranging impact of these developments, as the soldier uses the first-person form to redefine the qualities of virtue, honour, and exemplarity in accordance with his own experience. Textual features that initially appear excessive, contradictory, or incoherent may be rendered more intelligible by reconstructing the cultural context of the work's production and circulation, including the evolving status of soldiers in the sixteenth and seventeenth centuries as well as the literary forms available to them for narrating violence. Paredes's self-presentation in the *Breve suma* reflects and responds to sixteenth-century concerns, and became part of the cultural milieu in which seventeenth-century soldiers wrote their autobiographies. As a protean figure whose name became synonymous with both the perfect soldier and the *soldado fanfarrón* (the braggart soldier), Diego García de Paredes produced in his *Breve suma* not only a model of conduct for his son but also, even if unintentionally, a model of a soldierly "coronista propio" (self-chronicler), in the priest's turn of phrase, that later soldier-autobiographers might selectively appropriate or disavow.

~

Paredes was born in 1468, and his life and career effectively parallel the beginning of the precipitous alteration in the tactics, strategies, scale, and conceptualization of warfare that, as several scholars have argued, would spur simultaneous developments in the realms of finance, bureaucracy, and state configurations (G. Parker, *Military Revolution* 1–3). As theorized by Roberts, Parker, and others, the military revolution of the early modern period was a process that would have far-reaching consequences. The extensive use of explosive weapons would reshape the physical geography of Europe, with the advent of trench warfare and the construction of massive fortifications more resistant to cannon fire. Likewise, the social geography of emerging nation states would be reconfigured as the newly constituted armies provided unprecedented opportunities for social ascent.

Before the advent of standing armies, one way in which the burgeoning armed forces of early modern Europe acquired manpower was through the enlistment of mercenary soldiers. Paredes's role as a soldier for hire in the various conflicts that rocked the Italian peninsula at the turn of the century underscores both the importance of mercenaries in the long process of military professionalization and the ambivalence with which they were regarded by their contemporaries, an ambivalence that would later extend to recruits and conscripts populating national armies. While mercenaries, including entire companies for sale, had been common in Europe throughout the Middle Ages, the employment of such forces increased throughout the sixteenth and seventeenth centuries with the expansion in the scale, speed, and duration of warfare (G. Parker, "Dynastic" 150). Both their ubiquity and the unsettling spectacle of social ascent achieved by even the most low-born condottieri contributed to a widespread distrust of such freelance warriors.

For theorists such as Niccolò Machiavelli, mercenary armies were militarily inferior and morally questionable. Whereas native militias and companies of knights had served in times of war either out of self-preservation or to honour an oath of fealty, mercenaries served purely out of self-interest. Thus, in *The Prince* Machiavelli warns that mercenary armies "are useless and dangerous; if a prince continues to base his government on mercenary armies, he will never be either stable or safe ... [T]hey have no love for you nor any cause that can keep them in the field other than a little pay, which is not enough to make them risk death" (47). The very act of receiving money in exchange for military service represented the commodification, and therefore debasement, of warfare; the only men who would provide such labour were, in Machiavelli's words, "not the best but rather the worst of a region; because if any there are of bad reputation, lazy, uncontrolled, without religion, fugitives from the authority of their fathers, swearers, gamblers, in every way badly brought up, they are the ones who are willing to serve as soldiers" (*Art* 582). As we will see, beginning with Paredes's account of his arrival in Italy in 1496, the *Breve suma* unapologetically embraces and redefines as virtuous some of the worst qualities that Machiavelli and many of his contemporaries denounced.[6]

The *Breve suma* does not begin with a description of the author's family or birth, a significant feature of most early modern autobiographical works. Rather, the narrative begins *in medias res*, like an epic tale, with an episode in which Paredes exemplifies the insubordination, belligerence, and physical superiority that will become his most notable characteristics: in stealing a horse from a relative, he singlehandedly injures (and perhaps kills – the text is unclear) the older man as well as three of his squires. Confirming Machiavelli's criticism of the mercenary as a rebellious youth who defies patriarchal authority, this homicidal act presages Paredes's conversion from a young hidalgo to a professional soldier. Paredes and his brother Álvaro subsequently flee to Rome, hoping to find employment as mounted fighters in one of the formations that were constantly being mustered, but their hopes are dashed when they find the city enjoying a period of relative tranquillity. One of the manuscript versions of the text highlights the mercenary aspirations of the brothers as well as the unsavoury way in which they made a living until they could find military employment:

> No hallamos quién nos diese de comer, por la falta de la guerra, que no había. [...] A ocho de marzo del dicho año se vieron mis compañeros y yo más necesitados que solíamos, y andábamos tan alcanzados con el poco partido, que era forzado ir de noche a buscar ventura de enemigos, y lo que se ganaba íbamos a vender a Nápoles, y así, teníamos también mozas ganando el vestido.
>
> (For the lack of war, we couldn't find anyone to feed us. [...] On 8 March of the same year my companions and I were particularly destitute, and we had used up almost all of our scant resources, so it was necessary to go out at night looking for enemies, and what we won from them we went to Naples to sell, and along with what we made off a few wenches we made a living.) (*Suma* 41–2)[7]

After a few months of this arrangement, Paredes makes peace with a powerful relative, Cardinal Bernardino de Carvajal, who is instrumental in arranging his first post as a captain in one of the companies formed under the condottiere Próspero Colonna. From the beginning, Paredes portrays his youthful rebelliousness as the mark of a self-made man who exploits his natural abilities and social connections to forge a spectacularly successful career. Likewise, he presents warfare as a means of escaping financial pressures, with military service providing an entrance to a parallel society that protects men from outright banditry, even as some of the same skills and social structures are transferred from the criminal underworld to the soldiers' barracks.

Paredes was neither the first nor the last hidalgo to embrace the professional practice of arms out of necessity. Later throughout the sixteenth century, with the coalescing of a permanent infantry under the banner of the Spanish monarchy, at least 15 per cent of the recruits were members of the petty nobility. A much smaller percentage belonged to the higher echelons of the aristocracy and received special remuneration in honour of their status; the smallest percentage was comprised of nobles of the highest rank, identified as *homini da bene*, who could afford to serve without the expectation of pay (Sherer, *Warriors* 21). Like the mercenary armies that preceded it, the bulk of the Spanish professional army that began to form at the turn of the century was made up of men from varied social classes and backgrounds. This social heterogeneity was precisely one of the characteristics that critics of mercenary armies denounced; not bound to a common aristocratic code, and without any allegiance beyond their own profit, mercenaries could not be expected to act honourably or cohesively in the heat of battle. Thus Machiavelli warned that such professionals were dangerous because they were "disunited, ambitious, without discipline, disloyal" (*The Prince* 47). Whereas mercenaries were viewed by some as a motley collection of men united only by their individual greed, Paredes's self-presentation counters such criticisms, as he describes actions motivated both by a potent sense of personal honour and strong intergroup loyalties.

By the seventeenth century, one of the institutions that would contribute to a sense of unit cohesiveness in the new professional army, despite its motley social composition, was the *camarada*, a tradition that Paredes in the *Breve suma* gestures to in its prototypical form. The *camarada* was an informally constituted group of soldiers who chose to eat, sleep, and spend their leisure time together, regardless of individual rank or regional affiliation. The emotional bonds and quotidian concerns shared by the *camarada* were a key element in creating a common military identity, particularly in a period when military administration and discipline were still evolving. Although the precise origins of the *camarada* are uncertain, it appears that the tradition – which would be codified by Philip III in the first quarter of the seventeenth century – stretches back to the early years of the Spanish military presence in Italy and the self-regulating structure of mercenary armies (Sherer, "When" 394–5; O'Donnell y Duque de Estrada 390–1). In a military treatise dedicated to Philip II, Martín de Eguiluz suggests that certain aspects of the *camarada* are superior to the dynamics of the family unit in that each member contributes equally to the survival of the group:

> Entre padre e hijo se ve cada día, y así se apartan: por no venir en acuerdo. Pero las buenas camaradas pueden estar mejor y más conformes, porque cada uno trabaja su parte, así en presidio, siendo despensero el tiempo que le toca, como en campaña, que el uno trae de comer, y otro la paja en se echar, y el otro corta la rama para hacer la barraca, y el otro la haze; y el otro haze el fuego, y el otro de comer. En efecto cada uno haze lo que puede de su parte, y una buena camarada se govierna desta suerte, haziendo cada uno lo que le toca, y comiendo juntos conventualmente.

> (Between father and son you see this every day: they grow distant because they can't reach an agreement. But good *camaradas* can be better and in greater accord, because each member has his own job, both in the garrison – serving as storekeeper when it's his turn – as well as on campaign. One brings the food, one supplies the straw, one cuts the branch to make the hut, and the other one sets it up; one lights the fire, and the other prepares the food. Each one does his part, and a good *camarada* is governed in this way, each one doing a task, and eating together communally.) (4v)

The institution of the *camarada* was also much admired abroad; French captain and military theorist François de la Noue dedicated a chapter of his *Discours politiques et militaires* to enumerating its benefits. In addition to the financial advantages of the *camarada*, La Noue notes that the crowning achievement of the system lies in its constitution as a self-disciplining organism with the ability to enforce desirable behaviour among its members. In the course of arguing that the French should consider adopting a similar system, La Noue explains how the small group dynamics of the *camarada* encourage men to adhere to standards of honourable conduct: "chacun bride ses affections le mieux qu'il peut, pour ne commetre rien d'infame, de crainte de tomber en mespris & puis estre debouté du rang de ceux qui prisent l'honneur" (each [soldier] restrains his affections as best he can, to commit nothing infamous, for fear of falling into disgrace and being expelled from the ranks of the honourable) (427). Thus what began as a practical solution to the problem of supplying adequate housing and food for soldiers in a cost-effective manner would become a distinctive organizational feature of the Spanish infantry, one that would be credited with reproducing an ideal of communal honour and creating the close social bonds that would be crucial for success in the harsh conditions of battle.

In the *Breve suma*, a text that is conspicuously laconic and plagued by chronological inaccuracies, Paredes carefully records the names of his first companions in Italy, Spaniards from all corners of the peninsula who, like him, had relocated to Rome in search of financial opportunities and adventure.[8] Paredes notes how he and his brother Álvaro banded together with these men – including hidalgos and commoner ex-soldiers – to pool their skills and resources in organized crime. Later, this relationship of mutual dependence will be replicated when Paredes names these companions as officers when he is awarded his first company under Pope Alexander VI. From the beginning, Paredes describes lodging and, most importantly, fighting alongside this proto-*camarada*. Even before they are given official posts, Paredes and his gang distinguish themselves through acts of violence. Paredes relates how, armed with a javelin, he and his men kill five opponents wielding swords and wound another ten in a brawl occasioned by an insult. Subsequently they are released at the pope's order and their attackers, who happened to be members of the pope's guard, are charged "por el poco respecto que nos tuvieron" (for the scant respect they bore us) (255). This episode, which otherwise contains no explicit justification, is not simply a street skirmish among idle young men; the text conveys through the use of an unusual detail Paredes's spectacular strength, as he turns the javelin that he had been throwing as a game into a deadly weapon against multiple armed opponents. The episode also indicates Paredes's ability to lead his men, even at a disadvantage, which in turn generates a fearsome reputation for the group that is then transmuted into public honours and deference. As such, it foreshadows the soldier's first military victory, which is described in the *Breve suma* almost immediately thereafter. With the same group of men as his officers, Paredes recounts quashing an uprising in Montefiascone by means of a well-coordinated midnight assault. While one detachment is tasked with creating a distraction, Paredes and his men scale the battlements and slay the guards. Then Paredes, alone and reportedly using only his hands, pulls the bolt from the locked main gates, allowing the rest of the pope's forces to stream in and subdue the rebellion. Once again, the incident illustrates both the soldier's physical strength and his ability to act in concert with his men: "Eran por todos ocho banderas de infantería; fueron rompidos y la tierra saqueada, y la otra tierra se nos rindió de miedo" (There were eight infantry companies. They were defeated and the land sacked, and the other town surrendered out of fear) (256). As Paredes describes it, the company's daring action won the day against numerically superior forces, first through a combination of cunning and brute force, and then through the intimidating reputation they had acquired through victory.[9] For his company, the rewards are immediate; while the other mercenary forces mustered for the conflict are dissolved, their services rendered obsolete by victory, Paredes and his men are promoted to a coveted post in the papal fortress of Castel Sant'Angelo.

In a similar fashion, when Paredes recounts his participation in battle, he often moves between the first-person singular and plural. Though victories and defeats are described as collective, the use of the first-person singular highlights his role as a commander in providing strategic insight and courageous impetus. For example, in one of the more detailed accounts of one of a string of battles fought under the banner of Charles V's Imperial Army, Paredes writes:

> Ganamos de los frances a Urdabia, a Monleón de Sola y a Salvatierra. De allí fuimos a Tariz y fue quemada por los alemanes y saqueada; mas del vino quedaron tales, que los enemigos les tomaron el artillería que llevaban y yo iba de retaguarda con mis escopeteros y atravesé un monte y toméles el paso, donde venían con la presa cinco mil, y toméles descuidados y rompímosles y quitámosles el artillería y matáronse de ellos mil y prendieronse muchos.
>
> (We won from the French Urdabia, Monleón de Sola, and Salvatierra. From there we went to Tariz and it was burned by the Germans and sacked. But they were so drunk from wine that the French took the artillery that they were carrying. I was at the rearguard with my riflemen and I scaled a mountain and headed them off at the pass, where five thousand of them were coming with their booty, and I took them by surprise and we broke them and seized the artillery and a thousand of them were killed and more were captured.) (258)

Through the use of the first-person singular, Paredes claims credit for ordering his troops to scale the mountain to set up the ambush, while also acknowledging, with the use of the first-person plural, the collective effort necessary to win a battle against numerically superior forces. Although the *Breve suma* has been read as an atavistic account of individual heroism, episodes such as these emphasize personal qualities such as strength, courage, and tactical acumen while also delineating the structure of mutual dependence within which even legendary soldiers like Paredes moved.

Objections against the use of mercenary armies centred on the question of loyalty. The most dangerous aspect of employing them came down to the fact that a mercenary's service was a purchasable commodity rather than an expression of true allegiance. As such, critics like

Machiavelli contended that mercenaries were "valiant among friends, among enemies cowardly; [with] no fear of God, no loyalty to men" (*The Prince* 47). According to the account in the *Breve suma*, Paredes and his men are anything but disunited, undisciplined, and cowardly. In fact, Paredes presents himself as embodying the virtue of loyalty – but it is a loyalty that operates primarily on a horizontal rather than a vertical scale, arising out of a commitment first to his own honour, then to his men, and finally to the Great Captain. Thus one of the key events in Paredes's career is his desertion from the pope's guard and his defection to his erstwhile enemy. This incident, which might otherwise be read as the fulfillment of dark predictions regarding the divided loyalties of mercenaries, is told in the *Breve suma* both as a testament to the way in which honour motivates Paredes's actions and as a providential narrative of the soldier's eventual entry into the service of the Spanish monarchy.

The *Breve suma* describes the initial dispute that would eventually lead to Paredes's desertion as a disagreement over a battle cry. Ambushed by the forces of the Duke of Urbino, Paredes rallies his men to victory by roaring "¡España!"; this is a choice of words that leads to his chastisement at the hands of an Italian officer: "y porque peleando con ellos dije 'España, España' fui reprendido del capitán Cesaro Romano, diciendo que yo era traidor" (because in fighting the enemy I cried "Spain, Spain" I was reprimanded by Captain Cesaro Romano, who said I was a traitor) (256). The more well known version of the battle cry is "¡Santiago y cierra, España!" – a formulation that appears in its entirety first in late sixteenth-century texts, often in reference to the battles of the Reconquest (Linares par. 11–13). Here, however, in one of the earliest historical references to the slogan, Paredes recounts shouting only "Spain!" and thereby invoking the idea of a shared cultural if not yet fully political identity as a call to arms.[10] The battle cry is effective in that it succeeds in rousing Paredes's men to fend off the attack, but it is also dangerous as it points to their primary loyalty as a group of Spanish mercenaries. For the latter reason, Captain Romano publicly questions Paredes's allegiances and accuses him of treason. Paredes responds to the insult by challenging the officer in single combat. In direct contravention of the chivalric code and the norms of military discipline, Paredes readily admits to killing his surrendered opponent: "y Dios me dio victoria y le corté la cabeza, no queriendo entendelle que rendía" (and God gave me victory, and I cut off his head, refusing to accept his surrender) (256). While the Italian officer objects to the political dimensions of Paredes's invocation of Spain, Paredes understands the rebuke as an insult to his honour and reacts accordingly. When the pope has Paredes arrested for murder, thereby denying him both the right to the battle cry and the claim to revenge, the soldier considers their contract to be dissolved. That night, he single-handedly kills his guards and escapes to the camp of the Duke of Urbino. There he is well received and given the command of a company whose captain had died in battle the previous day – perhaps even by Paredes's own hand. While the pope had attempted to punish Paredes for his breach of protocol, the Duke of Urbino gladly welcomes Paredes and offers him "más mercedes" (more privileges) (256).

In a text that otherwise condenses into a single paragraph some of the most noteworthy battles in which he had a commanding role, Paredes chooses to narrate in detail how he switched sides and went on to use his privileged knowledge to defeat the armies of his former employer, but he does so in order to reframe apparent disloyalty as loyalty to a higher cause: principally, his own sense of honour. When the pope's forces attack the Duke of Urbino's encampment with renewed vigour in reprisal for having welcomed Paredes, the soldier himself devises a strategy to break the siege, "y como yo fui la cause de este cerco, procuré el remedio" (and because I was the cause of this seige, I found the solution for it) (256). Paredes draws on his knowledge of the pope's position to stage an ambush against an army of unsuspecting reinforcements, a move that is not only tactically clever but also guarantees that he will not be involved in direct combat with any of his former comrades. Paredes recounts how he led a detachment of six thousand Venetians to assemble in the trenches, where they were then mowed down by the Duke of Urbino's riflers; he recounts that two thousand died and many more were taken prisoner. Paredes's success in this particular battle also signifies the successful conclusion of the war between Montefeltro and the pope. Paredes attributes his success to "la voluntad de Dios" (the will of God) (256), a summary pronouncement that will be repeated throughout the *Breve suma*, as the author assigns a providential meaning to the outcome of each violent encounter. Though Paredes never offers an explicit exegesis on the deeper significance of each episode, by repeating the phrase "y Dios me dio victoria" (and God gave me the victory) (256), he endows this sequence of events with meaning, from his initial use of the rallying cry "¡España!" to his entry into the service of Montefeltro, which will eventually lead him to serve under the banner of the Spanish monarchy – even as this latter arrangement would prove to be far from perfect, a fact that the text elides. While Machiavelli and others criticized mercenaries for acting entirely out of crude self-interest, here Paredes suggests that his single motivation is his sense of personal honour, which he insists is further validated by divinely ordained victories and the eventual alignment of his personal and professional allegiances under the Great Captain.

Whereas critics of mercenaries labelled them as disloyal, disunited, and pusillanimous, motivated primarily by monetary gain, Paredes presents what could be the most problematic episode of his career as a moment infused with bravery, a testament to his commitment to a military identity embodied by the rallying cry "¡España!" Furthermore, Paredes makes clear that the incident was not motivated by financial gain but rather by a concern for honour, the right to define his reputation. In this way, Paredes frames his actions as a mercenary as virtuous, thus foreshadowing the coalescing of a professional mode of martial habitus characterized both by strong horizontal loyalties such as those forged in the *camarada* and by individualistic bravery prompted by the desire to project personal honour.

Even as the widespread use of mercenaries changed the complexion of armies and offered new opportunities for economic accumulation and social advancement, the chivalric values of the past persisted to some extent in the formulation of military honour. Among the definitions of honour offered by Covarrubias in the *Tesoro de la lengua castellana* is simply the external recognition of value: "[honra] vale reverencia, cortesía que se hace a la virtud, a la potestad, algunas veces se hace al dinero" (honour is the respect, courtesy that is shown to virtue, to power, and sometimes to money) (1068). The concept of honour that had informed medieval relations of power assumed a direct and divinely ordained correspondence between virtue and authority, such that the nobility's monopoly on arms simultaneously expressed and safeguarded their privileged position. As the nobility's participation in warfare declined throughout the early modern period, due to a variety of factors, a similar sort of logic would locate a symbolic ennoblement in the practice of arms itself, regardless of the circumstances of a particular soldier's birth. This could take the concrete form of an exceptional soldier being named to a hereditary or non-hereditary knighthood, as when Diego García de Paredes was inducted into the Order of the Golden Spur in 1530. On a conceptual level the identification between arms and ennoblement is manifested in the *Breve suma* in a parallel movement in which honour, traditionally defined as the external recognition of virtue, becomes a virtue in of itself. Just as Paredes interprets every victory and every privilege as evidence of divine favour, the text defines honour as both reward and effort, such that the performance of honour – its violent projection and maintenance, constantly safeguarded against real and perceived threats – becomes coterminous with honour itself. This understanding of honour informs the final lines of the *Breve suma*, in which Paredes claims exemplary status for the text of his life, "para que [Sancho de Paredes] en las cosas que se ofrecieren en defensa de su persona y honra, haga lo que debe como caballero" (so that Sancho de Paredes may do what he should as a gentleman, in defence of his person and honour) (259).

Paredes's *Breve suma*, which recounts more interpersonal conflicts than battle scenes, was disseminated in print as part of the *Crónicas*. Despite the fact that Paredes's personal library, like that of many soldiers of his rank, contained a copy of Caesar's *Commentarii de Bello Gallico*, the legendary soldier's autobiography circulated not as a *comentario* (like that of the early seventeenth-century account of the soldier Diego Duque de Estrada), but rather as a *suma*, a summary account of those personal deeds the author judged most important for his son Sancho to know and draw upon as a model of conduct.[11] The genre indicated by the *suma* is that of a didactic summation; when applied to the story of a life, it is often that of a religious figure worthy of emulation.[12] In this way the title accentuates the author's exemplary aim as indicated in the text's final dedication, which in one of the mansuscript versions invokes, by the lexical choice of the term *espejo* (mirror), the didactic genre known as the "mirror of princes": "Dejo estas cosas a Sancho de Paredes, por espejo en que haga sus obras conforme con éstas, en servicio de Dios" (I leave these things to Sancho de Paredes, as a mirror with which to perform deeds such as these, in God's service) (*Suma* 48). Timothy Hampton explores the term "espejo" in Pietro Paolo Vergerio's *De ingenius moribus*, which councils its young masculine readers to begin the process of self-betterment first by looking in the mirror and then by looking to the lives of heroes to identify virtuous actions to imitate (10). In order to understand the ways in which the *Breve suma* redefines exemplarity in terms of the professional soldier's sense of honour, it is necessary to understand the broader landscape of contemporary exemplary writing, as well as what Hampton has identified as a "crisis in the representation of exemplarity in the late Renaissance" (x), as an increasingly inaccessible gulf separated ancient models from early modern readers.

Perhaps the kind of exemplary writing closest to Paredes's *Breve suma*, in terms of structure and content, were the chivalric novels that were wildly popular in the first half of the sixteenth century. The reign of Charles V (1517–55), who self-consciously styled his court after an idealized vision of the medieval past, coincided with their peak of popularity with a new novel appearing at the rate of one a year (Eisenberg, *Romances* 40–1). Because of the spectacular way in which the pseudohistorical heroes of romance embodied chivalric virtues, *libros de caballerías* "were perceived as manuals of courtesy and general social comportment" (Harney 153). Though Paredes may not have owned any of these extraordinarily popular serials of adventure, the military and courtly circles in which he moved were thoroughly saturated with chivalric themes. He could not help but be aware of the characteristic tropes of the chivalric novel, as the *Breve suma*'s episodic structure, organized around violent tests of personal strength and honour, attests.

The prototypical *libro de caballerías* is Garci Rodríguez de Montalvo's *Amadís* (Zaragoza, 1508), a fictitious biography of an extraordinarily virtuous young nobleman of spectacular fighting prowess. In Daniel Eisenberg's succinct analysis, "the *Amadís* defined what the romance of chivalry would be in Spain. From *Amadís* the other romances took their basic framework: the travelling prince, the constant tournaments and battles, the remote setting in a mountainous, forested (never desert or jungle) land, the interest in honor and fame" (*Romances* 31). This is a familiar European landscape even as the actual armies of the period marched through the deserts of North Africa, northern Mexico, and Chile, and the jungles of West Africa, Central and South America, and the East Indies. Though ostensibly set in places and times that are remote, the novels displace onto a fabulous yet recognizable cartography the ceaseless wars of the period, while enshrining the quest for honour and victory as appropriate motivations for action. As Hampton has argued, this structure has its own limitations even as it articulates a new representation of exemplarity, one that attempts to account for the increasing awareness that ancient history could not provide fully adequate models for contemporary conduct:

> In humanist exemplarity the contingencies that weighed on the acts of the ancient exemplar generated a moment of unfamiliarity and shock, a second of recoil, during which the reader was led to reflect on the distance between himself and his model, between modern and ancient. This moment of self-consciousness was seen as the effect of the encounter between humanist ideals of public action and the alterity of ancient history itself. Because the romance text neutralizes historical and social reality, it permits the reader to bypass this mediating reflective moment and turns reading into mere wish fulfillment. (247)

It is precisely this aspect of fantasy or "wish fulfillment" that Cervantes cunningly exploits in *Don Quixote*, as the conditions of the contemporary world render ridiculous the would-be knight errant's attempts to imitate chivalric heroes.

Despite its distance from contemporary social reality, the basic framework of the chivalric novel paralleled certain aspects of military life, such that the genre provided one avenue through which medieval-chivalric values might be mapped onto and transformed into particularly martial virtues. As Raffaele Puddu has argued, the martial honour developed by the new professional armies of the period would take as its model chivalric honour – the aristocratic code of conduct that provided a limit to (and apologia for) the nobility and the monarchy's shared monopoly on violence. According to Puddu, allowing the socially heterogeneous ranks of the new armies to partake in the chivalric code (articulated through the ideology of honour) had the effect of "dissipating the most subversive aspects" attending to the massification of these forces (10).[13] Likewise, the work of Irving Leonard attests to the widespread popularity of the genre, particularly among soldiers, who may have found a point of wishful identification with the idealized warrior-heroes of chivalric romance.[14]

Paredes's *Breve suma* echoes the chivalric novel's itinerant trajectory, episodic structure, and emphasis on violent, supernaturally ordained encounters, even as it condenses the power inscribed in the chivalric novel's magical trappings into the soldier's own hands. Though the professionalization of warfare meant the creation of new fighting technologies, including firearms and explosives, as a gentleman and a high-ranking officer, Paredes does not mention handling firearms in his autobiography. Although the military revolution would eventually usher in significant changes for soldiers of all ranks, Paredes's *Breve suma* illustrates how the military aristocracy still styled itself along medieval chivalric lines. When not engaging in hand-to-hand combat or performing astounding feats of strength, Paredes most frequently appears dressed in armour, armed with a sword, and riding on a horse. Though he describes being wounded by gunfire on several occasions, he never depicts himself using a gun – although he does wield a javelin, a door bar, and other makeshift and memorable weapons. At a time when more battles were beginning to be won by the brute force of cannon fire, Paredes's self-presentation in the *Breve suma* recalls the figure of the classical and medieval warrior characterized by physical courage and strength. In this sense, the image that Paredes presents is consonant with those of the virtuous men in the *de viris illustribus* tradition and their fanciful manifestation in chivalric romance.[15]

As in the chivalric novel, the exemplarity of the text lies in its performance of a military-aristocratic sensibility that is communicated and safeguarded primarily by expressions of violence, including, but not limited to, the duel. As we have seen, the first episode in the *Breve suma* is one such violent encounter. While Paredes's self-presentation is characterized by an emphasis on physical strength and courage, many of the scenarios exemplifying these qualities are discordantly banal and brutal. In this respect, the text's opening gambit is particularly illuminating. Paredes's justification for horse theft is not made clear, but its position at the opening of the text signals its importance: in terms of narrative development, the "birth" of Paredes as autobiographical subject is accomplished in a homicidal act, in which he seizes an animal replete with material and symbolic significance.[16]

As recounted in the text, each subsequent conflict takes on a sanctioned status, as each is a stage upon which Paredes successfully performs the attributes of strength and bravery, accruing more honour and renown in the process. This string of challenges culminates in an exchange, a version of which Lope de Vega would immortalize in the play *Las cuentas del Gran Capitán* (1638). The scene, recounted to different effect in both the *Crónica del Gran Capitán* as well as in the *Breve suma*, dramatizes the conflict between arms and letters, the warrior class and the new bureaucratic elite. In the *Crónica*, the Great Captain, Gonzalo Fernández de Córdoba, is called to court by King Ferdinand's treasurers, who demand a post-victory financial account of his expenditures in the conquest of the Kingdom of Naples. Fernández de Córdoba responds to the request with a sardonic list:[17]

> En el primer capítulo asentó que había gastado en frailes y sacerdotes, religiosos y en pobres y monjas, los cuales continuamente estaban en oración rogando á Nuestro Señor Jesucristo y á todos los santos y santas, que le diesen victoria, doscientos mil y setecientos treinta y seis ducados y nueve reales. En la segunda partida asentó setecientos mil y cuatrocientos y noventa y cuatro ducados á las espías, de los cuales había entendido los designos de los enemigos, y ganado muchas victorias, y finalmente la libre posesión de un tan gran reino.
>
> (In the first section he claimed that, for friars and priests, poor folk and nuns, to continually pray to Our Lord Jesus Christ and all the male and female saints for victory, he had paid the sum of two hundred thousand seven hundred and thirty-six ducats and nine *reales*. In the second section he claimed seven hundred thousand nine hundred and ninety-four ducats paid to spies, from whom he had found out the enemy's designs, and thus gained many victories, and finally gained possession of such a great kingdom.) (qtd. in Rodríguez Villa 284)

According to the *Crónica,* King Ferdinand was chastened by the exasperated wit on display in the Great Captain's response: "Entendida del Rey la argucia, mandó poner silencia al infame negocio; porque quién sería aquél, si no fuese algún ingrato, o verdaderamente de baja o vil condición, que buscase los deudores y quisiese saber el número de los dineros dados secretamente de un tan excelente capitán" (The King understood and ordered that this infamous business not be brought up again; only an ingrate or a person of truly low and base condition would search out his debtors trying to find the exact sum of money given secretly to such an excellent captain) (284–5).

Paredes recounts a similar episode in the *Breve suma* in a way that recalls the fierce interpersonal loyalties originating in the *camarada* and inhering in the structure of command. When Paredes arrives at court, accompanying Fernández de Córdoba, he encounters a roomful of murmuring nobles who gossip about the Great Captain's extravagant expenses. In response to these complaints, Paredes throws down his glove and challenges any man who dares defame the captain out loud. As Paredes tells it, the courtiers fall silent, knowing that Paredes has never lost a duel. After a few tense moments, King Ferdinand himself picks up the glove and returns it to the soldier, stating that he agrees that the Great Captain is "el mejor criado suyo y de mejores obras" (the best of his servants, who had committed the greatest deeds) (257). While in the historical account of the *Crónica* Fernández de Córdoba silences the king's trifling treasurers by acquiescing, in a parodic mode, to their request, Paredes resorts to the starkly performative gesture and language of the duel. In Paredes's account, his valour, supported by the weight of his fearsome reputation, precipitates King Ferdinand's public recognition of Fernández de Córdoba. By challenging a roomful of nobles in front of the king, Paredes stakes his honour on that of his captain, and ultimately elicits from the king himself an implicit rejection of the newly financialized conception of military service as a contractual relationship mediated solely by money.

The tensions attending the transformation in the social organization of armies, characterized by a greater reliance on mercenaries and local recruits contracted for their service, and by codified laws that subordinated soldiers not to a particular lord but to the Crown, are reflected in this episode. In both the *Crónica del Gran Capitán* and Paredes's *Breve suma* the soldiers convince the king – in the Great Captain's case through wit and in Paredes's case through the verbal threat of violence – to affirm the mutual bonds of service and recompense uniting the monarchy and nobility.

Diego García de Paredes's *Breve suma* marks a transitional moment, as the author presents himself as embodying a traditional military-aristocratic notion of personal honour, even as the realities of sixteenth-century warfare began to favour collective over individual action and to emphasize subordination to military discipline over all other considerations. In fact, as Thomas Devaney has argued, a similar shift in the concept of nobility had already begun to take place in fifteenth-century Castile. In his reading of Fernán Pérez de Guzmán's *Generaciones y semblanzas* (1450), Devaney notes that the author praises the historical figures that are the subject of the text for manifesting a host of equally important individual virtues, including courage, fortitude, prudence, and generosity. In contrast, more than three decades later, a similar work of historical biography, Fernando del Pulgar's *Claros varones de Castilla* (1486), subordinates these virtues to a single overarching quality: that of loyalty and submission to the Crown. As Devaney concludes,

> What it meant in practice to live a virtuous life varied considerably over the course of the [fifteenth] century. In particular, we can see a turn away from those aspects of traditional chivalric behavior that esteemed the individual – including adamant personal honor, independence, and the pursuit of fame – and towards those that we might characterize as focused on the collective: loyalty, religious fervor, and pride in Castilian identity. ("Loyalty" 125)

At the crossroads of these developments, in his autobiography Paredes often embraces both individual valour and valour in a collective like the *camarada*, always ready to remind the sovereign (first the pope, then King Ferdinand) of the pact of mutual honour that constitutes the conditions of service.

While the *Breve suma* incorporates many of the structural elements and tropes of the chivalric novel, particularly in its emphasis on the violent accumulation and maintenance of honour, the autobiography differs from these textual antecedents in several key respects. First, despite Paredes's recurring formula of assigning providential significance to his victories, he makes no explicit claims for any virtuous motivation for his action, beyond the desire to acquire and maintain honour itself. Paredes's self-presentation in this regard is markedly different from that of the heroes of chivalric romance. To take one example, the protagonist of *Cirongilio de Tracia*, one of the two chivalric novels found in the innkeeper's library in *Don Quixote*, is described in the novel's prologue as a virtuous exemplar, and the principles underlying his conduct are explicitly framed as worthy of imitation: "No se movió con yra a las batallas, mas con misericordia y clemencia que tuvo de los afligidos y voluntad de deshazer los tuertos y agravios, donde todos los príncipes deste tiempo pueden tomar enxemplo para más buenamente governarse" (He was not moved to battle with anger, but with mercy and clemency towards the afflicted, and with the will to right wrongs and offences; in this all of the princes of this age can take his example to govern better) (Vargas 6–7; qtd. in Eisenberg, *Romances* 12). Secondly, masculine exemplarity in the novel of chivalry depends in part on deference to women who, as Eisenberg notes, are the literal and metaphorical "spectators at the tournament" (12), whose gaze endows the actions of the hero with meaning. Love for an idealized lady is for the chivalric hero both a source of strength and a mark of refinement, indicating that the aristocratic monopoly on violence is divinely sanctioned and operates within defined limits. Even as Paredes's *Breve suma* claims divine favour for the soldier's actions, there appear to be no limits to his violence, and his victims include women and other non-combatants. The most controversial episode in the *Breve suma* is patently anti-chivalric, and appears to contain no underlying principle of ethical conduct worthy of imitation. It is also the episode with the greatest number of textual variants, which may indicate that it was somewhat problematic for contemporary copyists.[18] The overall contours of the scene, however, are consistent across the manuscript and printed versions of the text: in travelling to Coria, in Paredes's native Extremadura, the soldier exacts a gory revenge against a group of harassing civilians.

On the way to his home in Trujillo, Paredes stops at an inn, where two indulgence sellers, two pimps, and two prostitutes sneer at the sight of the breastplate glittering beneath his travelling cloak. As in *Don Quixote*, the inn is a liminal space in which people of different classes and professions mix. The result is not a humorous sharing of stories and perspectives but the eruption of animus. Each character in the episode is defined by his or her profession – that is, by what he or she sells, and the initial provocation arises when the civilians taunt Paredes by asking if he is a "mercader de puercos" (pig merchant) (258). The group continues to insult Paredes until one of the men approaches to tug on his balaclava. Paredes, recalling the event, explains that he sent word to the company of riflemen who were behind him on the road, ordering them to act as if they didn't know him: "Envié secreto el paje a ellos, avisándoles que hiciesen que no me conocían, por ver en qué paraba la fiesta" (I sent my page secretly to them, warning them to act as if they didn't know me, in order to see how the party might play out) (258). Far from the chivalric hero's desire to "right wrongs and offences," Paredes seems to highlight boredom as a principal motive for purposefully occluding his identity, thereby setting the stage for a spectacular outburst of violence.

Paredes, wielding the bench upon which he had been sitting, attacks one of the men "y abríle la cabeza" (I cracked open his head) (258). Next, he describes shoving the other five civilians into the fireplace, where one of the women is burned alive and the other four barely escape, their hands and faces scorched. Both the language and content of the episode reveal the gruesome pleasure with which the soldier recalls meting out punishment, resonating with what Ruff has identified as another outcome of the military revolution: "the violence inherent in the relationship between growing numbers of soldiers and the civilian population" (52). Two somewhat theatrical details reinforce Paredes's disregard for his victims. First, he claims that he and his men sat down to eat the dinner that the group had abandoned. Second, when the incensed townspeople threaten to first invade and then burn down the inn with Paredes and his men inside, Paredes (perhaps in parallel to the tale of his first military victory in Montefiascone) describes yanking the bar from the inn door and brandishing it against the counter-attack – despite the fact that the men now accompanying him are armed with rifles. Just as Paredes's performance in battle and in the duel is explicitly interpreted as evidence of divine favour, the episode at Coria is resolved with the intervention of a powerful relative: "Al ruido y alboroto vino el Obispo, que era mi deudo y sosegóse todo" (The Bishop, one of my relatives, came, alerted to the noise and disruption, and he calmed them down) (258). While some scholars have doubted Paredes's authorship of the *Breve suma* based on this episode, near-contemporary readers such as Tamayo de Vargas apparently had no such reservations. For Tamayo de Vargas this brutal encounter was entirely consonant with the military-aristocratic ethical imperative: the violent defence of honour and the exercise of control by means of physical and social superiority.

Indeed, in his biography of Paredes the royal chronicler gingerly admits to his subject's violent excesses, only to excuse them as a necessary element of the warrior's disposition. In a historical work that is meant to enshrine Paredes in imperial history and galvanize contemporary Spaniards to similar feats, this choice is significant. Tamayo de Vargas, a *letrado* of relatively humble extraction and a student of Juan de Mariana, uses the prologue of the biography to link his labour – writing history – to that of Paredes – making history:

> Io refiero lo que e podido rastrear ... con estilo ahora mas militar, que (como en otras obras mias) cuidadoso ... porque mas hermosea a Hercules

> la piel de Leon sangriento, que la vista de la purpura flammante, i mas el descuido de los nudos de la clava tosca, que el artificio del sceptro de oro.
>
> (I recount what I have been able to verify ... with a style more military than meticulous, as in other works of mine ... because the hide of the bloody lion beautifies Hercules more than the sight of splendid purple, as do the careless knots of his heavy club more than the artifice of the golden sceptre.) (n.p.)

Tamayo de Vargas goes on to state that, because the raw material of Paredes's life does not initially seem to advertise the virtue of prudence – understood here as moderation or judiciousness – the historian's task has been to sprinkle the biography with "raros preceptos" (choice precepts) that allow the reader to extract moral significance from the text.[19] This apparent lack is both recognized then lightly dismissed with a rhetorical question that equates Paredes with none other than Alexander the Great: "Alexandro, ¿que puede ser sino guerra?" (What else could Alexander signify than war?) (n.p.). Thus, Tamayo de Vargas straddles the binary of arms and letters in the biography, modulating his language to match the military content – here identified with the bloody hide and coarse club, objects that stand in sharp contrast to the fabricated splendour associated with the symbols of power – even as he supplements the account with edifying adages. Tamayo de Vargas concludes the prologue with a defence of Paredes's seemingly immoderate deeds that is also an implicit justification for the historian's own intellectual work: "parecían a los más tímidos i tardos imprudencias porque siempre condenamos lo que menos podemos" (to the timid and dull-witted, his deeds seemed reckless because we always condemn what we cannot accomplish) (n.p.).[20]

In his analysis of memoirs written by Renaissance noblemen from England, France, and Spain, Yuval Noah Harari maintains that "Renaissance military memoirs establish a threefold connection between honor, violence, and history. Rightful violence was the supreme way of gaining honor; honor in turn gained on the right to use violence; and history guaranteed this transaction by recording honorable violence" (170–1). In contrast, in his *Breve suma* Paredes asserts the right to define his memory, not as history, but as a new kind of writing suited to a new historical moment. In his biography, Tamayo de Vargas recognizes the distinction, explaining that, unlike Caesar's *Commentaries*, the legendary soldier "escribióla ... con menos ambición, i más como soldado, que solo pretendía hacer relación de sus cosas, no adornarlas, sin reparar en el computo de los tiempos, ni en las successión de los acaecimientos, porque fuera de anteponer los que eran últimos, dexó muchos de no menor nombre" (He wrote it ... with less ambition than Caesar, and more like a soldier, who only desired to recount his experiences, not to adorn them, and without noting the computation of the years, nor the order of events, because outside of putting first those that happened last, he left out many things of no less renown) (n.p.). Paradoxically, these chronological inaccuracies, gaps, and a tightly circumscribed personal frame impress Tamayo de Vargas (and, indeed, the priest in *Don Quixote*) for their unpretentiousness. Events like the brawl at Coria have no immediate relevance to larger royal or national narratives, and the evident pleasure that Paredes takes in recalling this and similar events seems to speak more to the fantasy function of fiction than to the sober, "ambitious" realm of history. All of these textual qualities are read by Tamayo de Vargas as a marker of truth – personal (or autobiographical) truth, if not historical precision.

While the exemplary pose adopted in the concluding lines of the *Breve suma* may be initially jarring, it is congruent with what Hampton articulates as "the understanding of the self in terms of narrative" (29) implied by the very concept of exemplarity. At the same time, beyond the dubious morality of some of the actions that Paredes recounts, there is a contradictory energy that animates the text. The claim of having lived a life worthy of imitation sits uneasily beside the extravagant, practically inimitable episodes that Paredes strings together in the *Breve suma*. The nature of exemplarity, as Harari notes, is that exemplars "are never unique ... for they may always be replaced by other exemplars" (112). Rather than emphasizing any universal ethical principles underlying his actions, Paredes insists upon his extraordinary strength and valour, which are in turn both the basis for and the most striking outward signs of his singular honour. The soldier's self-novelization inheres in the narrative choice of sometimes bizarre and sometimes banal details that serve to transmute the historical person into a larger-than-life persona. In this way, in addition to leaving a model of conduct for his adolescent son, Paredes granted the soldiers of the following century a compelling set of ideas: that the practice of arms was intrinsically ennobling and related to the kind of exceptionality associated with chivalric heroes, and that despite the incursions of new technologies of war and the incipient commodification of military labour, a soldier's life experiences (including formal battles as well as interpersonal conflicts around the performance of honour) were worthy of inscribing in written narratives that would stand alongside the literary and historical record.

Chapter Two

Professional Honour and the Production of Knowledge

Following the beginning of the move towards professionalization in the preceding century, the sixteenth century witnessed the creation of military science; that is, the matter of war in all its historical, technological, and philosophical dimensions became an object of knowledge in its own right. The printing presses of Venice, Brussels, Madrid, and other cities in Spanish dominions spewed out a vast quantity of material in various formats, covering every aspect of the conduct of war, from history and strategy, to the intricacies of drilling with firearms, and meditations on the qualities of the perfect officer. These works were eagerly devoured by a heterogeneous readership composed of members of the upper echelons as well as rank-and-file soldiers keen to improve their skills, their chances of survival, and perhaps their possibilities for career ascent. Both implicit and explicit in these texts was a new concept of martial honour as a professional habitus, a set of skills and a code of conduct subject to military discipline and (at least theoretically) open to all. In his *Diálogo de la verdadera honra militar* (Venice, 1566), for example, Jerónimo de Urrea offers a revised definition in which "true honour" and virtue are inseparable and intrinsic to the subject: "La honra mora con la virtud, y el virtuoso es el honrado, a este honrado, nadie le puede quitar la honra, sino le quita la virtud, donde ella mora, pues la virtud uno a otro no la puede quitar, solo el hombre propio es el que puede a si propio quitar su honora, con apartar de si la virtud, abraçarse con los vicios, y maldades" (Honour resides with virtue, and the virtuous man is honourable. No one can take away the honour of an honourable man, unless he takes his virtue, wherein honour resides, because one cannot take virtue away from another, only from oneself, by putting it away and embracing vice and evil) (5v). Operating from this definition of "true honour," Urrea denounces the trappings of chivalric honour, in particular the duel, as "allende que es vanagloria, es ignorancia" (in addition to vainglory it is ignorance) (5v–6r). In the dedication to the Spanish infantry, he decries the duel itself as a "desordenada [desvariada] y bestial costumbre" (disorderly and bestial custom) (n.p.). In contrast to the "vainglorious" man who seeks out violent encounters for personal glory, Urrea argues that a good soldier's honour consists primarily in performing two duties: following his flag into battle, wherever that might be, and obeying his superior officers. In this, he recognizes that the most difficult task – the one most worthy of honour – consists in overcoming the natural desire for comfort and safety. Furthermore, Urrea claims that the virtue that begets true honour arises from actions performed from a dispassionate disposition: "Dizen que la virtud, no es potencia del alma, ni afecto alguno, sino un abito en bien obrar con elección, y un medio entre los estremos de los afectos, y pasiones" (They say that virtue is not a faculty of the soul or affect, but rather consists in choosing to act well, in the middle of the extremes of emotion and passion) (78r). Against an older model of military aristocratic honour characterized by the violent imposition of one's will on others, Urrea erects a model defined by the principle of rational self-mastery.

This chapter shows how virtue and honour are conflated into two practically identical properties that are the province of the individual alone. The individual must control himself in order to attain "true honour." This formulation of honour connects to a new martial habitus, one that is inevitably gendered as masculine. Such a formulation would prove attractive to writing soldiers, as it provides a stable ground from which to issue critique or claim reward – or accomplish both objectives at once, as the resulting text is framed as an intellectual service made possible by the soldier's military experience. Both the life described therein and the resulting text are figured as a *servicio* (service), a gift that requires recompense.

The petitionary mode of life writing that I identify in this chapter is a narrative form structured by the social dynamics of suppliance. As such, it is an intersubjective exchange defined by inequality: the dedicatee or intended reader has the power to change the writer's fortunes for better or worse, and the text is intended to encourage the best possible outcome. Both the life described therein and the resulting text are figured as a service. As such, it is perhaps best understood in the broader context of what Folger has called the early modern "economy of *mercedes* (grants or privileges)" (14) and the documentary culture that enabled it.[1] The expansion of bureaucracy – the proliferation of official reports, accounts, and testimonies that accompanied territorial expansion – meant that there was a host of models for the communication of information, including self-presentation, and a variety of rhetorical strategies for initiating requests. As discussed in the introduction, a key intertext for soldiers' autobiographies may be found in the *relaciones de méritos y servicios*, the forms of official self-presentation required for royal preferment. Like military life writing, the drafting of these documents was a material practice anchored in a hierarchical intersubjective relationship; that is, it was a transaction carried out among multiple people who had different points of access to power. Whereas the bureaucratic *relación* follows a standard generic format and is characterized by the multiplicity of voices testifying to the petitioner's worthiness for public honours and financial reward, soldiers' life writing subordinates a wealth of experiences to a single, idiosyncratic authorial point of view.

While the larger context of Renaissance humanism and lettered culture discussed in the previous chapter illuminates the growing tensions between exemplarity and autobiographical self-fashioning, this chapter turns to another realm of writing that may be thought of as the realm of knowledge work, particularly that centred on the autobiographical "I." In a neat mirroring of two kinds of *relaciones* – *relaciones de sucesos* (accounts of events) and *relaciones de servicios* (accounts of service) – in the following texts the soldiers' autobiographical experience is marshalled for didactic and illustrative purposes in order to produce a work that itself is rendered as a service. By the first quarter of the seventeenth century, Urrea's *Diálogo* had seen three editions, indicating the popularity of its revisions to the idea of honour. In the context of a welter of similar works, the life writing of Diego Suárez Corvín (1552–post-1623) and Domingo de Toral y Valdés (1598–post-1635) similarly embraces a cerebral formulation of martial virtue and honour. Both autobiographical texts portray honour as a professional, lettered attribute that each soldier has acquired through experience and study. As such, in these texts honour provides a kind of authority, outside the accident of wealth or social position, from which to issue wide-ranging critiques, including the critique of certain aspects of the military organization (as in the case of Toral's *Relación de la vida*) and a revisionist history of Spanish imperial policy (as in Suárez's autobiographical paratexts). Rather than primarily seeking to amaze or entertain, Suárez and Toral present their lives as evidence of a new paradigm of professional achievement in which intellectual skills are considered as commendable as fighting prowess; thus, the value of their autobiographical texts is framed as the production of knowledge. The autobiographical narrative is a performance of rational deliberation as each author interprets the "text" of his life. Critique is the ultimate endgame for this ratiocination, and it is where the didactic element of the texts lies. Both texts, albeit to different degrees, are subordinated to a larger petitionary purpose; Suárez's autobiographical paratexts preface a longer historiographical work that he hoped would secure patronage, while Toral's life story contains an implicit request for a much-promised but long-deferred reward. The preferment sought by both soldiers hinges on fashioning their military experience as a source of insight, such that the service rendered is figured as both (ephemeral) military labour and (more durable) intellectual work.

~

Born in Asturias in 1552, Diego Suárez Corvín (sometimes referred to as Diego Suárez Montañés) was a soldier and a prolific writer who produced poems, a military treatise, a policy paper dedicated to Philip III, at least two autobiographical paratexts prefacing longer works, and a monumental history of Spanish military intervention in North Africa.[2] This history, which was never completed, runs over six hundred folio pages long. Two autobiographical sketches, which Suárez states are based on a longer autobiography (since lost), were written to accompany different versions of his North African history, which he split into more manageable parts for the purposes of seeking patronage. Both paratexts tell the same story with small but significant differences, particularly relating to the circumstances under which Suárez arrived in the fortress outpost of Orán. The more extensive of the two autobiographical works, *Discurso verdadero de la naturaleza, peregrinación, vida y partes del autor de la presente historia*, surfaced in the governmental archives of Algiers in the nineteenth century, where it was transcribed by French Hispanist Alfred Moral-Fatio.[3] While the manuscript of the *Discurso* has since been lost, the overall arc of the life it describes is identical to the prologue and first chapter of Suárez's *Historia del Maestre último que fue de Montesa de su hermano don Felipe de Borja*, a lengthy fragment of the soldier's even longer African chronicle (Suárez 14–20). While Morel-Fatio indicated that he believed readers would be amused by the soldier's description of a quasi-picaresque youth, in this chapter I focus rather on the proposition that Suárez sets out at the beginning of the text: that he writes in order to demonstrate his own capacity for intellectual labour, despite his lack of formal university training.

A sonnet prefacing Suárez's *Historia del Maestre* pleads for the comprehension of a benevolent reader, issuing a standard apology for the soldier's clumsy style, while also proclaiming the superior truth value of his words. Comparing his poetic abilities unfavourably with "fino oro" (fine gold), Suárez notes in his defence that he spent thirty years in the wars of Orán "sufriendo trabajos muy extraños / derramando oscuro sangre de sus venas" (suffering foreign travails / spilling dark blood from his veins) (54). Here Suárez collapses the binary cliché of arms and letters by linking the "baja escoria" (dross) of his literary style to the "oscuro sangre de sus venas" (dark blood of his veins), shed during decades spent on the North African frontier. Suárez contrasts the ivory towers of "famosas academias" (famous academies) with the watchtowers ("la atalaya") of North Africa (54). The precious materials and refined locations that Suárez disavows are clear markers of class and status; yet what renders the soldier's style as low and unlovely is precisely the basis of his authority for writing history, and furthermore is a sign of his work's authenticity. A few pages later, in the "Prólogo al benévolo lector," Suárez paints a picture of himself as both a practiced soldier and a productive writer: "juntamente con el ordinario trabajo y ejercicio de las armas, interpolé siempre el de las letras, leyendo libros y borrando papel en el poco tiempo que me sobraba o, por mejor decir, hurtaba a mi mismo reposo" (along with the usual work and exercise of arms, I interposed that of letters, reading books and blotting paper in the short time that was left over, or rather, that I robbed from my own repose) (73).

The first chapters of both the *Historia* and the *Discurso verdadero* attempt to anchor the validity of the history that they precede in a truthful and thorough accounting of the author's life. While many soldier's autobiographies similarly insist on the veracity of the stories they recount, thus recalling their origins in the bureaucratic and juridical forms of the service report and sworn testimony, Suárez is particularly vehement in his assertions of truthfulness. For him, credibility not only constitutes personal honour but is also an integral part of a constellation of virtues that in turn authorize him to undertake the weighty task of historiography. Suárez explains his motives in appending the *Discurso verdadero* to the history of North Africa:

> El hombre que tiene ánimo y atrevimiento para tratar de vidas agenas de otros, muertos y vivos, deve, antes que se meta en tan peligrosos trances, rrepresentar y mostrar la suya, quien es por si mesmo, su naturaleça de patria y sangre, discurso y carrera de la vida que a tenido hasta la ora que saco la obra a luz, no rrecatandose ni escondiendo la verdad de oficio puesto, ni trances altos ni vaxos que aya tenido en su vivienda, para que de esta manera su travaxo y obra sea mas estimada de los prudentes letores, que pocos gustan de los que en su entroduçiones y prologos venden grandeças mentirosas.

> (The man who has the desire and daring to write of the lives of others, the living and the dead, should, before undertaking such a dangerous task, describe and show his own life, showing who he is, in his own words, his country and his family, the course and trajectory of the life he has lived up until the present moment of writing, not camouflaging or hiding any part of the truth, neither the high or the low parts, so that in this way his life and work will be held in even greater esteem by prudent readers. Because very few readers enjoy reading introductions and prologues full of great lies.) (*Discurso* 146)

Likewise, the autobiographical paratext to the *Historia del Maestre* is also concerned in marking the distance between fiction and history, particularly chivalric romance, which masquerades as stories of war. Suárez draws a sharp distinction between historical writing and fiction, which he dismisses as useless. He distinguishes between ideal readers – "discretos y prudentes" (discreet and prudent) – and the readers for whom the book is not intended: readers of "marañas patrañeras de que otros tienen apetito y reciben gusto, como de *Olivante de Laura, El caballero del Febo, El caballero de la Cruz, Don Quijote de la Mancha* y otros semejantes libros" (tangled tales that others enjoy, like *Olivante de Laura, The Knight of Febo, The Knight of the Cross, Don Quixote de la Mancha*, and other similar books) (77). Suárez's evisceration of chivalric romance is not limited to the reader's perspective; underlining the difficulty of his own historiographical labour, he claims that the research and writing of history is a "much harder" task than inventing fictional tales:

> Es muy mayor trabajo y peligro inquirir y hacer una historia de cosas verificadas de guerra estando a la cara testigos de ella, que forjar y componer otra de mentiras afeitadas con estilo y color de la verdad, como hay muchas, de que muchos gustan y pierden el tiempo sin fruto ninguno, ni se les pega nada que puedan ejemplificar con verdad, como podrán desprender los que la presente historia leyeren.

> (It is much more work and more dangerous to research and write a history of verified matters of war, face to face with witnesses of it, rather than forging and composing a story of embellished lies, adorned with the style and colour of the truth, of which there are many examples, which many people like and waste time with, without ever coming across any truthful and moral examples, like those who read this history will be able to find.) (77)

The first chapter of the *Historia* provides Suárez with an autobiographical space in which to comment on literary genres and to relate his own life to the work he has undertaken. In contrast with the widespread impression within Spain that the North African frontier was no longer a space of economic productivity or cultural importance, Suárez begins his revisionist history by supplementing this perception of lack with an autobiographical sketch that highlights his own assiduous work ethic and intellectual capacity.

In many respects, the life story that Suárez recounts traces a trajectory similar to that found in much contemporary military life writing. Suárez was a second son of the petty nobility who, after acquiring a basic education, left home partly out of a desire, he says, to see the world, and partly due to a falling out with his elder brother. Thus began a period of itinerant wandering through Castile and Andalusia, serving various masters, from shepherding to serving the head baker at El Escorial. In 1577 (at the age of twenty-five), Suárez relates in the *Discurso verdadero* how a dishonest recruiting captain convinced him to enlist with promises of honour and fortune in the Italian peninsula. Seduced by the beguiling stories of veterans returned from the Italian campaigns, Suárez happily signed up. On Easter Sunday, his transport ship docked, not in Naples, but off the coast of North Africa, in Orán. Suárez would remain there, against his will, for the next two decades. Orán, a key strategic asset on the northwestern coast of Algiers, had fallen to Castilian forces in 1509, but with the opening of commercial trade routes in the Atlantic and the decline of overland travel between Europe and Asia, the once vibrant city had slowly sunk into a dusty imperial backwater. As such, it was one of the least attractive posts for a soldier at the time. Like many before him, Suárez quickly discovered that in Orán he would find neither fame nor fortune, as he spent the next few years essentially performing manual labour, building the city's defensive walls.[4]

Like many Spanish soldiers stationed in North Africa, Suárez expended a considerable amount of energy attempting to be transferred elsewhere. Unlike many of his peers, he tried to escape through legal channels, making the customary petitions to the appropriate authorities rather than simply deserting, as many soldiers did. All of these petitions were denied. Having exhausted the options for leaving lawfully, Suárez resigned himself to life in the garrison; he successfully lobbied for a position as sexton and clerk at the Iglesia de San Bernardino, and he married the daughter of a high-ranking garrison official, which allowed him to join one of the oldest Spanish families in the city.

It is at this point, according to the *Discurso veradero*, that Suárez began to write his monumental history. In the autobiographical sketch he admits his lack of formal training for such a task, while stressing that this deficiency is more than made up for by his "natural yngenio" (natural wit and disposition) and his meticulous methods and work habits:

> Sirviendo yo desta manera a su Magestad y aquella santa casa, por no perder tiempo ni estar ocioso me aficione a escrivir esta historia de sucesos de guerra que an pasado en aquellas plaças de Marçaelquivir, Oran, Argel, Bugia y en todo su reino de Tremecen antigua y modernamente, sobre que fue mi motivo, sin tener genero de gramatica ni curso della, si solamente ayudado de mi natural yngenio, juntamente con aber considerado el estilo de algunas otras semexantes historias.
>
> (Serving in this way His Majesty and that holy house, in order to not waste time or be idle, I began to write this history of the wars of Mazalquivir, Oran, Algiers, Bugia, and all of Tremecen both in the olden days and more recently, as was my desire, without having studied grammar, only helped by my natural wit, together with having considered the style of similar histories.) (152)

Rather than give himself over to unproductive pursuits, Suárez describes using his free time to pore over records, perform and transcribe interviews with eyewitnesses to the North African campaigns, and consult "similar histories" in order to absorb their lessons on structure and style. As Bunes Ibarra and Alonso Acero have noted, Suárez's purpose in writing his monumental tome is to discursively resituate the North African theatre of war at the centre of imperial policy, claiming for it the same historical and spiritual significance as that of the Americas (Suárez, *Historia del Maestre* 15–18). Finding himself virtually exiled to a "forgotten frontier,"[5] Suárez turns to the writing of history in an attempt to literally and figuratively improve his situation.

Suárez's project is informed by the new methods and concerns of early modern historiography: rather than a cycle governed by fallen human nature, history was now often perceived as a linear trajectory (Bentley 237). In the broadest terms, the roots of early modern historiography may be traced to multiple factors, including the establishment of global empires, increased contact with other cultures and civilizations, religious schisms and crises, and the scientific revolution, which reframed the natural world as an object of knowledge (236–7). The anxieties – and possibilities – provoked by these expanded horizons led to practical and theoretical shifts in the writing of history. According to Sabine MacCormack, early modern historiography began to focus on shorter spans of time, emphasizing phenomena "capable of sustaining comparisons and the description of historical patterns or laws" (59). In other words, rather than necessarily drawing a broad picture of historical development across centuries or even millennia, historians began to focus on discrete events, such as the War of the Alpujarras, the subject of Diego Hurtado de Mendoza's sixteenth-century *Guerra de Granada*, in which the author describes and analyses events that he had witnessed first-hand. As MacCormack argues, the constrained temporal frame of much early modern historiography was coupled with a new emphasis on "the interplay of forces beyond the individual's control" (59); rather than referring to the ancient past for precedent, early modern historians could now draw on the well-documented events of the relatively recent past in order to see the roles played by the institutions and circumstances contemporaneous with the event being analysed. In the case of Mendoza's *Guerra de Granada*, MacCormack perceives the historian's emphasis on "the isolating and impersonalizing forces of government by *letrados*" as a contributing factor in the conduct and outcome of the suppression of the Morisco revolt (57).

Particularly in its preoccupation with the discourses of objectivity, Suárez's *Discurso verdadero* echoes new models of historiography. As MacCormack notes, among the defining characteristics of early modern historical writing are a new stance towards the Graeco-Roman past, revised standards of evidence, and, for some writers, a conscious desire for impartiality (46). MacCormack describes the pragmatic orientation of much early modern history: "For [early modern scholars], the historian's task was not so much to preserve truths enshrined in a long textual tradition but rather to understand for the first time since the end of antiquity how the Romans had acquired and administered their empire" (46). In order to accomplish this task, historians increasingly turned to sources outside the textual tradition, including "inscriptions, coins, architectural remains and even ancient works of art" (46), all objects that supplemented an ever more dubious legendary history. In addition to the historical analysis of classical material culture, scholars attempted to emulate the example of ancient historians when recording events closer to their own times. For a historian such as Pedro López de Ayala, whose fourteenth-century *Corónica del rey don Pedro* recounts a regicide he helped to orchestrate, the classical virtue of impartiality was paramount. As MacCormack points out, in the prologue to the *Corónica* Ayala stresses his own impartiality as a historian, despite – or perhaps because of – his role in Pedro I's fall (40). In this particular case, the historian's declaration of unbiased truthfulness points to classical precedent, in addition to containing an element of practicality. As a prudent courtier, Ayala doubtlessly understood the need to tread lightly in describing a historical event in such close proximity to the present (40). In the same vein, Suárez openly acknowledges the "dangerous" nature of writing history, and thus uses the autobiographical space of the sketch to prove his own credibility and worthiness for the task.

Recruited under false pretences, Suárez had hoped to serve his king from the sumptuous cities of Italy; when he arrived in Orán he immediately understood that he had been virtually exiled to an almost-forgotten corner of the empire. The chronicle of North Africa, for which he unsuccessfully attempted to secure patronage for publication, was intended as both a path to preferment and a revalorization of the strategic and historical importance of the region in which he had spent the bulk of his career. It also further polished and projected the reputation of the Velasco family into which he had married – descendants of one of the original Castilian conquerors.

In fact, in describing his marriage to María de Velasco, Suárez includes an unusual statement regarding the circumstances of the union:

> Tenía yo treinta y seys años, y ella diez y siete, y con aber yo caminado por España, Andalucía y otras partes estava virgen sin aber tocado a muger ninguna, preçiandome siempre en todo de limpieça, huyendo de ocasiones que en esto se me ofreçian muchas veces, por ser yo de moderado talle y conversacion onesta.
>
> (I was thirty-seven years old, and she was seventeen. And despite having wandered all throughout Spain, Andalusia, and elsewhere, I was a virgin, having never even touched a woman, taking pride in my purity in everything, continually fleeing temptations – which were offered to me on numerous occasions – because I have always been one for moderation and honest conversation.) (152)

The statement itself is somewhat unusual, in the context of prevailing stereotypes that equated masculine honour with sexual experience. Suárez's choice of words (virgin/*virgen*) is also notable. In the Spanish of the sixteenth and seventeenth centuries, significant semantic and symbolic associations appear to tether virginity to femininity. In Covarrubias's *Tesoro de la lengua española*, for example, the term *virgen* is defined in purely feminine terms:

> Por otro nombre la llamamos donzella; deste estado, y de la virginidad, y su castidad avia mucho que dezir, pero es lugar comun: y asi me contento con lo dicho, y con remitir al lector curioso a un emblema mio, cuya figura

> es una açucena rodeada de un seto rompido, y ella destroncada con la letra: *Nulla reparabilis arte.*
>
> (A synonym for virgin is damsel; of this state and of virginity and chastity, there is much to be said, but it is common knowledge; and so I content myself with this, and point the curious reader to an emblem of mine, which depicts a lily that has lost its petals, surrounded by a broken hedge, and underneath the words: *Nulla reparabilis arte.*) (1010)

By defining a virgin as a damsel and referring to a visual emblem of deflowerment, Covarrubias indicates that virginity is a purely feminine property – a state that for all intents and purposes is identified with the intact hymen. Likewise, the vast majority of contemporary literary and visual representations of virginity reveal the same principal: that is, virginity is a virtue that only makes sense with respect to a female body.

Why does Suárez insist that he had married as a virgin, in seeming contraposition to the feminine signifying system within which virginity was embedded, and against established secular expectations of male sexual behaviour? The work of anthropologist Mary Douglas on purity and danger may illuminate the larger significance of Suárez's claim. According to Douglas's research on the organization of social life in both premodern and modern cultures, impurity represents danger through disorder. Dirt, for example, she defines as simply matter out of place, that which is formless in nature and therefore has the ability to modify existing boundaries (41). At the symbolic level, anything defined as impure or transgressive is dangerous precisely because of its explosive power to threaten the established order. Conversely, the crossing of boundaries is itself fraught with danger, as such movement threatens to redefine that which is pure as impure, and vice versa. Within this symbolic system, virginity (the maintenance of a man's or woman's sexual integrity) is a key guarantor of existing boundaries – the boundaries between castes, classes, religions, and cultures (159).[6]

In this regard, the North African context in which Suárez writes may provide an additional clue for understanding why he emphasizes his previously virginal state. The fortress cities of Orán and Mazalquivir were surrounded by high walls not only to repel Ottoman Turkish attacks but also to prevent the soldiers garrisoned there from the allied dangers of illicit contact with locals and outright desertion. Marriages such as Suárez's – to a fellow Spaniard who had grown up in the city – were encouraged by military authorities, who feared both the prospect of religious apostasy and the degradation of discipline if soldiers became involved with local Muslim and Jewish women. In declaring that he had entered marriage without having previous sexual experience of any kind, Suárez attempts to demonstrate an exemplary ability to withstand temptation, a virtue that was made particularly relevant in the context of Catholic Spain's uneasy occupation of Muslim territory.[7]

At the same time, with his declaration of virginity, Suárez tacitly rejects the prevailing association between soldiers and unruly conduct. In the same sentence he links his virginal adolescence and young adulthood to the related virtues of moderation and self-control. In this way, virginity functions as only the first and most attention-grabbing detail in a more comprehensive ethical self-portrait, one in which the qualities of "onestidad" and "moderación" are key. As Mar Martínez Góngora has demonstrated, it is precisely these qualities that came to be associated with the modes of masculinity espoused by Renaissance humanists and men of lettered professions in Spain (*Utilización* 124). By embracing this more cerebral model of manhood, in which bodily self-control – rather than excess – is valued, Suárez is able to point to an alternative martial masculinity, and assuage the fears of cultural and religious disorder attendant upon military action. In this way, despite his lack of formal training, Suárez argues that he is the best suited to tell the story of Spanish imperialism in North Africa, as an exemplary soldier whose life has always been characterized by integrity.[8] And so he concludes the *Discurso verdadero*:

> E querido mostrar antecipada y sumariamente en esta historia mi naturaleza y inclinacion y curso de vida, para enterar los letors de mis partes y vivienda, en que el curioso que lo quisiere saber y aberiguar lo hallara asi sin descrepar punto de la verdad, de que siempre me e preciado.
>
> (I have desired to show in advance and in a summary fashion in this history, my nature and inclination and life story, to inform readers so that those who are curious and who wish to know and verify who I am, may find that I have not differed in a single point from the truth, because it is the truth that I have always valued above all.) (157)

In concluding the *Discurso verdadero* with this reiterated commitment to truth, the curious detail of Suárez's virginity becomes a somatic stand-in for the historian's probity and trustworthiness. The stereotypical soldier's amorous conquests become a self-conquest, in the subjection of the body's desires, and virginity itself becomes a masculine virtue that not only discursively protects the racialized and religious boundaries threatened in the course of military action but also guarantees the authenticity of the historiographical work that tells the story of imperial expansion.[9]

~

Like Diego Suárez Corvín, in his autobiography Domingo de Toral y Valdés redefines honour as a matter of maintaining rational self-control in order to establish critical authority. Born in 1598, he wrote his *Relación de la vida* in 1635; the text was not published in Toral's lifetime and contains no paratext or other explanatory material.[10] The *Relación* recounts Toral's youth and the most significant events of his military career, including his service in Flanders, a disastrous expedition along the African coast, and his overland trek across Persia. In addition to vivid descriptions of Toral's travels, the autobiography includes striking episodes of intercultural exchange as the author praises the Jews and Muslims who assist him on his journey. Also striking are the text's markedly critical stance towards the Spanish military hierarchy and the deep sense of hopelessness with which the author regards the future. Using multiple narrative techniques and foci, the *Relación* presents the soldier as a talented and conscientious commander, often in stark contrast to the noblemen under whom he serves. As the autobiography unfolds, Toral's experiences are variously rendered in the language of historical exposition, travelogue, biographical sketch, and military treatise, while interrogating the relationship between work and reward, a process that shuttles between describing and performing leadership while meditating on the benefits and obligations that define it. Though the few scholars to study the autobiography have unanimously remarked on Toral's pessimism, none have analysed it as the *Relación*'s defining feature, nor questioned its use as a strategy of self-fashioning.[11] In this chapter I situate Toral's critique within the lettered discourses upon which it draws, and I analyse the gendered dimensions of the text's despondent tone as a Baroque structure of feeling arising from a crisis of military leadership and statecraft attributed to alternately deficient or hyperbolic masculinities.

As in most soldiers' autobiographies, the first few lines of the *Relación* identify the author's parents and the time and place of his birth. Accordingly, Toral reports he was born in 1598 in Asturias, into an impoverished family of the petty nobility. His childhood was marked by poverty and loss; following his mother's death in childbirth, Toral recounts that his father, reacting both out of grief and in the hope of securing a stable income, decided to move with his two oldest children to Madrid. There Toral was placed in the service of a wealthy gentleman for four unremarkable years, after which, for unknown reasons, he left his master to spend another four years wandering the country "como otro Lazarillo de Tormes" (another Lazarillo de Tormes) (497). The incident that would provide the catalyst for his enlistment came not long after his return to that same master. The man – who is unnamed in the text but referred to as occupying one of the pre-eminent positions in the country (497) – received him like a prodigal son, inspiring the jealousy of Toral's fellow servants. Upon learning that one of them had criticized him in front of his master, Toral assaulted him. Convinced that he had killed the man, he fled Madrid and found himself in Alcalá de Henares, where troops were being raised for the war in Flanders.

Despite his youth and the attempts of the recruiting lieutenant to dissuade him, Toral joined the company and was immediately confronted with the miseries of military life. After losing two fingers and all of his money in a fight, he waited, along with the rest of the newly formed company, to be deployed: "Dos meses estuvimos esperando sin socorro ninguno, buscando la vida con los modos a que da licencia la soldadesca cuando no hay superior que lo estorbe ni remedio a la necesidad" (Two months we waited without any help, fending for ourselves the way soldiers will when there's no superior officer to get in the way, nor any other way to meet our needs) (497). Finally, Toral's company and forty-two others were packed into impounded merchant vessels and shipped to Dunkirk. As Toral bitterly notes, the horrific conditions of the voyage claimed more than seven hundred men before they even reached the battlefield. This episode, the first treated in detail, establishes the critical intent of Toral's autobiography. In supplying the exact dates and numbers of men involved, Toral asserts the accuracy of his testimony; similarly, by concluding the episode with the names of the presiding officers, he offers a condemnation of their incompetence.

The rest of Toral's time in Flanders is equally unsuccessful. After a long lull in the hostilities Toral recounts a surprise attack that goes awry, leaving the army no other alternative than to begin the long process of building fortifications from which to launch another offensive. After parenthetically noting that during this time he received his first promotion (to *cabo* or corporal), Toral goes on to describe the difficulty of constructing these fortifications during winter. In addition to being practically immobilized by the rain and mud, the soldiers were ill-equipped to handle the cold; without adequate clothing, many of them lost limbs or died from exposure. Following the pattern established in the previous episode, Toral states the casualties and ends with the name of the highest ranking official to oversee the failed operation: "de

9000 que entraron en el puesto se apuraron en 2000, sin haber muerto el enemigo" (the nine thousand men that entered this post were reduced to two thousand, without the enemy sustaining any casualties) (501).

Toral left the Army of Flanders with positive recommendations and, after a period spent raising other armies, he set sail for the East Indies at the rank of Captain. Under the command of Count Miguel de Noroña, the new viceroy of the East Indies, Toral's once-promising career begins to slowly stagnate as he is ordered to take on increasingly dangerous assignments with little potential for reward. Eventually, the viceroy – who has become Toral's enemy – arrests him on trumped-up charges and releases him only when his skills are required. Aware of his tenuous situation, Toral arranges to return to Spain, travelling overland in a caravan through Isfahan to Aleppo, sailing to Cyprus and then Malta on his way back to the Continent. The autobiography concludes with Toral having returned to Madrid and having successfully cleared his name against the viceroy's accusations in an audience with King Philip IV and his advisor, the Count-Duke of Olivares. But, exhausted from his journey and without an adequate source of income in reward for his service, Toral sees only a bleak future ahead. In one of the few evocations of emotion in the text, Toral finishes by indicating that the many dangers he has survived abroad are nothing in comparison with his present and future state of necessity.

While Toral's *Relación* begins with his birth and ends with his present, penurious circumstances, it obeys the injunction included at the end of the text: "el hombre ni en bien ni en mal es bien que hable mucho de si" (whether for good or ill, it is not good for a man to talk much of himself) (547). Instead, Toral's self-presentation is accomplished in his description of the battles he witnessed, the men with whom he served, and the cities he visited. In this way, both in the choice of subject matter and the language of reportage, the *Relación* enfolds within an overarching autobiographical frame the discourses of historical narrative, travel writing, and biography, as well as the technical vocabulary and persuasive function of the military treatise. As Alessandro Cassol has suggested, that parts of Toral's *Relación* were revised and circulated as history indicates the close connection between the text and the content and rhetoric of historical writing. Although Toral's explicit purpose in the *Relación* is not to provide a definitive account of any single event, his privileged position as a first-hand witness to a number of important occasions immediately imparts documentary value to the text.

The historiographical impulse of the text, as seen in its focus on serious events – sieges, battles, the death of important men – rendered in precise and quantitative detail, is indicative of the *Relación*'s motives and interlocutors. Though there is no paratext to Toral's *Relación* and no trace within the autobiography of the names of its intended readers, persistent references to the soldier's financial need, in sharp contrast to his accomplishments, point to the *Relación*'s status as a quasi-professional document. Furthermore, the historical content of the text and its solemn rhetorical mode suggest that Toral expected readers to judge his case both by the significance of the events in which he participated and the shrewdness of his analysis, in addition to his exemplary conduct as an officer.

Cassol has located seven fragments of the *Relación* dispersed among five different manuscripts, all currently located in the Biblioteca Nacional in Madrid. The fragments include Toral's descriptions of the fortresses at Hormuz Island and Diu, which appear in the manuscript miscellany *Descripción de la India Oriental*, as well as his account of sieges in Flanders, an offensive in Mombasa, and the death of don Rodrigo de Costa, all of which are inserted into volumes of *Sucesos* titled by the year of their occurrence ("Entre historia" 316). Cassol notes that each passage was copied in the same hand some time after 1635, the date of the *Relación*'s composition. Additionally, the manuscript of the *Relación* contains marginal annotations in the same script, perhaps indicating that the copyist had further designs upon the text (Cassol conjectures that the copyist may have been preparing a summary of Toral's life) (313). What is certain is that, in order to introduce Toral's various accounts into the manuscript miscellanies, the copyist revised them, changing Toral's first-person narration to the third person and deleting elements deemed to be excessively personal. Although the anonymous copyist attributed the authorship of the fragments to "Capitán Domingo de Toral y Valdés, castellano de nación" (qtd. in Cassol 314), each episode is scrubbed of its autobiographical traces, including references to the author's prior military experience, his commentary on strategy, and the scant emotional responses he records.

These editorial changes were easily accomplished, as the *Relación* already carried many of the hallmarks of historical exposition. Toral's account of the siege of Bergen op Zoom provides a good example of a complex episode drawn precisely, with well-chosen detail, and culminating with incisive analysis. The siege was a key event in the ongoing conflict between Spain and the Dutch Republic; Toral's account was extracted in the *Sucesos de 1622* as one of the low points of that year (Cassol, "Entre historia" 316). The siege was one of many carried out during the Eighty Years' War, a conflict that had begun in 1578 with the defiance of the Spanish Netherlands against Philip II and that would eventually become the most protracted armed struggle of the period

(González de León, "Doctors" 63). The first part of the war concluded with the Dutch Republic essentially gaining independence in 1609. Far from pursuing the glory of imperial ambition, Spain approached the second half of the war primarily out of economic necessity, as the expansion of Dutch trade and navigation in the East and West Indies was widely believed to be a contributing factor in the country's economic decline. After a twelve-year truce expired in 1621, one of the first major actions of Spanish forces under the command of the Marquis of Spínola was the siege of the fortified city of Bergen op Zoom in Dutch Brabant (Israel 1–9). Toral's account relays the multiple factors responsible for the attack's spectacular failure, and in this way illuminates an event that was acknowledged as pivotal even at the time. While Toral's analytical ability and technical expertise render his account valuable, it is his graphic description of trench warfare that gives it particular resonance. The following passage records the horrific casualties sustained by just one company of the multinational Army of Flanders in a single day of fighting:

> Servía entre nosotros un tercio de ingleses que también se halló en todo lo que se ofreció; de ellos y de los nuestros estaban las trincheras llenas de cuerpos muertos que no se podía poner los pies en la tierra, si no es en ellos, pisando los unos que retirándose murieron otros que allí mataron; reputáronse 500 los muertos.
>
> (Among us served a tercio of Englishmen who were present in every battle; the trenches were so full of corpses, our men and theirs, that one's feet didn't touch the ground, stepping on the ones who died in retreat and the ones who were killed there; the dead numbered around five hundred.) (506)

These brief lines provide an indelible image of human destruction coupled with a quantitative assessment of the damage. Later, Toral goes on to describe the impersonal nature of trench warfare, as the trenches of the enemy slowly approached their own until the distance between the two lines literally became a stone's – or a grenade's – throw away:

> Ibase poco a poco con las trincheras; cada palmo que se adelantaba costaba mucha gente … estaban cerca las del enemigo de las nuestras, que las granadas se echaban con la mano de una en otras, y con ellos hacían daño notable, porque en cualquier miembro o parte donde daba le hacía pedazos.
>
> (It went little by little with the trenches. Each handspan that we advanced cost many lives … the enemy's trenches were so close to ours, that grenades were

> thrown by hand from one to the other, and this caused considerable damage, because whatever limb or part they touched shattered to pieces.) (506)

Though Toral does not pause to meditate on the honourability of this faceless mode of warfare, his description here and elsewhere makes clear that he regards the trenches as, at the very least, grossly inefficient. In a theme that is repeated throughout the *Relación*, Toral condemns the lack of correspondence between the enormous amount of lost labour (and lives) in Flanders, in comparison with the territory won. Toral's desire to bring effort and reward into equilibrium – as seen in the *Relacion*'s appeal for the soldier's own recompense – is manifested in his professional concern for strategy and provisioning, both procedures for maximizing gains while attenuating losses.

In addition to technical descriptions of the city's fortifications and eyewitness accounts of some of the individual skirmishes that culminated in the defeat of Spínola's army, Toral's evocation of the gruesome conditions of war would likely have been of interest to readers who encountered this episode in the miscellany as well as in the *Relación*. This siege, in which an army of just over twenty thousand appeared to evaporate in just a few months, prompted a serious reconsideration of Spain's policy in the Netherlands, with the final result that Spain opted to pursue a largely defensive strategy (G. Parker 180; Israel 9). As Jonathon Israel describes it, "the setback caused a considerable shock in Madrid and indeed provoked a marked reaction against the whole concept of using the army to put pressure on the republic ... The Council of State reckoned that in Flanders in 1622 it had spent to no purpose some 3,700,000 ducats from the Spanish and Italian revenues" (10). The enormous cost of attacking the fortress cities dotting the Dutch Republic, as well as the heavy casualties, disease, and desertion that cut down the Army of Flanders by almost half, marked a turning point in Hapsburg policy towards the Netherlands, which allowed Spain to more fruitfully pursue other political and territorial objectives elsewhere. Toral's account of death and dismemberment in the trenches, as well as his tacit condemnation of the terrible conditions and lack of provisions, only confirms that this decision had been correct, if belated. Toral concludes the episode with a disheartening observation:

> Se tuvo noticia que el enemigo con todo su poder venía por tierra a socorrer aquella plaza, y antes que llegase nos partimos nosotros; caminamos a media noche; este fue el fin del sitio de Bergas, donde se colige desta y el de la Inclusa y de la navegación de la Isla, a que las cosas de España se consideran su fin por el principio.

(We heard that the enemy with all of his might was coming by land to aid that plaza, and before they arrived we left; we marched at midnight; this was the end of the siege of Bergen op Zoom; one gathers from this and from the siege of Sluis, and the navigation of the Island, that the matters of Spain are over before they've begun.) (508)

Toral's final analysis of the unsuccessful siege is marked by bitterness; in invoking the midnight retreat under the shameful cover of darkness, Toral alludes to the dishonour of defeat. And by referring to the battle together with its initial, equally ill-fated phases, Toral is able to extrapolate a frank and wide-ranging critique: not only the projects of the Army of Flanders but also all of "las cosas de España" are potentially condemned to failure at inception (508). The *Relación* goes on to demonstrate the accuracy of this prognosis as the same faulty planning characterizes the joint Spanish-Portuguese forces deployed in the East Indies, even as the backdrop shifts from the marshes of the Low Countries to the torrid zone off the African coast.

This change in scenery is accompanied by a change in the command structure; now as a captain charged with escorting the new viceroy of the East Indies to his post, Toral has more responsibility but less actual fighting to accomplish. Accordingly, this portion of the *Relación* is more descriptive and focuses on evoking the dangers and privations of the voyage, along with the disposition of the cities and ports along the way. Cassol suggests that this shift in emphasis can be understood as a shift in genre, from an autobiography focused on the author's military service to an example of travel writing. Though these episodes may share the characteristics of travel writing, as Cassol goes on to note, Toral's point of view is always that of a soldier, and his descriptions therefore tend to include information about the fortifications or strategic value of the locations he visits (143). Similarly, when Toral is not describing a particular place, he reports on the process of travel in practical terms. Beginning with the port of departure, Toral gives the latitude and longitude of each major stop along the way, stressing the effect of climate and provisions on the passengers' health. As the fleet draws near to the equator, the days become marked by suffocating heat and stillness, and many become ill. Although the difficulties of navigating in the torrid zone were well known, Toral indicates that, once again, poor planning contributed to the human wastage:

Con las grandes calmas y mudanza de clima enfermó casi toda la gente; ayudaba a esta la poca comodidad con que se navegaba, porque en una nao iban seiscientas personas, todas debajo de cubierta, salvo los que se acomodaban en los castillos de proa y popa, y el calor de la gente de unos con otros, los calores grandes del sol, la falta de agua y mal acondicionados bastimentos, como tocino salado, sardinas y pescado, y lo recio del vino que también abrasaba los hígados, todo fuego y provocativo para beber y causar una sed inaccesible, fue todo esto causa de que muriese mucha gente.

(From the great stillness and the change in climate almost everyone became ill; this was exacerbated by the little comfort that we had in sailing, because a single ship was packed with six hundred people, all below deck, except those who lodged in the forecastle and sterncastle, and the heat of the close quarters, the great heat of the sun, the lack of water and poorly prepared food, like salty bacon, sardines, and fish, and the harshness of the wine that also burned the liver, all fire and incitement to drink with an unquenchable thirst, all of this caused many people to die.) (512)

Toral paints a nightmarish picture of the days in the torrid zone. Plagued by scurvy, the ship's passengers grow weak, begin to lose their teeth, and finally die in droves; eventually the planks are covered with the blood of the dead and dying: "los bordos de las embarcaciones estaban de sangre que por ellos se echaba, rojos, que a lo largo, desde otras embarcaciones, se conocía el estar la tablazón cubierta de sangre" (the shipboards were red with the blood they lost, so that, from a distance, from the other ships, it was known that the planks were covered in blood) (512). Along with many others, Toral became so weak that he was briefly pronounced dead. In this intermediate stage in the voyage, in the time and space preceding landfall and the eventual encounter with the enemy, Toral describes how, at the height of his illness, he came to a realization:

¡Oh, qué buenos que somos cuando enfermos, como en esta ocasión, entré en cuento conmigo, y conocí cuántos trabajos nos da quien grandezas nos promete! ¡Cómo trocara el estado en que me hallaba, no por lo que el Virrey me había prometido, mas por el del más miserable del que estaba en tierra!

(Oh, how good we are when we are ill, as on this occasion, I reckoned with myself, and I comprehended how many trials are given us by those who promise great things! How I would exchange the circumstances in which I found myself, not for what the viceroy had promised me, but for those of the most unfortunate person on earth!) (512)

In this, one of the few exclamatory passages in the *Relación*, the voyager's encounter is substituted by the pilgrim's enlightenment, brought about by what appears to be a deathbed examination of conscience. Curiously, the *desengaño* (disenchantment) that Toral recounts is not of a transcendently spiritual quality, as might be expected. While the first exclamation might be understood as Toral's acceptance of the earthly trials and tribulations that prepare individuals for the afterlife, the second phrase anchors Toral's desires in the present. Though the experience of illness has revised these desires – from the *grandezas* falsely promised in reward for his service to the simple wish to be elsewhere, even if poor – Toral's aspirations are resolutely worldly. In keeping with this practical sensibility, Toral ends this passage as in his description of the siege of Bergen op Zoom: the episode concludes with the numbers, informing the reader that the torrid zone is forty-seven degrees wide, and that in traversing it the fleet lost five hundred men (512).

In a few brief lines, the *Relación* demonstrates the author's grasp of geography and meteorology as necessary tools for both navigation and logistics; while avoiding the torrid zone was impossible, Toral indicates that the voyage would have been more successful with the proper provisions, particularly adequate supplies of food and water. Without assigning blame to any specific person (perhaps because an accusation against Noroña, the viceroy, would have been discarded, based on their difference in rank and their mutual antagonism), Toral appears to attribute the losses to impersonal, bureaucratic forces as much beyond his control as the searing sun at the equator. Nevertheless, the choice of a single vivid detail – the ships with their bloodstained planks visible from afar – adds weight to Toral's testimony and immediacy to his complaint.

In Cassol's estimation, the passages dedicated to Toral's experiences at sea, particularly the harrowing voyage from Portugal to Mozambique, constitute the finest example of writing in the text ("Entre historia" 309). Certainly, as we have seen in the episode above, the combination of empirical information, visual detail, and autobiographical exposure lend authority and interest to the account. From the sweltering conditions in the South Atlantic to the heavy winds and rain of the Indian Ocean, Toral portrays the atmospheric effects and the reactions of his fellow passengers in dramatic detail. The tempest encountered by the fleet as they approach the Cape of Good Hope is recalled in an arresting series of images that further suggest the tropes of the travelogue:

> Corrían algunas veces vientos tan recios que levantaban unas sierras de mar, que ellas mismas subían la nave hasta los cielos, y luego las mismas

> le bajaban a lo profundo de un valle que formaban dos sierras opuestas; parecía que la una, venciendo con sus olas a la otra que sostenía la nave, la quería tragar y caer sobre la plaza de armas, y cuando con violencia venía sobre la nave la volvía a subir al cielo, con estas admiraciones tan costosas a la experiencia, tan pesadas a la vista, fuimos llegando al Cabo de Buena Esperanza.
>
> (Sometimes the winds blew so strongly that they lifted up mountains out of the ocean; they raised the boat to the heavens, and then dropped it to the depths of the valley formed by two opposing precipices; it seemed that one mount, conquering with its waves the other, wanted to swallow it and crash upon the middle of the upper deck, and with violence come upon the ship causing it to rise again to the sky; with these wonders, so costly to experience, so oppressive to the sight, we made our way to the Cape of Good Hope.) (513)

The topographical metaphor – the heaving sea throwing up successively larger and deeper mountains and valleys – indicates Toral's literary skill; likewise, the anaphora of the last line reflects his characteristic economy of expression, as its brief repetition manages to communicate both the passengers' distress and the long duration of the storm. Beyond the inclusion of this episode either to maintain readers' suspenseful attention or elicit their sympathy, Normand Doiron has suggested that descriptions of storms at sea are an integral part of early modern travelogues (163). According to Doiron, regardless of the veracity of such accounts, stories of storms at sea occur with such persistence that they are practically obligatory in the travel literature of the period (170). In the persistence of such stories Doiron perceives an element of ritual; in describing the voyager's helpless confrontation with the forces of Providence or nature, storm narratives point to the ontological and eschatological uncertainties to unfold over the course of the journey. Passengers are faced not only with their own death but with "la fin du temps" (168), as the confusion brought about by the storm prefigures the new maps and revised histories resulting from the voyage of discovery: "La confusión, notamment celle de la mer et du ciel, le désordre et souvent la discorde que suscite la tempête constituent alors des cas extrêmes de la diversité que les voyageurs découvrent partout dans la nature et dans les moeurs" (The confusion, especially that of the sea and the sky, the disorder and often the discord that the storm arouses constitute extreme cases of the kinds of diversity that travellers discover both in nature and customs) (169). Indeed, as the *Relación* follows Toral back to relative safety on land, it becomes clear that the violence of the storm foreshadows the soldier's chaotic experiences in Africa and India under the viceroy's command. And yet it is not a confrontation with the inexplicable codes of behaviour adopted by an exotic Other that prompts Toral to self-examination; instead, it is his poor treatment at the hands of the viceroy and, later, his fortuitous rescue at the hands of Muslims and Jews that inspires him to exclaim "¡Sea Dios alabado que todas las naciones hizo capaces de razón!" (Praise God, who made all nations capable of reason!) (540).[12]

In addition to the thematic and narrative elements of travel writing sketched above, the *Relación* reveals an affinity for the early modern travelogue's empirical mode of description. While travel writing and historiography are now generally accepted as two divergent modes of organizing knowledge, the early modern period established no such clear distinction. First because, much like autobiography, "travel writing" was not defined as a genre; for this reason, the term refers to a necessarily capacious category, encompassing any text that emphasizes descriptions of foreign lands and their inhabitants. In an age when most travel was motivated by political, military, or mercantile concerns, such descriptions often take on the dimensions of history. In fact, Toral's portrayal of the architectural features of Hormuz Island in the Persian Gulf and Diu Fort on the western coast of India were excerpted in the volumes of *Sucesos*, indicating that contemporary readers were as interested in first-hand depictions of important battles as they were in acquiring knowledge of the exotic corners (or former outposts) of the empire. This desire for information drove the reception of both historical writing and the array of texts containing topographic, chorographic, anthropological, and ethnographic details gleaned by travelling abroad. In tracing the genealogy of "sightseeing," Judith Adler notes that the ascendance of "eyewitness" accounts over "hearsay" in judicial contexts mirrors the preference for the eye over the ear expressed in sixteenth- and seventeenth-century travel sermons (11). As Adler puts it, in the early modern period "auricular knowledge and discourse, identified with traditional authority, Aristotelianism and the Schoolmen, are devalued in favour of an 'eye' believed to yield direct, unmediated, and personally verified experience" (11). As Anna Suranyi notes, the seventeenth century's emphasis on the traveller's "I/eye" laid the groundwork for the following century's "scientific and classificatory projects that evolved into the new scientific disciplines of biology, 'race,' and natural history, [and] the political discourses of modern nationalism" (20). In describing and classifying the people and places they encountered, early modern travellers engaged in a process of representation that created the category of the observed Other, and in so doing engendered their own identities. According to Mary Louise Pratt, beginning in the early modern period, travellers' accounts "textually [produce] the Other without an explicit anchoring in the observing self" ("Scratches" 139–40). Put differently, the Other is a fantasy of the objective "eye/I" who is unaware of the limitations of his perspective. Though, as Pratt indicates, much of the literature of discovery represents native populations in this fashion, the *Relación* is striking for the way in which it avoids this discourse of the Other.

Although Toral traverses a relatively well-known path as he moves up the western coast of India, through present-day Pakistan, Iran, Iraq, Syria, and Turkey on his way back to Spain, his account bears a certain relationship to those of travellers to the Americas. While the first records of the discovery and conquest of the New World invoked fabulous riches and either unimaginably docile or savage indigenous inhabitants, later records focused on the prosaic realities of colonial administration. Joan-Pau Rubiés charts this evolution from "the medieval sense of the marvellous" that structured the accounts of the first colonial explorers, to what he terms "the discovery of the futile" in colonial texts, as the projects of evangelization, imperial expansion, and economic growth proved to be difficult to reconcile (76). The sense of futility first made evident in the summary of the siege of Bergen op Zoom is heightened in two episodes following Toral's discharge from the viceroy's command; in contrast to the perception of failure identified by Rubiés in the documents of colonial consolidation, as Toral makes his way alone and on foot back to Madrid, he confronts the disappointment of imperial ambitions as he encounters human and material reminders of Spain in the unfamiliar landscape beyond the empire's borders.

The first encounter is recorded in Toral's admiring description of the Persian city of Isfahan. Situated on one of the key trade routes to Asia, at the time of Toral's arrival this thriving metropolis was both the new capital of the Safavid Empire and one of the largest cities in the world, notable for its riches and its remarkable architectural features. Yet Toral only briefly mentions the famous network of boulevards and bridges connecting the different parts of the city; most striking to him is the city's cultural and religious diversity, including enclaves of Greek Orthodox Christians and Roman Catholics. In addition to the churches and convents associated with the Eastern Church, Toral notes the presence of three Catholic religious orders: Portuguese Augustinians supported by the king of Spain, Italian Discalced Carmelites maintained by the pope, and French Capuchins provided for by King Louis XIII. In this way, these orders with their different missions all function as peaceful representatives of a warring Europe. In addition to the assortment of religious practitioners in the city, including a variety of Christian religious orders, Muslims, Jews, and the Persians themselves, described only as "herejes en respecto de los turcos y de la ley de Mahoma" (heretics with respect to the Turks and the law of Mohammad) (538), Toral indicates the cultural differences among the city's inhabitants and visitors as seen in their various items of clothing. While cultural conformity was required by law in Spain, through legislation regulating dress and language, Toral describes Isfahan as a kaleidoscope of sartorial style. This diversity is both a product and condition of the city's status as a commercial metropolis: "porque los persianos no tienen otra ganancia ni el Rey otra renta que la del comercio … por esto pueden pasar por su tierra de todas naciones como andan vestidos a su uso" (because the Persians have no other profits nor their King any other income than that of commerce … for this reason, people from all nations can pass through their land dressed according to their own custom) (537). In the midst of this heterogeneous, seemingly apolitical (at least with respect to the conflicts in Europe), and profit-oriented city, Toral comes upon a startling monument. In the centre of Isfahan's famously wide central plaza, newly completed at the time of his visit, Toral finds the remnants of Spanish artillery captured in the English-Safavid occupation of Hormuz Island:

> La plaza es muy grande y espaciosa, y en ella tiene más de veinte piezas, medios cañones, todos labrados en España y llevados de Ormuz, que de allí sacó cuando la ganó, y hoy los tiene por trofeo y señal de su grandeza, con todos sus letreros de los fundidores y Generales de la artillería en cuyo tiempo se hicieron, con las armas reales, que yo vi y leí con harto dolor de mi corazón.
>
> (The plaza is very large and spacious, and in it there are more than twenty pieces, half cannons, all forged in Spain and taken from Hormuz when they captured it, and now they have them as a trophy and a mark of their greatness, with the names of the smelters and Generals of the artillery from when they were made, along with the royal arms, which I saw and read with much pain in my heart.) (537–8)

In 1622, while Toral was occupied with the unsuccessful siege in Flanders, the Portuguese outpost at Hormuz Island was taken by joint Anglo-Persian forces eager to control the flow of trade in the Persian Gulf. The island had been a Portuguese possession for over one hundred years, and was therefore held by the Spanish monarchy as part of the Iberian Union (Ruthven and Nanji 80–3). Toral's surprise and sense of dislocation at encountering the fortress's cannons far from their intended place gives way to melancholy; in the context of Isfahan's central plaza, the once-powerful weapons have become a souvenir of Spanish destruction while the high-born names engraved on them are legible only as a list of shame. As this passage makes clear, for Toral the most unsettling aspect of his travels is not meeting with an exotic and inscrutable Other; instead, it is his encounter with a vision of imperial failure that provokes nostalgia and regret. Following this expression of emotion, Toral quickly reverts to descriptive and empirical language, concluding the passage on Isfahan with a brief line on its walls and disposition: "Las murallas de Ispam son de tierra con algunos cubos huecos, a trechos, está en 34° de altura de la parte del Norte; esto es, Ispam" (The walls of Isfahan are made of earth with a few empty cubes, in sections; it is at 34 degrees latitude; this is Isfahan) (538).

While Toral's awareness of the significance of the events he had witnessed is indicated in his mode of historical exposition, the passages of the *Relación* dedicated to travel (rather than battle) record moments of realization and self-recognition; in traversing the space between his stated destinations, Toral's encounters with illness, death, and imperial failure are elaborated in the language of interiority, including a deathbed self-accounting ("entré en cuento conmigo" [512]) and pain felt "de mi corazón" (538). Implicit in episodes written in the registers of history and personal testimony is a critique that Toral makes explicit in moments that most clearly connect to the concerns of contemporary military treatises. The works of early modern military science comprise one among the many textual models and resources that were available to literate soldiers of the period. These treatises, which arose simultaneously with developments in military technology and strategy, served a didactic as well as a persuasive function; in addition to providing technical information on fortification and artillery, they also argued for new protocols of leadership (González de León, "Doctors" 63). These protocols – and the gendered language in which they are embedded – are echoed throughout the *Relación* as Toral repeatedly calls for promotion based on combat experience while exemplifying the qualities necessary for command.

According to Fernando González de León, the first half of the sixteenth century witnessed a proliferation of Italian works on military science; the defining characteristics of these works include "a scientific approach to warfare … and a shift in military ethics, away from the chivalric code of honor, towards a more ruthless and utilitarian moral system perhaps best exemplified by Niccolò Machiavelli's *Art of War*

(1521)" ("Doctors" 62–3). In contrast to the early sixteenth-century renaissance of military science in Italy, it was only with the advent of the Eighty Years' War in the second half of the century that Spanish contributions to the genre began to multiply. Faced with technological and strategic challenges that altered the social composition of the army, military theorists began to develop new guidelines for all aspects of warfare; in light of what was perceived to be a decline in standards at the highest level of the Army of Flanders, a significant number of these treatises attempt to establish the qualifications and experience required for promotion (64). By determining the character and education of its leaders, the army – which, particularly in Flanders, faced problems of discipline at least partially brought on by a lack of economic resources – could become more efficient and effective. In this way, as González de León notes, "Flanders … thus became Spain's (and indeed Europe's) academy of military science" (64).

The treatises that the *Relación* most obviously resembles belong to the genre of the *espejo militar* or portrait of the ideal officer. Modelled on the *espejo de príncipe,* didactic works defining the virtues and obligations of the monarch, these treatises were most often written by seasoned military professionals and were quite popular, judging from the various editions and translations that have survived (González de León, "Doctors" 64–5). One of the most striking characteristics of such works is their promotion of practical skills. Bernardino de Escalante's *Diálogos del arte militar* (1583) outlines the necessary knowledge for the successful *maestro del campo,* or tercio commander; according to Escalante, these officers should know to "combatir una ciudad y defenderla, o hazer guerra en campaña, dar batalla a los enemigos, hazer correrías, retirar escaramuzas, hazer puentes sobre ríos, y fortificarse en campañas, y conducir Artillería, y otras muchas cosas" (attack and defend a city, or make war on campaign, give battle to the enemy, perform raids, retreat from skirmishes, erect bridges over rivers, and to fortify the army on campaign, to conduct artillery, and many other things) (56; qtd. in González de León 68n35). In addition to dominating the different fields of war (in offensive or defensive positions, in city sieges or open country), the ideal officer has basic surveying, engineering, and logistical skills. While the military thought of previous centuries had stressed the nobility and elite education of the officer class, treatises like Escalante's emphasize "el arte militar" as the practical application of geographical, mathematical, and historical knowledge (67). For Escalante as well as many other military professionals of the period, skills such as these could only be acquired in the crucible of war (68); for this reason, they protested against the prevailing practice of promoting officers based on nobility rather than merit, a tradition that Toral, too, denounces.

Toral, as a member of a proud but impoverished *hidalgo* family, concurs with the ideas propagated in the ideal officer treatises, insisting on various occasions in the *Relación* that there is no substitute for battlefield experience. As we have seen, the concept of experience is integral to Toral's self-presentation; in a relatively brief and varied text, the word *experiencia* appears twenty-four times, and the notions of witnessing and participating bolster the authority of the *Relacion* as both historical and personal testimony. Toral alludes to the painful imprint of experience on the soldier's flesh; in describing his time in the Army of Flanders, Toral states: "dos años que había dormido con la gola puesta, que con el asiento de las armas y de la pica la tenía señalada en los hombros" (two years I had slept with my gorget on, and with the weight of arms and pike it was imprinted on my shoulders) (508–9). This reference to the way his armour had (mis)shaped his body is not a complaint; instead, Toral suggests that experiences such as these are, or should be, part of the ideal officer's education.[13]

The value that Toral places upon experience – and the disdain with which he regards noble but unseasoned officers – becomes explicit in an episode following a failed attack off the coast of Africa. Not only was the attempt beyond the forces and abilities of the viceroy's men, it was also under the inexpert command of don Francisco de Mora, who Toral describes as "muy buen caballero, cortés y bien hablado, amigo de hacer todo bien, fácil en la persuasión, muy palatino y cortesano" (a very fine gentleman, courteous and well spoken, he liked to do everything well, easy upon persuasion, a man for the palace and court) – and yet completely ill-prepared to perform the task he had been given (532). In stark contrast to Mora, whose qualities seem more suited to the court than to a combat zone, Toral expounds on the kinds of expertise necessary to wage war, including technical as well as social skills, as leadership requires "el gobernar y sujetar con tanta opresión tanta cantidad de gente, de tan varios naturales" (the governance and conquest with such oppression such a number of people, of so many different temperaments) (532). All of these skills taken together comprise "el arte militar," which Toral vigorously maintains can only be acquired through experience:

> El arte militar … no se aprende en una sala cerrada de libros, ni en la urbanidad de la corte; más apréndese en una campaña y otra, y en un sitio y otro sitio, con un trabajo y otro, arriesgando una y cien veces la

vida, ya con el trabajo personal ya con el riesgo de perderla, teniendo una sagacidad profunda, un natural claro, una privación de toda pasión.

(Military art … is not learned from books in a closed room, nor in the urbane atmosphere of the court; rather it is learned in one campaign and another, in one siege and another, in one trial and another, risking life one and one hundred times, in hard labour and risk, acquiring a deep sagacity, a clear temperament, a lack of all passion.) (532)

Much like the military treatises of the period, this passage presents an affinity for the Neostoic virtues of fortitude, temperance, and rational deliberation (González de León, "Doctors" 70). Based on Justus Lipsius's *De Constantia* (1584) and associated, in Spain, with the writings of Francisco de Quevedo, Neostoicism represented a masculine ideal characterized by impassivity (*apatheia*) and self-mastery as a means of confronting an inconstant fortune. According to Pavla Miller, Lipsius's writing produced a new mode of masculinity in which self-discipline became intimately associated with a more robust state and a powerful military: "[The] new man would go beyond the Christianity of the Middle Ages to embrace the old Roman values, and demonstrate the importance of rationality in character, action, and thought. In the fortunes and misfortunes of political life he must retain his constancy, follow reason, curb his natural instincts, and be ready to act and fight. He must be actively involved in life but maintain an inner emotional and intellectual detachment" (117). Toral's opening statement in the passage on "el arte militar" – that the soldier's education occurs not in the enclosures of the library or court, but in the open field (532) – indicates that he understands military virtue to participate in a gendered economy very similar to that described by the Neostoics. While the *Relación* never explicitly claims these virtues for the author, it does recount his long record "en una campaña y otra, y en un sitio y otro sitio," from the sieges at Flanders to the raids on the African coast. Furthermore, from Toral's analysis of the failure of the siege at Bergen op Zoom to his evaluation of the poor provisions aboard the viceroy's fleet, his interpretation of events demonstrates "un conocimiento de las causas," a capacity for insight and discernment. Most importantly, the ideal officer's "privación de total pasión" reflects Toral's rational mastery over his emotions and desires; accordingly, the *Relación* does not register any unseemly instances of fear, anger, or love. Instead, the prevailing sentiment of the text is a sadness verging on melancholy, a productive passion associated with contemplation rather than brash action.[14]

Although Toral never explicitly defines his own virtues in these words, his identification with the perfect officer is established indirectly, both in this abstract representation as well as in the biographical sketch he includes of his mentor, the Portuguese admiral Ruy Frere da Andrada. As Toral notes towards the end of his description of "el arte militar," experience is particularly important in developing a dispassionate disposition that allows the ideal officer to confront the vagaries of fortune. For nine months of his tour under the viceroy, Toral was dispatched to the command of Ruy Frere da Andrada, a Machiavellian figure whose abundant experience and prudent impassivity made a significant impression. Toral begins his profile of the admiral by indicating his experience and practical knowledge: "era uno de los soldados más bien entendidos que había en la India; tenía larga noticia y experiencia en las cosas de aquellas partes" (he was one of the most expert soldiers in all of India; he had much knowledge and experience in the ways of those parts) (522). An intellectual man, the admiral's greatest friend and counsellor – according to Toral – was the first-century Roman historian Tacitus, and he preferred to exercise his mind over physical exertion. By cultivating an inscrutable affect and an inflexible rule, Ruy Frere inspired obedience. His leadership was accomplished by a virtuosic self-mastery that extended beyond restraining his own passions to dissimulation: "Hacía particular estudio en el disimular, tanto, que lo que parecía que amaba, aborrecía, y lo que parecía que aborrecía, amaba; procuraba no darse por entendido de muchas cosas" (He made a particular study of dissimulation, such that what it appeared he loved, he hated, and what it appeared he hated, he loved; he managed to act as if he didn't understand many things) (522). This purposeful opacity extended from his personal preferences to his official correspondence. Although it must have been exasperating for Toral at the time, he recounts with admiration how Ruy Frere's orders were always written cryptically, "de suerte que al bien y al mal dejaba siempre una aldaba de que asirse" (so that for better or worse he always left himself a way out) (522).

In addition to his shrewdness, Ruy Frere's iron self-discipline inspired both fear and respect in his men; the Admiral rarely drank alcohol and never permitted himself to mingle informally with subordinates. Though he was generous and would happily grant the petitions of deserving soldiers, he could be cruel. Toral recounts how Ruy Frere was swift to impose the harshest penalties on those who disobeyed him, including beheading an officer whose only crime had been to spare a female captive from death. While admitting the Admiral's remorselessness, Toral explains:

> Tenía opinión de que el temor hacía más bien las cosas que el amor; decía, que el temor traía consigo miedo y respeto; y el amor facilidad; y que de estos dos extremos, el temor era el mejor para conseguir cosas de trabajo y dificultoso; fundábalo en que ninguno tenía tanto amor que sobrepujase al propio, y que siempre antepone su particular primero.
>
> (He held the opinion that fear was more effective than love; he said that fear brought dread and respect; and love a quality of overfamiliarity; and of these two extremes, fear was better to acquire hard and difficult things; he based this on the idea that no one had so much love that it would overcome his own self-interest, and that one would always put himself oneself first.) (522)

Though Toral's portrait of Ruy Frere betrays his own misgivings about some of the Admiral's methods – indicated by the choice of modifiers like "cruel" (522) and "más política que cristiana" (more political than Christian) (522) – his respect for the man is evident. Toral excuses the length of the passage dedicated to Ruy Frere by noting, "de los que he conocido el tiempo que he servido al Rey, era él que tenía más enseñanza y daba más admiración en el modo de gobernar" (of those that I have met during the time I have served the King, he was the one who had the most learning and was most worthy of admiration in his way of governing) (523).[15]

Both Toral's description of the ideal officer and his pen portrait of Ruy Frere indicate the "tactical uses of Neostoicism" that González de León perceives in early modern military treatises ("Doctors" 70). By aligning himself with a mode of masculinity associated with men of rational action and deliberation, whose merit was based on conduct rather than birth, Toral presents himself as an appropriate candidate for a position of responsibility. Indeed, while in the *Relación* Toral's experience and examples are drawn from his military career, his perspective is compatible with that of the *letrado* class, the educated functionaries who increasingly advocated for advancement based on the quality of their work rather than nobility, and who espoused an ideal of masculinity rooted in self-discipline (Martínez Góngora, *El hombre* 210–11).

In addition to Toral's identification with the self-discipline shared by the ideal officer and the perfect *letrado*, his cultivation of the registers of historical reportage and travel narrative, as well as his mathematical and geographical knowledge, demonstrate his versatility and worthiness for reward. Yet at the end of the *Relación* the solid certainty that Toral has espoused throughout seems to melt away as he contemplates an unfavourable future. Following an interview at court in which he does not manage to receive recompense for his service, Toral suspects that the relationship between work and reward – justice itself, as he says several times – has ruptured. The economic crisis that manifests itself in the denial of the soldier's request becomes, at the end of the *Relación*, an epistemological crisis, signalled in the stuttering repetition of the verb *saber*: "Lo que sé de cierto con tanta experiencia que no sé más que al principio, y esto es evidencia, que pues no he sabido para mí, ¿qué puedo saber estando hoy más lleno de trabajos y con más necesidad, y menos fuerza para poderlo buscar?" (What I know with certainty on the basis of so much experience is that I don't know any more than I did at the beginning; and this is the proof, given that I have not known for myself, what can I know today being more full of travails and with more need, and less strength to seek knowledge?) (547). The discourses of knowledge and experience so painstakingly elaborated throughout the text collapse here into an expression of helplessness and uncertainty. The Neostoic impulse to master one's circumstances through the application of reason leads only to a single, dark assurance with which the text concludes: "Que por mi se puede decir, según tantos trabajos he pasado y peligros de la vida, y al presente en más necesidad, que el día siguiente siempre es el peor" (As for me, one could say, in light of so many trials and dangers, and my present state of need, the next day is always the worst) (547). For a soldier like Toral, who had risen as high as his merit could take him, embracing melancholy is both a final critique of his circumstances and an embrace of an alternative model of self-worth, an ideal of martial honour that, like the Neostoics, rejects both frenzied action and heroic Christian suffering, preferring the consolation of contemplation. Suffering for Toral would appear to have neither exchange value nor redemptive value.

The pessimism of these final lines indicates the failure that unites the autobiographical projects of Diego Suárez Corvín and Domingo Toral y Valdés. While fragments of Toral's autobiography would circulate as historical writing, stripped of any personal details, the soldier himself seems to have slipped from history. Whether his petitions were granted is unknown. Needless to say, Suárez's dream of assigning the North African frontier a newly significant status in Spanish historiography and imperial policy would never materialize. Unsuccessful at securing patronage, Suárez's monumental, unfinished manuscript contains a blank space where he hoped to include the year of publication. The distinctive strategy of self-fashioning adopted in both texts, though it may not have yielded any immediate material benefits, nevertheless allowed the authors to express a sense of their own significance and leave a record of labour that they feared was otherwise ephemeral.

Chapter Three

Spiritual Honour and Religious Authority

Completed in 1603 and licensed for publication the following year, Jerónimo de Pasamonte's *Vida y trabajos* opens with an epigraph that simultaneously signals the author's hermeneutic intent while visually evoking his wounded and infirm body: "Dicen en nuestra España que no hay mejor maestro que el bien acuchillado" (They say in our Spain that there is no better teacher than he who is well experienced) (5).[1] Covarrubias's *Tesoro de la lengua castellana* records a version of the adage under the entry for "acuchillar" (literally, to slash) and interprets it as extolling the superiority of experiential knowledge as it is incised into the subject. This homespun proverb, which appears in a variety of contemporary texts, is emblematic of an age in which authority was increasingly invested in experience.[2] As discussed in chapter 2, the early modern emphasis on personal experience is reflected in the realms of historiography and military science; likewise, this emphasis is manifested in a heightened interest in eyewitness testimony, experimentation, and affective piety, as well as in the unprecedented number of autobiographical texts produced in the period. In the case of the soldier and would-be cleric Jerónimo de Pasamonte, the proverb serves to foreground his injured body as both epistemological site and symbol of expert authority. Pasamonte, who was felled by gunshot in the Ottoman reconquest of La Goleta, describes in his *Vida* almost two decades spent in captivity and the subsequent years of penury following his release. Written in response to accusations of adultery and heresy levelled against him by his wife's family, Pasamonte's *Vida* mounts a multilayered self-defence emphasizing the author's sexual purity and spiritual integrity. The scars of his experience – from the gunshot at La Goleta to the beatings he endured as a galley slave and, then, the attempts at poisoning and other attacks on his person and honour after his release – are a repeated motif throughout the text. While the wounds sustained in Turkish captivity are presented as signs of special discernment, a spiritual knowledge acquired through somatic means, the assaults against his physical integrity and reputation are framed as a debt of honour that he argues should be paid, not in heaven, but on earth.

Like many of the soldiers swelling the ranks of the Spanish tercios, military service was not Pasamonte's primary vocation. As an orphaned younger son of the Aragonese lower nobility, his social and economic possibilities were circumscribed by what his elder brother chose to endorse and fund. Equally limiting was Pasamonte's poor eyesight, which barred him from undertaking a life of religious study as he would have preferred. Despite having pledged to take the habit and enter a Bernardine monastery at eighteen, when his brother denied him the financial support necessary to follow his monastic inclinations Pasamonte found himself with few other viable options for employment. Shortly thereafter, he enlisted in a company under the command of don Juan de Austria, where his impaired vision was outweighed by his imposing stature, and within days he was sent to Italy. After several years of service throughout the Mediterranean, in 1574 Pasamonte was wounded by gunshot and taken prisoner at the battle of La Goleta. The bullet that tore through his neck and back saved his life; unable to fling himself into a final, suicidal attack against the enemy, Pasamonte was captured and enslaved. During the eighteen years he spent as a captive of the Ottoman Turks he suffered various punishments for his part in unsuccessful uprisings and escape attempts. Upon returning to Christendom in 1592, Pasamonte began a period of spiritual doubt allegedly brought on by his subjection to witchcraft and sexual persecution at the hands of his co-religionists. More than a decade later, the embittered soldier set down the story of his ordeals and dedicated it to two highly placed ecclesiastical officials in Rome, evidently hoping they would exercise their power to punish his enemies and rescue him from a dishonourable domestic situation that he describes as a second captivity.

Denounced as heretical, both the *Vida* and its author were subjected to scrutiny by the Holy Office in Naples. After a period of four months, during which the author and his scribe were called to appear before the tribunal, the text eventually passed Inquisitional censure and was licensed for publication. Nevertheless, as Pasamonte states in his letters of dedication, the *Vida,* like much early modern life writing, was intended for private circulation. Written from a military outpost in Naples to two highly placed Spanish clerics stationed in Rome, the *Vida* represents an aspirational attempt to map the author's position in social space and project his spiritual authority beyond that typically accorded to middle-ranking soldiers. As we will see, an appeal to personal experience is key to this endeavour, as is a reformulation of martial honour that accentuates the virtue of perseverance and the capacity to suffer.

The purpose of Pasamonte's *Vida* is first indicated in the letters prefacing the manuscript, which dedicate the story of his life to Jerónimo Xavierre, master general of the Dominican Order, and Bartolomé Pérez de Nueros, a Jesuit who had helped to organize Pasamonte's release from captivity more than a decade earlier. In these letters of dedication, Pasamonte frames the autobiographical material of the text as merely illustrative of his larger objective, which is to call on the Church as represented by Xavierre and Pérez de Nueros to judge the sins described therein. Excusing himself as "unworthy" (5) to pen a longer introduction, Pasamonte briefly explains that the motive of his autobiography is not one of individual desire or personal ambition; instead, he is divinely compelled to write in the service of a greater good. Significantly, the sins that Pasamonte reports are not his own, but rather those of his fellow Catholics, whose spiritual well-being is presented as the sole motive of his writing. In the letter to Xavierre, Pasamonte states: "suplico humilmente por las llagas del Hijo de Dios se dé remedio a tantos daños como hay entre católicos, y sólo por esto he escrito toda mi vida y intención, sin pretender ni haber ninguna vanagloria" (I plead humbly by the wounds of the Son of God for the remedy for the great harms among Catholics, and for this only I have written of my whole life and intention, without claiming or having any vainglory) (5). While the first letter leaves the exact nature of these sins unspecified, in the second letter Pasamonte identifies the transgressions his autobiography will denounce at the same time as he establishes his authority for issuing judgment:

> En el tiempo que he estado entre turcos, moros, judíos y griegos, he visto su total perdición por tratar con ángeles malos, y después que estoy entre católicos ha permitido Su Divina Majestad que yo haya padecido tantas persecuciones por malas artes, que si tengo vida es por la inmensa bondad de Dios. Y he venido en la cuenta cómo la ruina de toda la cristiandad es por dar crédito a estos malos espíritus.
>
> (In the time in which I have been among Turks, Moors, Jews, and Greeks, I have seen their total perdition for communicating with evil angels; and now that I am among Catholics, His Divine Majesty has allowed me to suffer so many persecutions by evil arts that if I am still alive it is only because of the immense goodness of God. And I have come to realize that the ruination of all Christendom is due to giving credit to these evil spirits.) (5)

According to this second letter, it is the sin of witchcraft, doubly debased by its association with Muslim, Jewish, and Greek Orthodox practitioners, that Pasamonte seeks to condemn. Following his disavowal of any self-interested motivation for writing, Pasamonte only barely gestures towards the standard humility topos, concentrating instead on professing his experiential authority as a soldier who has lived faithfully among infidels. Having cited the sin, the text of the autobiography will slowly accumulate proofs taken from the author's life demonstrating the harm perpetrated on the innocent by those dabbling in "malas artes" (5). In this way, the rhetoric of Pasamonte's autobiography, with its detailed demonic as well as earthly torments and barely delineated dark prophecies, and its structure, shaped by a pattern of persecution met by divine justice, is meant to provoke its intended recipients to action. In the face of the evidence amassed in the text, further legitimated by the virtuous representation of the author's life, Xavierre and Pérez de Nueros were evidently meant to recognize the extent to which witchcraft had taken hold among Catholics – especially women – and to punish the guilty by consigning them to the spiritual death of excommunication, while Pasamonte himself might be praised for his steadfastness.

Despite being licensed to print, the manuscript would not be published until the early twentieth century; only since then has the *Vida* been the object of sustained critical interest. In fact, the same supernatural elements that provoked an Inquisitional investigation continue to arouse critical curiosity; most scholars have read the author's persistent recurrence to the supernatural as evidence of a kind of pathology, exceeding the limits of textual decorum and straining the reader's credulity.[3] Revealed in descriptions of the author as "passive and will-less" (Cossío viii), suffering from "a possible loss of mental health due to his moral and physical debilitation" (Pope 131), which in turn manifests in "persecution mania" (Levisi 31), these historical and literary approaches to Pasamonte's *Vida* respond to the autobiography in the register of diagnosis. Pointing to the signs presented by the narrator, many critics have concurred in a negative assessment of the author's mental health, an assessment that accounts for otherwise anomalous features of the text.

How might Pasamonte's intended readership have reacted to the *Vida*? What frameworks would have guided a contemporary reception of this hybrid narrative, part autobiography, part spiritual manifesto, and part judicial accusation? Although no record of the clerics' response has been found, the Inquisitional approval and subsequent preservation of Pasamonte's carefully copied manuscript would seem to indicate the partial success of the narrative. In order to address these questions, this chapter examines the intersection of corporeal discourse and experiential epistemology to show how physical mutilation and illness acquired in military service are rendered legible in this text, as signs of spiritual honour and insight. Here honour corresponds to one of the definitions registered in the *Diccionario de Autoridades*: "estimación y buena fama, que se halla en el sugeto y debe conservar" (esteem and good reputation, which is found in the subject and must be preserved). I argue that the *Vida* represents an attempt to recover a sense of honour that the author fears has been fractured by circumstances beyond his control, as he frames his military experience as key to a superior spiritual identity, beginning with the tale of his captivity.

Pasamonte's account of captivity presents fascinating parallels with that of Miguel de Cervantes, particularly in the daring yet unsuccessful escape attempts both men claim to have coordinated. Born in 1547 and 1553, respectively, both Cervantes and Pasamonte fought in the battles of Lepanto, Navarín, and Tunis, and even served in the same tercio under Miguel de Moncada for a period of eight months (Ríquer 23). Pasamonte, who was among the seven thousand men left behind to guard the fort of La Goleta following the Spanish victory at Tunis in 1573, was captured only a year later when vastly superior Ottoman forces retook Tunis in what was to be the decisive battle in a long history of Spanish and Ottoman disputes over the region. Cervantes was aboard the fleet of ships sent to reinforce the beleaguered Spaniards at La Goleta but, delayed by storms, by the time the fleet arrived it was already too late: the city had fallen and the only survivors were, like Pasamonte, gravely wounded men who were immediately pressed into labour. Years later, in two sonnets and "La historia del cautivo," Cervantes would criticize the failure of the Spanish Crown to protect its interests in North Africa, a strategic error that created the geopolitical conditions for Cervantes's own capture in 1575 when his ship was attacked by Barbary pirates off the coast of Naples.

Although their imprisonment took place in different corners of the Muslim world (Cervantes was held in Algiers, while Pasamonte spent time in all the major ports of the Ottoman-held Mediterranean, including Constantinople and Alexandria), both Pasamonte's *Vida* and many of Cervantes's works are inflected by the trope of captivity.[4] Yet, as Ruth El Saffar has noted, Cervantes's work is characterized by a singular resistance to first-person narratives; even while playing with the themes of the picaresque novel, the typical "I" of Cervantes's narrative speaks not directly to the reader but to other characters within the text (191). Despite this persistent elision of the first-person perspective, several scholars have suggested that the imprint of a specific life event (captivity) on Cervantes's literary production indicates the centrality of the autobiographical form to his work. While the vast and varied array of Cervantes's literary production is of course quite distinct from Pasamonte's *Vida*, both are marked by references to prisons. Cervantes's work is full of captives, from Captain Viedma of "La historia del cautivo" to the kidnapped coastal dwellers of the play *El trato de Argel* and the lovers of *Persiles*, and many of his works take up the question of an ethical response to freedom and its antithesis. María Antonia Garcés and other scholars attribute the frequency of this theme and the authenticity of Cervantes's many fictional representations of life in Muslim captivity to the five years that the author spent as a captive in Algiers. Likewise, images of slavery haunt Pasamonte's *Vida*, both in the descriptions of the heavy chains he was forced to wear while he rowed in the galleys and, less literally, in his suspicion that evildoers had attempted to bend his will into sinning. Although Pasamonte and Cervantes may never have met, or even known of each other's writing (*pace* Ríquer and Martín Jiménez; see note 4), a comparison between the ways these two contemporaries employ the autobiographical event and cultural trope of captivity is illuminating.

The majority of scholars agree that the most clearly autobiographical elements of Cervantes's oeuvre refer to his imprisonment in Algiers; how then did Cervantes, who populated his works with a variety of perspectives, broach the pitfalls and possibilities of the singular, first-person form? As El Saffar has perceptively argued, both the overarching narrative structure and the interpolated stories of the *Quixote* may be read as Cervantes's commentary on the limits of autobiography (192). Referring to Don Quixote's knightly transformation and his wish to inspire a scribe to commemorate his deeds, El Saffar writes that, "to become the subject of narrative ... one must first of all adopt a persona distinct from one's given identity, and one must entrust the narrative that will follow to an Other who turns out to be not only enemy, but who literally writes in an alien tongue" (192). In the *Quixote* one of the guises of the Other is the scribe Cide Hamete, whose manuscript the narrator of the prologue claims to have found and translated. That Don Quixote is produced as a subject of the narrative – not through the direct address of the first-person form, but rather in a palimpsest of memory, inscription, and translation – is integral to El Saffar's claim that the text is a meditation on the nature of writing itself: "As the author makes clear through his multiplication of narrators, translators and scribes, something invariably gets lost in the translation" (192). In the case of autobiography, what cannot be transmitted is the ontological status of the original subject, as the subject of narrative is inevitably shaped by the language used in its creation; but, if the original subject is lost, a new subject arises in his or her place. Accordingly, Cervantes's narrators are never "creators of their own personae" who speak directly to the reader (193). Instead, these characters develop dialogically, especially as they relate their life stories to one another. Captain Viedma's tale, which relates his captivity and miraculous rescue at the hands of a beautiful Moorish woman, culminates in his reunion with his brother, whose position – much like that of Pasamonte's elder brother – indirectly influenced the Captain's capture, as his birth order directed his choice of a dangerous profession. El Saffar cites Cardenio's story as a further example: "Telling his version of himself, however erroneous … has the result of bringing him to the place where he can finally hear himself in the story of another, in the story of the debased and yet somehow redemptive woman his own story cannot name" (194). Seen in this light, both these interpolated stories and their place within the larger structure of the novel illustrate the point that "the story of the self may only be found in the story of the Other or, more radically, that the truth about the self can best be told by that which the self rejects or refuses about itself" (194).

Pasamonte's *Vida* is constructed in opposition to the Cervantine notion that the story of the self is best told through the voice of the Other. In fact, as we will see, by transcribing both the aspersions and adulation spoken by his Muslim masters and sinful co-religionists, he appropriates the voice of the Other (the Afro-Portuguese renegade, the crippled woman, the *morisca*) into his own self-authorizing discourse. Nevertheless, the dialogical structure of Cervantes's first-person narratives is replicated – as it is to a lesser extent in all soldiers' autobiographies – in the written address of Pasamonte's *Vida*, which is formulated with two specific individuals in mind. Unfortunately, unlike in Cervantes's fiction, the effect of Pasamonte's address on his interlocutors, and their response to him, is unknown.

~

While Jerónimo Urrea, in his *Diálogo de la verdadera honra militar*, defined honour for a modern soldier as obedience and bravery, Pasamonte defines honour for the Christian knight as the deference accorded to the virtue of long suffering. Pasamonte first describes himself as a *miles christianus* – a Christian knight, an allegory of virtue elaborated in martial language – in chapter 18, which introduces his account of the years he spent in Muslim captivity: "¡Eya, Pasamonte! Quesistes ser soldado sin pensar que el apóstol San Pablo lo fue, y San Sebastián, y otros sanctos. Y aquellos ilustrísimos Macabeos con tanto derramamiento de sangre defendieron y pelearon" (Hey, Pasamonte! You wanted to be a soldier without thinking that the Apostle Paul was one, and Saint Sebastian too, and other saints. And those illustrious Maccabeans who with such bloodshed defended and fought) (9).[5] By aligning himself with the righteous warriors of the Bible, Pasamonte implies that his original monastic vocation is not at odds with his soldierly occupation, particularly as his religious fervour and physical fortitude – both defining characteristics since early childhood – are tempered in the crucible of captivity. While as a young boy Pasamonte describes himself enduring painful accidents and beatings due to a combination of divine intervention and his own physical toughness, it is during almost two decades of slavery that he will become more than a simple soldier, following in the footsteps of Saint Paul, Saint Sebastian, and the victorious army of Judas Maccabeus. In marked contrast to the chapters describing the periods before and after his enslavement, Pasamonte seems not to suffer from his otherwise ceaseless fevers and ailments during this time. Instead, he finds lesser pains "cured" by the beatings inflicted on him by his Muslim masters. While Pasamonte's body and its experiences of pain still take centre stage in his description of captivity, that body now takes on a new meaning as it becomes the locus of resistance to spiritual temptation and physical violence.

The transformation takes place at the beginning of his enslavement when, facing a long recovery from the gunshot that felled him at the battle of La Goleta, Pasamonte describes how he survived: "a puro palo me hicieron fuerte y se me quitó aquel dolor" (they made me strong with beatings and eventually that pain left me) (9).[6] Here, Pasamonte claims for himself a strength paradoxically derived from the same abuse meant to ensure his obedience. This strength has physical and spiritual dimensions, allowing him to attain a position of authority among his fellow captives while simultaneously steeling his resolve against the temptation of converting. Underpinning Pasamonte's self-portrayal as a holy soldier are his descriptions of the horrors he suffered in captivity. Depicting his body at the mercy of his captors is fraught with danger, however, given that several of the accusations later levelled against him by his mother- and father-in-law strike at the heart of his bodily integrity and masculine honour, as they accuse him of both impotence and failing to provide for his family. Accordingly, Pasamonte shows the integrity of his captive body threatened but never fully compromised, balancing descriptions of the spectacularly symbolic punishments meted out by his masters with triumphant accounts of how he was spared by his own ingenuity as well as by divine intervention.

Pasamonte presents himself as embodying the virtues of strength, courage, sagacity, and loyalty to the Catholic faith and to Spain – all elements most clearly chronicled in the episodes that narrate his multiple attempts to escape from captivity. In a domain occupied almost entirely by men, Pasamonte signals alterity by accentuating ethnic, religious, and national differences; accordingly, traitors and cowards are either "negro," "luterano," "griego," or "francés," a device that plays to the sympathies of the text's two Spanish readers while constructing the author's own identity in opposition to that of heretics. According to the autobiography, almost immediately after his capture Pasamonte devised a plan in which his fellow captives would occupy the castle they had been conscripted to construct, fire on the city from their position, take several boats, and escape to Christendom (10). Despite the months-long preparations required to carry out this daring strategy, Pasamonte and his men are doomed to failure when they are betrayed at the last minute, and one key player (a Greek) loses his nerve. The reprisals exacted for this slave revolt are terrible, despite Ottoman reluctance to diminish the financial resource represented by the captives and their forced labour. Because Pasamonte and his men agree to blame the plot on those who had already died, they mostly escape any further punishment; nevertheless, one slave is turned into a vivid example of the penalty for rebellion, his body dismembered and dispersed around the four corners of the encampment.

This punishment – which graphically illustrates the total destruction of the subject's physical existence both in the present and even for eternity, as dismemberment was widely held to pose a threat to the body's material resurrection after the Final Judgment – does nothing to deter Pasamonte, who describes participating in several more such attempts throughout the years of his captivity. Through his role in formulating and organizing attempts like these (despite their tendency to fail), Pasamonte demonstrates his heroic role as a leader among his fellow captives. The final scheme in which Pasamonte was involved before his legal release from captivity illustrates his position of authority, his courage, and his prudence. Despite spending a year in heavy chains due to his role in a previous uprising, Pasamonte overcomes his initial reservations when he is approached by a group of men who pledge to revolt and escape, but only under his guidance. The men devise a plot to arm themselves, but all is lost when their plans are betrayed by a man whose trustworthiness is suspect on two accounts, as a French Lutheran and as a barber surgeon (the diametrical opposite of Pasamonte, the Spanish Catholic soldier). Pasamonte describes his shrewdness on this occasion, while tacitly warning that those who refuse to heed his advice will suffer the consequences, stating that he had been wary of the man from the beginning, due to his nationality, occupation, and status as a Protestant. When his plea to leave "el luterano" (19) out of the plot is ignored, his collaborators are denounced, sentenced to one thousand lashes, and have their ears cut. Accused as one of the principal orchestrators of the attempt, Pasamonte prepares to die but is miraculously saved when his Muslim master recognizes him as a holy man. Following an exchange with his master, in which Pasamonte sees divine intervention, Pasamonte is exempted from the worst punishments. In one of the few occasions where Pasamonte portrays himself with the boastful swagger of a typical *miles gloriosus* – rather than his more usual stance as a *miles cristianus* – he triumphantly describes his return to the prison where the slaves, including the Frenchman and his accomplices, reside: "Viérades nuestro Pasamonte, que tenía la muerte tragada cuando vino al propalo, entrar por la puerta del baño con la mitad de los palos que los otros y con sus orejas" (See our Pasamonte now, he who was at the brink of death, entering through the dungeon door with half the beatings of the others and with his ears) (23). Directing himself to the Frenchman and his fellow traitors, Pasamonte whips off his hat with a flourish, exposing his intact ears, saying, "aún traigo mis campanas" (I've still got my bells) (23). In episodes such as these, Pasamonte indicates that, as a holy soldier, experiences of pain, privation, and betrayal serve only to harden his resolve in matters temporal and spiritual, particularly as divine justice safeguards the essential integrity of his body and rewards his courage in speaking the truth.

Pasamonte's role as a leader of uprisings and revolts is complemented by his portrayal of the spiritual endurance he evolved during the years of his captivity, finally culminating in his attaining the status of a preacher "en tierra de enemigos de la fe" (in the land of the enemies of the faith) (60), an achievement he returns to at several moments in the autobiography in the course of justifying the position of spiritual authority from which he makes his claims for excommunication. Having spent far longer than the average number of years as a captive, in his autobiography Pasamonte faces the challenge of accounting for his physical and spiritual deeds while in Muslim territory.[7] Much like the corporal discipline that ultimately fortified his body against pain, Pasamonte relates how the limitations of living among Moors and

Turks invigorated him in the practice of his faith; unlike the renegades – Christians who converted to Islam in captivity – Pasamonte describes himself as proudly clinging to his Christian identity, praying, preaching, and acquiring religious books, despite the many material benefits of apostasy.

Had he chosen to convert to Islam, Pasamonte would have earned an exemption from rowing in the galleys, a particularly punishing form of labour that, in the Muslim world as in Christian Europe, was reserved for the least desirable members of society, including criminals and slaves. This, in addition to periods spent building fortifications and other public works on land, is how Pasamonte spent most of the years of his captivity. On one occasion, following the discovery of yet another escape attempt, Pasamonte is accused as the mastermind of the plot, and is shackled and placed in a position of arduous "authority" over his fellow captive rowers, forced to coordinate their efforts in order to move their masters' ship. Surprisingly, Pasamonte does not spend much time detailing the gruelling conditions in the galleys. Towards the end of his captivity, he notes only that when the ship's captain would insist on towing other vessels, thereby increasing the weight pulled by the galley slaves, "era el trabajo tanto y la privación del sueño, que me dieron tres veces de palos porque cantaba, que no tenía otro alivio" (the work was so difficult, and I suffered such sleep deprivation, that they gave me three times the beatings because I sang, because I had no other relief) (23).

Pasamonte had little need to report extensively on the conditions in the galleys or in the *bagnios*, given that captivity narratives were abundant, and religious orders charged with the redemption of captives often publicized in lurid terms the horrors to which Christians were subjected in Muslim lands (Friedman 72). Especially given the fact that one of the principal addressees of the autobiography had intervened in his redemption years earlier, Pasamonte could be assured that his readers were well aware of works like Antonio de Guevara's 1539 *Libro de los inventores del arte de marear, y de muchos trabajos que pasan en las galeras*, which warned of the starvation threatening captives sent to the galleys, detailing the inadequate rations they would receive even as they were forced to row in shifts lasting as long as twelve hours:

> No buscad agua limpia, fresca y de buen sabor. Bebed sin prestar atención un agua caliente, turbia, fangosa, casi fétida ... En cuanto al pan, contentaros con un bizcocho negro, duro, lleno de gusanos, muchas veces cubierto de moho y roído por las ratas. La carne estará mal cocida, más dura que la madera y más salada que la sal, más difícil de digerir que una piedra.

> (Do not search for clean, fresh, and good tasting water. Drink water without paying attention to the hot, turbid, muddy, almost fetid liquid … As for bread, be content with a black biscuit, hard, full of worms, many times mouldy and rat-bitten. The meat will be poorly cooked, harder than wood and saltier than salt, harder to digest than a rock.) (qtd. in Barrio Gozalo 102)

In addition to the twin spectres of malnourishment and dehydration, slaves were exposed to the elements and vulnerable to the diseases that spread rapidly aboard the galleys. Particularly when the ships participated in battle, the slaves bore the brunt of the effort required to manoeuvre the vessels quickly. As one galley slave later recounted:

> Cuando dábamos caza a una nave con el aullido del contramaestre ordenando acelerar, el esfuerzo se hacía tan intenso que nuestros músculos se tendían hasta romperse. Después estaban duros y doloridos, el aire enrarecido nos quemaba el pecho, creíamos perecer ahogados. Y si por desgracia nuestra presa se escapaba recibíamos de inmediato los golpes del vergajo, pero ya estábamos tan destrozados que apenas si sentíamos dolor.
>
> (When we pursued a ship with the call of the boatswain ordering us to speed up, the effort was so intense that our muscles stretched to the breaking point. Afterwards they were hard and painful, the congested air burned our lungs. We thought we would die by drowning. And if by some misfortune our prey escaped we immediately felt the blows of the whip, but we were already so destroyed that we barely felt the pain.) (qtd. in Barrio Gozalo 103)

In comparison with vivid accounts such as these, which explicitly address an audience (through the use of the second-person plural) or describe shared experiences (through the use of the first-person plural), Pasamonte's laconic description of the "trabajo" and "privación de sueño" (23) that accompanied his stint in the galleys typifies the autobiography's overarching emphasis on the author's singular experiences – in this case focusing as much on miniscule acts of bravery as on his misery. In referring to the temporary relief from exhaustion and physical agony that he achieved by singing at the oars, Pasamonte reminds the reader of one of the opening episodes of the text in which, as a young child, he sang his way through a delirious fever, inspiring admiration in all who heard him: "me tomaba la calentura y yo cantaba con mucha gracia, que cuasi todas las señoras del lugar venían a ver esta maravilla, y estuve bueno" (I was taken with a fever and I sang so gracefully that practically all of the women of the place came to witness the miracle, and I was healed) (6). In the context of the first part of the autobiography, which recounts several similar miracles from Pasamonte's childhood, this early episode frames his response to illness as a "maravilla," and his suffering body becomes a minor spectacle of God's grace. Similarly, during his captivity, it is Pasamonte's active role in responding to the conditions in which he finds himself that allows him to escape association with an abject masculinity identified with slavery. In this way, the *Vida* begins to weave together the threads of physical misfortune, miraculous intervention, and spiritual fortitude that distinguish Pasamonte from his peers and that will ultimately allow him to claim an experiential authority that justifies the boldness of his claims.

Considering the frequency with which Spanish men – soldiers and civilians – were taken captive, both in military actions and piracy, it is unlikely that the fact of slavery in itself was considered emasculating. Nevertheless, contemporary accounts illustrate that, especially for men who chose to renounce their religion in favour of Islam, the physical consequences of such a choice held strong implications for (Christian) understandings of renegades' masculinity. Describing the process by which the Inquisition ascertained the religious fidelity of returned captives, Olga Fernández notes that a thorough inspection of the captive's body often uncovered the undeniable evidence of masculine apostasy: "En ocasiones, la evidencia del cuerpo funciona en contra de los declarantes, quienes tienen que justificar la presencia de una marca específica sobre sus cuerpos – la circuncisión – que era considerada prueba inequivoca de que se habían convertido al Islam" (On occasions, the evidence of the body worked against the declarants, who had to justify the presence of a specific mark on their bodies – circumcision – that was considered unequivocal proof that they had converted to Islam) (57). Although these "retajados" (castrated [men]) (57) might explain that they had been circumcised by force, the mark of the male renegade could easily be read as a kind of symbolic castration: given that, as Friedman notes, the friars of redemptionist orders were often instructed to attempt to free women and children first because they "were regarded as weakest in the faith, and most likely to apostatize under pressure" (146), the man who renounced his faith and submitted his body to the knife evinced a shameful weakness, both in his inability to maintain his Christian beliefs and to preserve his corporeal integrity.

Although Pasamonte does not explicitly treat the renegades he encounters in such gendered terms, it is clear from the autobiography that, even among the many kinds of traitors and heretics he confronted, the renegades placed in authority over Christian slaves were often the most reprehensible. According to Pasamonte, one of the cruellest men he encountered in Muslim territory was a Portuguese renegade: "Este negro portugués había dejado morir once o doce esclavos de cruelísima fiebre, sin quitalles la cadena, y a todos los hombres de mala vida y viciosos tenía desherrados, porque le pagaban" (This cursed Portuguese had let eleven or twelve slaves die of a cruel fever, without taking off their chains, and all of the bad and vice-ridden men he unchained, because they paid him) (26). Swayed more by expediency than by any sort of religious conviction, the renegades portrayed in Pasamonte's *Vida* are far more vicious and unreasonable than their masters. In this respect, Pasamonte's account of these years resonates with contemporary captives' tales, including that of Francisco Jiménez, who, in a conversation with a renegade, was told "It is a Turkish maxim … that a renegade can be considered a good Muslim only if he is rigorous with the Christians" (qtd. in Friedman 73). As Friedman goes on to note, in *Don Quixote* renegades such as Uchali are portrayed much more sympathetically (73). For Pasamonte's purposes, however, and in the context of an autobiography dedicated to two Catholic clerics, depicting the renegade – the embodiment of the temptation of apostasy – in the most negative light emphasizes the author's own unwavering spiritual commitment and integrity, thereby securing his status as a literal and figurative Christian knight.

Despite the horrors of life in captivity – physical pain, privation, and constant entreaties to convert – Pasamonte retrospectively casts his difficult experiences under Ottoman rule in a comparatively positive light. With the exception of religious renegades, many of his Muslim masters are portrayed as honourable men, particularly when they recognize Pasamonte as a man of God and treat him accordingly. While the threat posed by the religious alterity of Muslims had often been signalled by their effeminate if not sodomitic portrayal in Spanish literary and cultural discourse ever since the Middle Ages (Donnell 42–3), Pasamonte – unlike Cervantes and Diego de Haedo, for example (Camamis 78–81) – chooses not to depict them in this manner. In fact, before his release from captivity, Pasamonte appears to inhabit a purely masculine realm, devoid of both women and any trace of culturally defined femininity. In this world, the dangers are obvious, indicated by the strict hierarchy differentiating masters from slaves and by the religious differences that separate true Christians such as Pasamonte from treacherous heretics like the Lutheran informant. In contrast, upon his return to Christendom, Pasamonte enters a world teeming with conniving, lascivious women. Where the bagnios and galleys of the Ottoman-held

Mediterranean provided Pasamonte with the backdrop for daring escape attempts, the Spanish garrisons in Italy – Gaeta and Naples, where he was granted a stationary post – are rife with witchcraft and sexual sin. It is in this latter part of the autobiography that Pasamonte ceases to portray himself as a strong, spiritually and physically steadfast soldier and instead accentuates the aspects of virtuous victimhood that have accompanied his self-representation since childhood and throughout his captivity.[8]

Following his release from captivity, Pasamonte narrates a series of challenges to his honour on two fronts, as both his sexual honour and his spiritual integrity are threatened. Calling upon his experience of captivity as a marker of superior insight, the soldier's steadfastness in the face of entreaties to conversion (which would have entailed spiritual capitulation and circumcision, understood as a kind of emasculation) is newly tested.

While during the time he spent under Muslim rule Pasamonte portrays himself as a holy soldier, a defiant captive marked by physical and spiritual courage, widely respected by his fellow Christians and Muslim masters alike, following his release and return to Christendom in 1592, in his autobiography Pasamonte develops a persona that had only been glimpsed in previous episodes, that of the long-suffering martyr. While he was beaten and shackled as a Muslim captive, he was still strong, relatively healthy, and still had the use of his best eye; in the years after his liberation, Pasamonte describes endless bouts with illness and laments, "afligido de lágrimas" (afflicted with tears) (53), losing most of what remained of his eyesight. From a bold leader he is transformed in these episodes into a victim of diabolical plots against his physical, mental, and spiritual integrity, most of them hatched by wicked women and ostensibly occasioned by his own refusal to be drawn into sexual sin. Stating that although he could recount multiple examples of this type, Pasamonte claims for brevity's sake that he will only describe the first and the last, "para espantar a todo el mundo, que se vea el grandísimo daño que hay entre católicos" (to horrify the whole world, so that they might see the enormous harm that there is among Catholics) (41). In the first of these episodes, Pasamonte is stationed in Gaeta, where he boards with his friend Rodrigo de Dios and his wife, described as "una mujer morisca" (41), "una vieja muy burlera" (41) – a character already discredited on several counts by her inferior ethnic status, age, and unseemly behaviour. Finding himself tormented with strange pains and other unexplained physical sensations, Pasamonte comes to the conclusion that this woman is attempting to bewitch him with love philtres. Mindful of both his spiritual and physical well-being, he leaves his friend and finds lodging with a man named Castañeda. Even here, however, he is pursued by Celestinesque figures who attempt to draw him into ill-advised marriages and sexual entanglements: "pero las mujeres en aquella tierra todas son a una, y por no quererme yo casar ni estar en pecado (que tampoco soy santo), me procuraron la muerte" (but the women in that country are all the same, and because I didn't want to marry or fall into sin – not that I'm a saint – they tried to kill me) (41). The sexually disinterested mode of masculinity that Pasamonte assumes here reflects a sense of moderation and self-control associated not with common soldiery but rather with the ideal man as portrayed in the humanistic conduct manuals of the era (Poska 8; Martínez Góngora, *El hombre* 30–1). At the same time, perhaps because he considered himself a "fraile" (friar), Pasamonte describes himself consistently refusing the licentious advances of would-be wives and mistresses, even under the threat of death, thus exhibiting vestiges of the influence of what Maureen Miller has referred to as a kind of "extreme masculinity ... radically distanced from female impurity" (27–8).[9] While staying with Castañeda, Pasamonte becomes bedridden with a severe illness that he attributes to the poisoned provisions cooked for him by his would-be lovers, who have successfully managed to breach his bodily integrity by gastronomic means. (Later, Pasamonte explains that his deteriorating eyesight leaves him in the vulnerable position of having to ask his neighbours – in general, "malas mujeres" [71] and "descomulgadas brujas" [excommunicated witches] [59] – to cook for him.) Although even his friends counsel him to surrender and marry, Pasamonte claims to prefer death to such an attachment, even almost resorting to suicide in his despair. Saved on this occasion by his guardian angel, Pasamonte notes that tribulations such as his are the direct result of Christian – particularly feminine – commerce with the devil and, in tacit accordance with Church doctrine regarding women's vulnerability to demonic machinations, he asserts that only the ultimate threat of excommunication will curb such practices.

In the following episodes, Pasamonte continues amassing evidence for his call for excommunication, pitting his own martyred masculinity – victimized despite his unshakeable faith – against the schemes and subterfuge of various witch-like women, including a morisca from Tunis and another woman whose wickedness is hinted at in her physical disability as she is described as "una coja y qué tal" (a lame woman) (43). After moving house several times, leaving after discovering evidence of witchcraft in each, Pasamonte finds himself lodging with an Extremaduran soldier and his wife. Again, the wife of his landlord appears to be attempting to orchestrate a marriage between him and one of several widows of questionable virtue. When Pasamonte sternly tells her that he has no intention of marrying, she begs him not to look for housing elsewhere, claiming that her husband has sworn to kill her if they lose their lodger (and, most importantly, the rent he supplies). Pasamonte, betrayed by his own sense of honour and pity for the woman, agrees to stay until she slowly begins to poison him, reportedly taunting him at the height of his illness that he will die suddenly without being able to receive communion. This, followed by a vision of the woman surrounded by dozens of whirling demons dressed in the habits of San Francisco,[10] serves to convince Pasamonte of the seriousness of the situation; he describes leaving the house and following a regimen meant to purify both his body and soul: "En ocho días tomé tres purgas y otras tres veces los divinos sacramentos" (In eight days I took three purgatives and another three times the divine sacraments) (45). Having cleansed himself of spiritual and physical toxins, he tactfully tells the Extremaduran that the doctors have suggested that he move to another, less humid part of town, thereby invoking – intentionally or not – the early modern humoral model of sexual difference aligning femininity with the cold and clammy humours (Paster 416). True to his word, the Extremaduran, Pasamonte tells the reader, returned home to beat his wife, either assuming that she was the cause of Pasamonte's departure or simply in order to alleviate his anger at having lost a valuable source of income. When the woman resisted, she was killed with his sword. According to Pasamonte (who, in an unusual departure from his eyewitness narrative, relates the story second hand), the woman's death was doubly her fault, both for resorting to poison and for resisting her husband's chastisement. Speaking of her injuries, Pasamonte states: "Y de esta herida murió, que si se estaba queda no moría de las puñaladas" (And she died of this wound; if she had been still she wouldn't have died from the stabbing) (45). Pasamonte describes the woman's death as long and tortured, as she took a full twenty-four hours to expire. Incredibly, the author expresses no sympathy for the woman and no condemnation for the murder committed by her husband, declaring only that it was a fit punishment for her wickedness. Even the last, horrifying detail of the woman's demise evokes no compassion. When told by the doctor who attended her that the disembowelled woman's intestines were overflowing with worms, Pasamonte provides an allegorical interpretation of what would seem to be a straightforward medical fact, responding: "Señor, que no son sino dragones de la muerte que ella quería darme a mí" (Sir, these are nothing but the dragons of death that she tried to give me) (45).[11] Although he sees this violence as just, he tacitly fashions his own persona in opposition to men like Castañeda. Throughout the text, Pasamonte shows himself to prefer revenge through legal channels. His superiority is not physical or intellectual but spiritual: the evidence for this he presents in the text as making meaning out of the raw material of his life, not as history or treatise or philosophical meditation, but as theological speculation, or even angelology. On the basis of his superior knowledge, he calls for the appropriate authorities to intervene and clear his name by excommunicating his accusers.

Much like the early modern Catholic exhortations calling for women to regard their bodies as corpses filled with carrion (Perry, *Gender* 114), in these passages Pasamonte conflates the feminine with death, and sexuality with witchcraft. For this reason, when Pasamonte finally does decide to marry, the reasons he gives are entirely practical. Citing his deteriorating eyesight, which made it impossible for him to cook his own meals – and therefore left him at the mercy of potion-concocting neighbours – he reluctantly takes as his wife a young Spanish girl educated in a convent. Surprisingly, Pasamonte seems to take his new bride's chastity for granted; according to the text, the spiritual purity assured by her religious upbringing is the girl's most attractive feature: "Y por tener experiencia de las maldades del mundo, determiné de sacar una moza honrada de un monasterio y casarme con ella, pues allí no se imparan supersticiones ni artes malas" (And because I had experience within the wickedness of the world, I decided to choose an honourable girl from a convent and marry her, because there superstitions and evil arts aren't learned) (51). Soon, however, Pasamonte realizes his mistake in exchanging his well-guarded celibacy for the sexual and familial entanglements of marriage and the attendant dangers they pose to his physical and spiritual welfare; in a colloquial phrase that, in this context, offers an ironic counterpoint to the Pauline injunction that those incapable of sexual continence should marry ("mejor es casarse que quemarse" [better to marry than to burn] [1 Cor. 7.9]), Pasamonte states "huyendo de la sartén, damos en las brasas" (from the frying pan into the fire) (51). Despite his limited financial resources, Pasamonte's marriage brings with it the responsibility to provide food and shelter not only for his wife and children but also for her family. Although the particulars of this arrangement are different from those described by Allyson Poska in her study of masculinity in early modern Galicia,

Pasamonte's autobiography registers an impotent rage arising from the kind of "constrained … access to property and authority" (15) associated with uxorilocal residence. Though Pasamonte has nothing negative to say about his wife, perhaps because doing so would reflect badly on his own honour, the autobiography takes an unusual turn in chapter 52, which includes an itemized list of fifty "traiciones" (betrayals) (51) perpetrated on him by his wife's family. In this list, Pasamonte accuses his father-, mother-, and sister-in-law of a wide variety of sins, particularly witchcraft, lubriciousness, and avarice. This list constitutes a kind of self-defence, in that it appropriates accusations made against him by his wife's family into charges of their own depravity (according to Pasamonte, the family maintained alternately that he was enuretic, impotent, a fornicator, and had withheld money from them). This extensive and carefully recorded list of crimes, which is summarized at the chapter's conclusion into four main points, would appear to serve two purposes: more generally, it highlights Pasamonte's holy forbearance as he refuses to abandon his wife even though her family, he says, is literally killing him; likewise, the list presents in a judicial format the information necessary to exonerate Pasamonte and to call for the punishment of his most recent and persistent persecutors. At this point, the autobiography is nearly complete, as Pasamonte demonstrates that he has been martyred abroad and now at home, by a family of fellow Spaniards, no less – a fact stated in a moment of bizarre national pride: "pero nuestra nación, en lo bueno y en lo malo, es aventajada más que las otras naciones" (but our nation, in good and in evil, stands out among all the others) (51).

While the "traiciones" inflicted upon Pasamonte by his wife's family are varied, they overwhelmingly point to a betrayal that is as much social and economic as it is spiritual: they are devastating affronts to his honour. Alongside accusations of attempted murder by poison and witchcraft, Pasamonte claims that his mother- and father-in-law have slandered him on several occasions, publicly and to his wife, in an attempt to sow discord between the pair. The aspersions cast on Pasamonte's character threaten to irrevocably damage his reputation; rather than refute them, however, Pasamonte uses the autobiography to demonstrate their improbability, given his virtuous conduct in the past, while simultaneously denouncing their source. He recounts, for example, the contradictions inherent in many of their accusations, describing how his mother- and father-in-law first accused him of impotence – even going so far as to see a notary to find out how to arrange a divorce and seize half of his assets, only to later claim that Pasamonte was actively engaged in an amorous affair with a married woman. Later, after the birth of his children, Pasamonte was again accused of impotence: "dijeron que no era mi hijo y que yo había hecho empreñar a mi mujer por encubrir el impotente ... y otro que tengo de dos años han dicho también que yo había hecho empreñar mi mujer por otra persona" (they said that he wasn't my son and that I had had someone impregnate my wife to cover up my impotence ... and about another child of mine, now two years old, they also said that I had had someone else impregnate my wife) (54). Rather than explicitly repudiate this charge, Pasamonte prefers to render it ridiculous: "y agora que está mi mujer preñada, no sé de quién dirán" (and now that my wife is pregnant again, I don't know who they'll say did it) (54). Assuming that neither of these mutually exclusive accusations – of impotence and fornication – were true, why would Pasamonte's wife's family want to dishonour him in this way? As David Gilmore has noted with regard to present-day Mediterranean conceptions of masculinity, "la prueba última es la aptitud para la reproducción, es decir, preñar a la esposa" (the ultimate proof is the ability to reproduce, that is, to impregnate the wife) (90); as for the man incapable of reproducing, "se le considera un fracasado como hombre por ser sexualmente ineficaz" (he is considered a failure as a man for his impotence) (90). In the early modern period, too, impotence was taken as a sign of deficient masculinity, affecting both the subject's suitability for marriage as well as for entering the clergy; as Edward Behrend-Martínez notes: "Even when the Catholic Church accepted priests for ordination, it required them to be sexually intact and able" (1077). On the other hand, the charge of adultery would indicate a lack of sexual self-restraint associated with ideal, moderate masculinity (Martínez Góngora, *El hombre* 34–5). In either case, in these accusations of inadequacy and excess, Pasamonte's masculine identity was publicly placed into question and, if proven to be true, could have resulted in public humiliation and even the dissolution of his marriage. Rather than proclaim either his fidelity or his sexual prowess, Pasamonte instead includes more descriptions of his tearful suffering while simultaneously detailing the perversions practised by his accusers.

While his own wife's honour is described as irreproachable, Pasamonte paints a grim picture of her debauched sister Mariana, who, he claims, is prostituted by her mother and stepfather: "venden la hija y comen de su desgracia" (they sell their daughter and they eat from her disgrace) (59). Several of the fifty "traiciones" outlined in his "Memorial de las mayores traiciones" (Statement of the greatest betrayals) are dedicated to describing the scandals associated with her, including the rounds she made "de venta en venta" (from inn to inn) (54), the marriage that was arranged for her, only to be cancelled when her fiancé discovered her with another lover, and how she bore a child of dubious paternity not long after (55). While Pasamonte is tormented by visions of demons conjured by his mother-in-law and suffers in silence the concoctions of ground glass and mercury that she slips into his meals, the debased behaviour of his wife's family – even allegedly in his presence (54) – illustrates the inescapable, allied dangers of witchcraft and female sexuality. The most unusual episode of this sort parallels the tale of wife murder in Gaeta. Just as Pasamonte presents the death of the Extremaduran soldier's wife as a fitting punishment for her waywardness, the violence that is eventually inflicted on Mariana is described as spiritually beneficial, both for her and for her parents. In section 32 of the Memorial, Pasamonte recounts Mariana's unfortunate marriage to a lawyer, depicted admiringly by Pasamonte as "un letrado" (a lettered man) and "caballero" (gentleman) (55). In Pasamonte's words: "Pero [sus padres] hicieron un error, que fue casalla por virgen; y dicen que los paños de la sangre, por ponellos entre las piernas, se hallaron a la mañana en la cabecera de la cama, por habérseles olvidado" (But they made a mistake, which was to marry her as a virgin; and they say that the bloody rags, which were meant to be placed between her legs, were found in the morning at the head of the bed because they had been forgotten) (55). Rather than have the marriage annulled – without financial benefit – on the basis of Mariana's sexual status, Pasamonte recounts how his wily mother-in-law quickly accused the lawyer of sodomy.

Locked in a stalemate, the pair remain married and, after a short sojourn in Capua, return to Naples where they reside with her mother and stepfather. Not long after, however, in the course of a domestic dispute over Mariana's habit of gossiping and flirting from the window, she is assaulted and left for dead. When her parents return to find their daughter gravely injured, Pasamonte frames their response in economic terms: "Cuanto habían ganado y embutido, todo se acabó con las heridas y gasto" (All that they had earned and gobbled up, it was all gone with the injuries and the expense) (55); his own reaction to the incident also takes on a budgetary cast, but in the context of spiritual debts and credits: "y fue Dios servido no haya muerto por dalles lugar a enmienda" (and God was served that she didn't die in order to give them time to change their ways) (55). Although, as Elizabeth Foyster has noted, in the early modern period "a multitude of literary genres … taught that a man's honor depended on exercising control over the sexual behaviour of the women with whom he was associated" (207), it would seem that for Pasamonte the publication of his sister-in-law's already well-known dishonour is a strategy that is the lesser of many evils. Unable to conceal the disgrace of his wife's family, and finding it necessary to respond to their allegations, Pasamonte ends by stating: "Yo no pido justicia, sino misericordia" (I ask not for justice but mercy) (59). Asserting that their conduct threatens both his own life and that of his children, igniting in him a righteous anger that will drive him to murder, he begs the authorities to send his in-laws away to a prison in Puglia, "que por ventura allá no tendrán la commodidad que hay en este abysso de Nápoles" (there they would not have an easy time like here in this abyss of Naples) (59). In this way, Pasamonte's post-redemption narrative of domestic martyrdom portrays the author as enduring a series of hellish torments, as he sweats from love potion-induced fevers and suffers injuries to both body and reputation incurred by proximity to his wife's salacious family – all against the backdrop of infernal cities (Gaeta, Naples) that, he claims, breed evil as easily as the Ottoman strongholds of his captivity.

~

Both the allegations levelled against Pasamonte by his peers and the corresponding accusations elaborated in the *Vida* revolve around the question of heterodox beliefs and practices, particularly those having to do with angels and demons. Despite Pasamonte's self-presentation as a steadfast Christian soldier and martyr, his uncertainty about the orthodoxy of his own pronouncements is evident at multiple junctures in the text, both implicitly in the author's concluding statement that he has written only with the permission of his confessor, and explicitly when he anticipates his critics, stating "Dirá algún especulativo y mejor sofístico: '¿Quién le mete a este soldado necio sin estudio en estas disputas, pues la Iglesia de Dios tiene tantos doctores para defender sus causas?'" (Some speculative and sophisticated sophist will ask: "Who authorized this foolish unstudied soldier to enter into these disputes, when the Church of God has so many doctors to defend her causes?") (60). Pasamonte's answer is immediate and appeals to the superior nature of his painfully acquired experiential knowledge: "A eso respondo que el haber derramado más sangre que algunos en servicio de mi Dios, como se ve por lo escrito atrás, y haber predicado con su divino favor su santa fe en tierra de enemigos de la fe" (To this I respond that [I am authorized by] having shed more blood than some in the service of my God, as can be seen from the previous pages, and having preached with his divine favour his holy faith in the land of the enemies of the faith) (60). According to José María de Cossío, Pasamonte's numerous descriptions of angelic guardianship and demonic depredation advance "[una] especie de angeleología, tan elemental e ingenua que merece nota de simpleza" (a kind of angelology, so basic and naïve as to be simplistic) (x). Nevertheless, I would argue that what Pasamonte's *Vida* lacks in scholastic sophistication it makes up for in a wealth of vivid anecdotes that illustrate the author's contentions. As Trevor Johnson has noted, during the seventeenth century, "angelology" – metaphysical speculation regarding the nature and purpose of angels – was "modish ... both within and beyond the Society of Jesus" (191). In 1608, three years after Pasamonte sent a final version of his autobiography to a Dominican and a Jesuit, this trend was officially inaugurated with Pope Paul V's recognition and celebration of the existence of guardian angels in his proclamation of a feast day in honour of Los Santos Ángeles Custodios (192). While the early work of seventeenth-century theologians such as Francisco Blasco Lanuza tended to focus on the favours granted to humans through the intervention of such good angels, later writings highlighted the vicious nature of demons and expounded on the battles carried out between the forces of good and evil for the human soul (Tausiet, "Patronage" 233–4). Written shortly before this time, Jerónimo de Pasamonte's descriptions of his interactions with angels and demons reflect popular, long-cherished beliefs that nevertheless were not yet part of official Catholic dogma. Mindful of the physical and spiritual dangers of falling into error, in the autobiography Pasamonte generally avoids theological abstractions, always careful to draw only upon his own experience, which he swears "en confesión sacramental" to be true (72).

Pasamonte's attempt to make sense of the chaos and injustice of his lived experience and to sustain a convincing argument for the punishment of those he sees as his enemies is supported by a somewhat idiosyncratic theory of human and angelical interaction. Over the course of the autobiography it becomes clear that Pasamonte understood the borders between the physical and spiritual realms to be porous, crossed with particular ease by angels and demons. While, a generation earlier, Ignatius of Loyola and his all-male Society of Jesus had been quietly expanding the possibilities of Catholic masculinity, combining traditionally masculine and feminine qualities to fashion "an action-oriented mysticism [that] required a body made porous for the divine" (Strasser 57), the often abject state in which Jerónimo de Pasamonte describes himself – pursued by witches and laid low by demons – would seem to be at odds with the divine intimacy characteristic of the Ignatian mystical experience. Though Pasamonte credits his guardian angel with saving him on several occasions, most notably from attempting suicide when he found himself in despair (42), he is most concerned with charting the evils visited upon him by malevolent forces and in speculating on their purpose within a providential plan. In chapter 7, for instance, Pasamonte recounts how for the first time he was the target of obvious diabolical influence. He describes an incident that occurred when he was ten, when he was sent to board in the house of a doctor following the death of his parents: "este [el doctor] vivía en una casa que había un trasgo, y esta mala fantasma muchas noches venía encima de mí" (the doctor lived in a house that was haunted by a goblin, and this evil ghost came upon me many nights) (7). Tormented by a goblin-like entity, Pasamonte's strength was sapped and he eventually became mortally ill. In Pasamonte's words, "Yo vine a estar cuasi a la muerte y nadie me curaba" (I almost died and no one attended me) (7). Alone and sick, Pasamonte would only regain his health when his host, the doctor, passed away, occasioning his departure from the haunted house. Significantly, Pasamonte notes that his departure coincided with Lent, the period commemorating Christ's temptation in the wilderness; only at this time of heightened spiritual awareness, awakened by the faithful's fasting, abstinence, and penitence, was Pasamonte able to make confession, receive communion, and finally be cured of his infirmity. Although he does not explore in this chapter the connection between his practice of the sacraments and his physical healing, it is clear from this and later incidents that, for Pasamonte, the domains of the spiritual and material are coextensive; for this reason, the marks of angelical warfare can be read on his scarred, disease-afflicted physique.

Aside from this early childhood episode, most of Pasamonte's tales of demonic disturbance involve an active, human element facilitating the diabolical intrusion. Almost all the persecutions he complains of in the latter half of the autobiography are caused by human – usually female – collusion with evil spirits. In chapter 47, for example, Pasamonte recounts being tormented by an entity he refers to only as a "mala cosa":

> Estando en otra casa con un paisano mío, me sucedió … que una noche venía sobre mí una mala cosa. Y miraba yo durmiendo en visión una mujer que venía con aquella mala cosa, y conocía yo la mujer como si estuviera despierto, y no sé quién me batía al lado y me hacía decir: "Conjuro te per individuam Trinitatem ut vadas ad profundum inferni."
>
> (In another house with a countryman of mine, it happened that one night an evil thing came upon me. And in sleep I saw in a vision a woman who was with that evil thing, and I knew the woman as if I were awake, and

> I don't know who struck my side and made me say: "In the name of the Trinity I cast you into hell.") (42)

In this instance, it is Pasamonte's guardian angel that saves him, prompting him to rebuke the demon in the name of the Trinity. As Pasamonte explains, the woman accompanied by the familiar turns out to be a neighbour; when he sees her the next day, she confirms her identity by proclaiming that Pasamonte had only narrowly escaped death the previous night. As Pasamonte informs his readers, after this episode, "di en la cuenta qué cosas eran brujas y cómo cierto fue el ángel de la guardia el que me amonestó y defendió" (I realized what witches were and how it certainly was my guardian angel who admonished and defended me) (43). With this particular passage, and in the autobiography as a whole, Pasamonte attempts to convey the impression that he writes only in his capacity as a battle-hardened soldier, in order to share his hard-earned knowledge regarding witches and the demons that assist them, in the hope that the Church take more seriously the dangers that he knows they pose.

In these and similar incidents, Jerónimo de Pasamonte demonstrates his contention that angels exist primarily in relation to the human beings they help or harm. Having recounted a dozen such anecdotes, towards the end of his autobiography Pasamonte briefly ventures into the realm of theological abstraction. As to the existence of demons, Pasamonte can only surmise that God allows them (and, by extension, evil) to exist in the world in order to tempt mankind: "los ángeles de menos calidad, para tentar a los de menos calidad, y los de más calidad, para tentar a los hombres de más calidad, como son los más sabios" (the angels of lesser quality, to tempt those of lesser quality, and those of higher quality, to tempt those men of higher quality, the wiser men) (68). This notion complements the spiritual trajectory traced in Pasamonte's autobiography; while at age ten he was tormented by a single mischievous spirit, as an adult he would be assaulted by visions of a swarming multitude of demons, thus indicating the evolution of his virtue and wisdom. Within their divinely ordained role of allowing mankind to more fully practise the exercise of free will, as humans choose or refuse to indulge in the devil's "saber tan falso" (false knowledge) and "secretos admirables" (frightful secrets) (59), demons grant their human counterparts a limited and corrupt access to occult knowledge. While the constant recurrence of the phrase "¡O, secretos de Dios!" (Oh, secrets of God!) indicates Pasamonte's struggle to live within the metaphysical and epistemological limitations established by God, Pasamonte notes that recurring to demonic means to surpass these limitations can only ever bring harm. Returning to his own experiences, Pasamonte states that those who summon the forces of evil "por vía de estos malos espíritus quieren mudar los naturales a las personas y hacellos bestias y tenellos subjectos a todos sus gustos o matallos" (by way of these evil spirits they want to manipulate people's dispositions and make them subject to their whims or kill them) (69). Pasamonte's own dread of being besmirched by evil extends even to this brief discussion. At multiple points he interrupts the flow of his speculations to renounce Satan, as if even reporting on the nature of demons were enough to summon them. Defending himself from evil spirits (or, perhaps, from Inquisitional scrutiny regarding his motivations for detailing their exploits), he finally declares: "reniego del demonio y de sus obras, pero es verdad que lo hacen" (I renounce the devil and his works, but it is true that they do them) (69).

But is it demons themselves or their human interlocutors who most preoccupy Pasamonte? If the bulk of the author's experiences are any indication, it would seem that the latter are the true object of the text's critique. In reflecting on his own life, Pasamonte notes that Christians in collaboration with Satan have done great harm to the world, and he cites Martin Luther and Cardinal Wolsey as well-known examples of men led astray by diabolical influence (59). Because humans aided by demons needlessly persecute innocent victims such as himself and foment heresies and discord, the author demands that the most severe earthly punishment authorized by the Church be exacted against those who seek assistance from the devil. The culmination of Pasamonte's argument comes at the end of the text when, taking the entirety of his life experiences into account, he recommends the punishment of excommunication for those who, like his enemies, are in collusion with dark forces: "Y así digo que es necesario que Su Santidad y el Senado Apostólico, a público pregón y voz de trompetas, echen un bando que diga: 'Vistos los daños que entre católicos se siguen por tener y tratar y oír a ángeles malos, damos por descomulgados a quien tal tuviere u oyere o tratare'" (And so I say that it is necessary that His Holiness and the Apostolic Senate, publically and with a voice like trumpets, unfurl a flag that says: Seeing the harms among Catholics that arise for having and communicating with and hearing evil angels, we excommunicate whoever has and communicates and hears them) (60).

As María Tausiet has noted, by the seventeenth century the threat of excommunication was a fairly common disciplinary tool, implying not only spiritual condemnation but also a total expulsion from the Christian community meant to prefigure the subject's eternal separation from grace ("Excluded" 437, 450). According to Tausiet, "The list of crimes [punishable by excommunication] was headed by heresy and often included the possession of books on magic and other superstitious practices" (441). Excommunication could also be pronounced for sins as diverse as "the falsification of pontifical documents, aggression against a member of the clergy, and occupation of apostolic lands" (441). As Tausiet goes on to specify, in reality, any act construed as rebellious was theoretically subject to the Church's harshest penalty, if only to prevent further outbreaks of disobedience among the faithful (442). Although Pasamonte's argument for excommunication is explicitly framed in a general manner, it is clear from the multiple personal examples he cites that he has several specific people marked out for this punishment. And while the vast majority of the evidence supporting his call for excommunication falls under the rubric of superstition and the practice of magic, it may be significant that Pasamonte thought of himself as a member of the clergy due to an early but unfulfilled vow to join a Bernardine monastery: particularly considering a vision he relates in which a horde of demons rage at him, screaming "¡Oh el traidor, que es fraile!" (Oh, the traitor is a friar!) (59), it is possible that, in addition to their exercise of the black arts, Pasamonte wished his enemies to be tried for their attacks against him as a representative of the Church. Perhaps it is also for this reason that Pasamonte strives uneasily to combine his performance of a kind of Tridentine clerical masculinity, far removed from the stereotypical soldier's swagger in its emphasis on the author's asceticism and spiritual purity, with his later (and contradictory) role as a loving husband and father (Strasser 53–4).

Acutely aware of the unusual nature of his personally invested call for the excommunication of his enemies, which is supported by a conventional if not yet officially sanctioned understanding of human and angelic interaction, Pasamonte is careful to craft an authoritative persona for himself. Given the widespread belief that women were physically and spiritually susceptible to infernal influence, it is not surprising that Pasamonte emphasizes culturally sanctioned traits of masculinity in his autobiography as elements of self-legitimization. Augmenting the ever-present discourse of experiential authority, Pasamonte performs two divergent but ultimately related modes of masculinity in the autobiography, portraying himself alternately as a holy soldier, a triumphant hero of the faith, and a Christ-like martyr, a victim of spiritual torments that take on physical dimensions, including accidents, illnesses, and curses meant to provoke first sexual attraction and then death. In both cases, Pasamonte describes himself wearing the signs of these modes of masculinity imprinted on his body, as indicated in the proverb quoted twice in the text, once at the beginning and once towards the end: "no hay mejor maestro que el bien acuchillado" (6, 69). While Pasamonte the warrior describes himself sustaining wounds in battle and captivity that serve to fortify his courage and strength, Pasamonte the martyr relates tales of demonic illnesses that, while weakening his body, confirm his superior spirituality and grant him practical knowledge of the enemy's tactics. In both instances, the text betrays an acute anxiety as the author's bodily integrity – and therefore masculinity – is threatened during his captivity and finally breached through the ingestion of poisoned and bewitched food after his release. This anxiety simultaneously fuels and threatens to destabilize the delicate balancing act performed in the text, as the author must portray the porousness and vulnerability of his body only to the degree that it garners sympathy and esteem from the intended audience rather than engendering dishonour and disgust.[12] Perhaps for this reason in Pasamonte's account of his years of captivity the cruelties that he endured are balanced by references to the punishments that he escaped and the respect that he finally won from both his fellow captives and his Muslim masters.

While during his captivity Pasamonte's courage and strength was thrown into sharp focus by the cowardice of some of his fellow captives, in the latter part of the autobiography his victimization – through love magic, poisonings, defamation, and demonic visitation – at the hands of his enemies shows him to be a model of Christ-like martyrdom and holy anger, destined to receive restitution for his wrongs. If in the first part of the autobiography Pasamonte presents himself as warrior who, despite his captive status, possesses an intact body characterized by wounds that heal, ears that remain uncut, and a body and soul undefiled by the specific dangers of sodomitical penetration and apostasy, the events that unfold following his release illustrate the even greater dangers posed by the domestic demons conjured by his co-religionists, often within his own home. Symbolically feminized by supernatural beings, who render his tormented but intact warrior's body into an unruly and leaky vessel, plagued by flux and accused of impotence and incontinence, Pasamonte does not claim the usual martyr's reward of eventual corporeal reintegration and perfection. Instead, he uses the text, much like the soldier's petition, to demand restitution on earth. At the end of the autobiography, the strands of Pasamonte's argument come together as he pleads, on the basis of his understanding of angels and demons, backed by the credibility of his experiences of persecution both in captivity and in freedom, for the excommunication of all those convicted of having dealings with the devil. With his own religious purity guaranteed by the virtuous masculinity inherent in his self-portrayal as holy soldier and Christ-like martyr, Pasamonte begs the dedicatees of his autobiography to awake from their complacency and see the urgent need to punish the wickedness that threatens to engulf the Church: "¡Oh doctores sagrados!, poned el remedio en nuestros católicos, que veo el mundo perdido y cuasi ciego por estas maldades" (Oh holy doctors! Cure our catholics, as I see the world lost and almost blinded by this wickedness) (72).

In this way, in his *Vida* Pasamonte adopts the petitionary framework that characterizes much military life writing, even as he invests his martial experience with spiritual significance, and endows his supernatural encounters with the momentousness of great battles. Having established a pattern of persecution followed by divine justice in the autobiography, Pasamonte implicates his readers not only in his personal story but also in the wider narrative of God's justice carried out on earth. Yet within the economy of duties and privileges laid out in the text, the response of those readers to Pasamonte's appeal is, in some ways, insignificant: regardless of their reactions, the text's representation of the author's wounded body stands as a testimony to his experiential authority and privileged insight as a literal and figurative Christian soldier whose honour – despite entreaties to debauchery and apostasy – remains intact.

Chapter Four

Playing the *Pícaro*

The pseudo-autobiographical novel *Estebanillo González, hombre de buen humor* (Antwerp, 1646) is one of the chronologically latest and among the most widely read examples of the picaresque in the seventeenth century.[1] This controversial work, which has been characterized as both the exhaustion of the picaresque and its culmination, takes the form of a corrosively satirical soldier's autobiography that unfolds primarily against the backdrop of the Thirty Years' War (1618–48). In the dedication to General Ottavio Piccolomini, Duke of Amalfi and Governor of Arms in the Army of Flanders, Estebanillo claims that he has been moved to the risky act of autobiography by the dual desire to make himself memorable and to honour his protector with an entertaining tale: "yo, Estebanillo González, hombre de buen humor, hijo de mis obras y padrastro de las ajenas, y menor criado de Vuecelencia, quiriéndome hacer memorable, fiado en haber merecido ser el menor criado de V. Exc., me he puesto en la plaza del mundo y en la palestra de los combates dando a la imprenta este libro de mi vida y no milagros" ("I, Estebanillo González, a man of good humour, son of my own deeds and stepfather to the deeds of others, the least of Your Excellency's servants, having wanted to make myself memorable, trusting in having been fit to be Your Excellency's least servant, have thrust myself into the plaza of the world and the fray of combat by printing this book of my life and non-miracles") (I: 7). In the prologue to the reader, Estebanillo further clarifies that, though the printing press might transform his life story into merchandise, his aim is to render a service to Piccolomini and the other high-ranking members of his court by presenting them with a gift. But, Estebanillo adds, he wouldn't turn down any favours that he might receive in exchange for the laughter he hopes his tale inspires: "no lo doy a la imprenta para hacer mercancía dél, sino sólo para que sirva de presente y regalo a los príncipes y señores y personas de merecimiento;

y no volveré la cara ni encogeré el brazo a los premios que me dieren" (I don't turn it over to the printing press to make merchandise of it, but rather so that it can be gifted to princes and lords and worthy people, though I will not turn away or shrink from any prizes they might give me) (I: 15).

In a gesture familiar from the petitionary form of military life writing, influenced by the *relación de méritos* and spiritual autobiography, the fictional narrator stakes a claim for recognition on the value of his life experience, which is presented as a source of privileged insights in the autobiographical act. Here, however, dark humour veils deeply critical insights into the grotesque aspects of early modern military life. Even as Estebanillo boasts that soldiers will find the battle scenes in his *Vida* thrilling, he openly embraces his own dishonour when he recounts scenes of cowardice and desertion. In one episode, he describes hiding during the heat of battle, only to appear after the field has been won to theatrically stab the bodies of the dead and wounded enemy. Another scene encapsulates the way his inversion of military honour is played for laughs: accompanying Piccolomini to the field where the Battle of Nordlingen was fought – a battle in which the general had famously distinguished himself – Estebanillo is spooked by a burst of cannon fire and runs straight back to headquarters, where he dives into a hay loft and stays until he is summoned by his furious master. Piccolomini demands to know:

> —¡Pícaro! ¿Cómo sois tan cobarde que me habéis dejado, y a vista de una armada habéis vuelto las espaldas y puéstoos en huída?
>
> Yo le respondí:
>
> —Señor, ¿quién le ha dicho a Vuecelencia que yo soy valiente, o en qué ocasión no lo he hecho mucho peor que hoy? Si Vuecelencia me envió a llamar a Flandes para que le sirviese de soldado, está mal informado de mis partes, porque como otros son archiprestes de presbíteros yo soy archigallina de gallinas.
>
> Obligole la respuesta a convertir su enojo en placer y a disculparme de lo sucedido.
>
> ("Pícaro! Are you such a coward that you've left me, and in sight of the whole fleet you've turned your back and run away?"
>
> I replied: "Sir, who told Your Excellency that I'm valiant, and when have I not done worse than today? If Your Excellency sent me to Flanders to

serve as a soldier, you've been misinformed about my character, because just as there are archpriests of priests, I am the arch-chicken of chickens."

This response obliged him to turn his wrath to pleasure, and to pardon me for what I had done.) (II.9: 198)

This episode references the desertion common to the Army of Flanders and transforms it into a source of hilarity through which the wily Estebanillo wins pardon. Likewise, throughout the text Estebanillo exposes his dishonourable deeds with picaresque defiance, even going so far as to marshal them, towards the end of the novel, into an argument for preferment. In this way, the novel collapses the perspectives of pícaro and soldier to produce a protagonist who is as invested in the pursuit of material honour – the privileges and preferments that would bring economic stability – as he is uninterested in maintaining the standards of conduct that traditional honour requires. In fact, in transcribing his life, Estebanillo lampoons a textual form related to the soldier's recourse for recompense, as he mines some of his worst moments and attempts to exploit them for comic gold.[2]

It is this symbolic economy of fame and an established market for the picaresque as a form of entertainment that makes this genre a key resource for military life writing in the period. Despite a plethora of probable models (including the confession, saints' lives, sermons, historiography, and the burgeoning canon of commercial literature, including the chivalric romance), the picaresque novel is the category to which soldiers' autobiographies have most often been compared. Both share an episodic structure voiced by a first-person narrator who claims identity with the text's author. Both describe in anti-idealistic language the protagonist's often violent and sometimes comical experiences as he (or she) interacts with the diverse representatives of a highly stratified society. And both frequently articulate a trenchant critique of the various social ills that fall under their consideration. Likewise, the soldier's narrative and the pícaro's tale arise out of a common substrate of material need and social precarity.

For many soldiers, the picaresque provided a crucial intertext for novelizing the self precisely because it allowed them to exploit dishonourable episodes within their life stories. As the opening example of *Estebanillo González* indicates, the picaresque made space for the realistic representation of low-mimetic characters – a great source of the genre's popularity – as those characters struggled, to the evident delight of readers, to paddle against the current of their inherited impediments to a safe harbour of honour and good fortune. Whereas in *Estebanillo* the pícaro parodies military life writing, in this chapter I turn to the autobiographies of Miguel de Castro (1590–post-1617) and Catalina de Erauso (1592–1650), in which historical soldiers parody the tropes of the picaresque. Castro employs picaresque episodes as a strategy for narrating a fairly ignominious career as a military manservant and lover, though the purpose and ultimate circumstances of his writing remain unknown. Erauso, on the other hand, draws on the picaresque and on the religious figure of the *mujer varonil* as a means towards making her unusual, gender-changing story comprehensible and even exemplary for her contemporaries. Both authors, by contrast with the literary pícaro, write from a relatively middling position of social standing, but they are able to "play" the pícaro and produce themselves as cleverly insubordinate characters for whom the reclamation of honour can still be plausible. Thus, "playing the pícaro" performs the apparent fragmentation of martial honour (as defined in the reformist military treatises seen in chapter 2) in scenes of sexual excess, loss of self-control, and insubordination, in order to claim, not a picaresque outsider identity, but a distinctive and exceptional military identity that is at least partially defined by the power to claim the reader's attention.

The picaresque has been defined in various ways ever since the nineteenth-century birth of this taxonomy: in terms of its thematics (according to Alexander Parker, the key component of the picaresque is its "atmosphere of delinquency" [6]) and structurally (an autobiographical gambit, addressed to a powerful interlocutor, highlighting both the subject's attempts to exercise agency – of which the text is a piece – and the relative constraints placed on that agency by prevailing systems of caste and class). According to Howard Mancing, the author's sense that the novel belonged to a picaresque tradition – as indicated by means of titles and subtitles, shared vocabulary, and intertextual references to other picaresque tales – is the principal unifying factor (183). Whether it was too new to risk analysis or too lowly to merit consideration, early modern literary theorists make no mention of the kinds of literature we know as the picaresque (Eisenberg, "Does" 207). Still, seventeenth-century readers clearly recognized, if not a new form, then at least the filiation among books like *Lazarillo de Tormes* and *Guzmán de Alfarache*.[3] The engraving that served as the frontispiece of the first edition of *La Pícara Justina* (1605) demonstrates an awareness of this genetic relationship. The image, first commented upon extensively by Parker, depicts a ship labelled "la nave de la vida pícara" (the ship of the picaresque life) carrying Justina, Celestina, and Guzmán de Alfarache on a "río del olvido" (river of oblivion).[4] The ship is steered by Time and presided over by Bacchus, while a half-naked sleeping woman – Idleness – lounges below deck. At the bottom right Lazarillo de Tormes is seen manning a rowboat. The image is framed by blocks that spell out "el axuar de la vida picaresca" (the trappings of the picaresque life), each containing a smaller image that visually recalls specific episodes from exemplars of the genre, including dice, playing cards, a bunch of grapes, and a link of sausage. Even in the absence of a specific literary term to distinguish *La Pícara Justina*, the frontispiece of the first edition operates as a genre marker, confirming that contemporary readers recognized both the thematic similarities between texts like *Lazarillo* and *Guzmán de Alfarache* (as seen in the accoutrements of the picaresque life – the instruments of gluttony and intemperance – that surround the image that portrays them) as well as their parallels in form and diegesis (a narrative trajectory made visible in the river that bears the larger ship and Lazarillo's rowboat through the waves and towards their shared final destination: the Port of Death, signalled by a skeletal figure holding aloft a mirror). By combining text and image, the illustration effectively links Justina to her literary predecessors, a shrewd marketing move meant to capitalize on the popularity of such works, while simultaneously providing readers with a key to the text's interpretation.[5] In this way, the image, crowded with picaresque personages and mythological and allegorical figures, draws a "horizon of expectations" – to borrow Robert Jauss's descriptions of the function of genre (14–15) – in order to orient readers to the text's reception.

As Ulrich Wicks notes, the term *pícaro* made its literary debut in *Guzmán de Alfarache*; not long after, as we have seen in both the title and the illustration that opens *La Pícara Justina*, the word and its derivations definitively took on shades of shrewd insubordination, in addition to its previous, more neutral association with servitude (7). In a manner similar to this visual depiction in *Justina*, Estebanillo González inserts himself into the picaresque canon in the prefatory paratext, even as he swears that his is a true story: "te advierto que no es la fingida de *Guzmán de Alfarache*, ni la fabulosa de *Lazarillo de Tormes*, ni la supuesta del *Caballero de la Tenaza*" (I warn you that this is not the phony story of *Guzmán de Alfarache*, nor the fictitious tale of *Lazarillo de Tormes*, nor the supposed story of the *Knight of the Pincers*) (I: 13).

While excess, vice, and clever insubordination are hallmarks of the picaresque, the genre is also centrally, if counterintuitively, concerned with honour. According to Marcel Bataillon, it is this "preoccupation with decency, external honour, and social distinction" that gives rise to the picaresque's "multifaceted material" (214). On the one hand, an obsession with external honour is one of the many social ills that the pícaro-protagonists of various works encounter and critique. In the third chapter of *Lazarillo*, for example, the narrator briefly enters the service of an impoverished squire who spends what little money he has on keeping up the appearance of genteel leisure, even as he starves. This example causes Lazarillo to denounce "la negra, que llaman honra" (the vanity of honour) (84) – a convenient critique from a man who writes in an attempt to resolve his own personal *caso de honra* (case of honour). Similarly, Guzmán de Alfarache bitterly deduces from his experiences that what men call honour "más propiamente se llama soberbia o loca estimación" (is more correctly called pride or foolish estimation) (II.2: 267). Nevertheless, honour is a foundational concern for these narrators as their survival is dependent on their ability to navigate social space.[6]

Keeping in mind some of the complications of the generic classification sketched above, the autobiographies of Castro and Erauso share key similarities with the picaresque. Both texts unfold in a picaresque milieu that emphasizes the precariousness of the speaking subject's position in the social, economic, and gendered order. In contrast to the soldier's life writing studied in the preceding chapters, the autobiographies of Castro and Erauso respond to instability with what appears to be defiant exuberance, by accentuating the authors' insubordination and portraying them in many instances as dishonourable family members, untrustworthy friends, and bad servants. As such, these texts mark a distinctive strategy of self-fashioning in which a literary genre that is itself characterized by parody is inverted and parodied.

~

Around 1612 Miguel de Castro, a twenty-two-year-old ex-soldier, began to record the story of his life, though the purpose of his writing, beyond the clues in the text itself, remains unknown. Focusing on the period between 1605 and 1612, from his adolescence to young adulthood, Castro recounts his peripatetic adventures as a soldier engaged in combat in Italy and the Mediterranean, and his chequered career in the service of various noblemen. Alongside briefly recounted scenes of battle and copious catalogues of minutiae ranging from the contents of a certain supply ship to the intricacies of the military pay scale, Castro presents in dramatic detail multiple episodes of drunken street skirmishes and amorous conquests, punctuated by a handful of expressions of remorse. Due to the author's youth, irregular education, and liminal social status – forever on the verge of ascending to the ranks of the lower nobility but constantly threatened by the spectre of financial ruin – Castro's autobiography adds to this study an intriguing perspective on life in the Spanish tercios and the viceregal palaces of the Hapsburg empire outside the Peninsula.

Following the bibliographer and historian Antonio Paz y Meliá's first edition of the text in 1900 (*Vida del soldado español*), and the historian José María de Cossío's 1956 edition (*Autobiografía de Miguel de Castro*), several scholars have examined Castro's autobiography not only for its unique portrayal of certain historical incidents but also for the conflicted way in which it carries out the central task of authorial self-presentation. Whereas most previous criticism has principally been concerned with the ambiguous (Pope 197), failed (Cabo Aseguinolaza 593), and fragmentary (Levisi, *Autobiografías* 213–16; Juárez Almendros 164, 174) nature of the language used to construe the self at the centre of the narrative, I am most concerned with uncovering the context and meaning of the conventions Castro's *Vida* cites, especially as they converge towards an idiosyncratic rendition of the picaresque. In particular, the multiple sexual encounters described in the text foreground the importance of gender in the author's self-construction in a way that is unprecedented in the soldiers' autobiographies studied in previous chapters. While the discourses employed by García de Paredes (chapter 1), Suárez and Toral (chapter 2), and Pasamonte (chapter 3) telegraph certain specific attitudes towards gender, Castro explicitly names the destabilizing influences that the contemporary gender order was meant to contain. In this, Castro's text connects with the literary pícaro's disdain for traditionally defined honour, as well as the pícara's inevitable involvement in illicit sexual activity. By drawing upon the resources of the picaresque, Castro employs one of the most powerful rhetorical tools at his disposal, one that will allow him to mould his irregular past into a comprehensible, entertaining, and sympathetic story.

According to the first sentence of the *Vida*, Castro was born in Palencia in 1593 to parents whom he describes only as "legítimos" (1).[7] His early years are characterized by extensive travel as he accompanies his father and uncles – all highly placed ecclesiastical officials – on official journeys to Lugo, Orense, Valladolid, and Madrid. At the age of fourteen, and for reasons left unexplained, the author leaves home and joins the company of Captain Alonso Caro. After four or five days, however, he returns to stay with one of his uncles, the Bishop of Segovia. When the Bishop receives him coldly, Castro runs away again, this time joining up with the company of Captain Antonio de la Haya. As part of this new "family," Castro sets sail for Naples, thus beginning his adventures in Italy and the Mediterranean.

Castro conducts the greater part of his career in Naples and Malta, working his way up from soldier to *ayuda de cámara*, or one of a fleet of valets, attending to two different captains, the viceroy of Naples, and an assortment of Maltese gentlemen. In the course of his journeys, Castro plays a part in several Mediterranean military campaigns and meets a variety of intriguing women – from the virginal young daughter of a wealthy family to a beautiful Turkish slave – for whom he ruins himself and his career. Despite having risen to a relatively secure position in the service of the viceroy, Castro is driven to ever more desperate acts of negligence as he repeatedly escapes the palace and his duties in order to meet his mistress, the courtesan Luisa, several times a day. Although he is persistently punished for his delinquency, he seems unable to control his actions. Finally, he deserts his master, effectively ending his career, in order to have unfettered access to the courtesan. Their affair comes to an end not long afterwards; then, having squandered not only his own resources but also those of the woman he has subsequently found to maintain him, Castro is reduced to working as a servant for a few gentlemen of the lower nobility. At this point, the manuscript comes to an end, not long after a description of Castro's conversion and entrance into a religious order at the age of twenty-two. Though the last pages of the manuscript are missing, the text ends, mid-sentence, on a positive note, as Castro recounts an episode in which he is praised for his intelligence and writing abilities before several of his superiors.

There is a well-documented historical connection between the literary picaresque and the social and economic precariousness of the peripatetic soldier.[8] In Castro's *Vida* the discourses of soldier and servant intersect in the author's self-description of his years of scheming servitude. Not long after arriving in Italy, Captain de la Haya promotes Castro to his personal attendant, a position Castro will maintain, with various masters, throughout the course of the autobiography. Most importantly for Castro, this career move entails a new suit of clothes, one that sets him apart from the mass of soldiers who "iban tan rotos y desarrapados, y muchos sin camisas, [que] los patrones … les daban lo que podían, que fueron muchos a sus soldados cada uno alguna camisa vieja, para que se refrescase y limpiase el cuerpo de los piojos" (were so ripped and ragged, and many without shirts, that their patrons … gave them what they could, which was a lot for these soldiers, each one given an old shirt, to refresh himself and clean his body of lice) (9). Outfitted as a gentleman's attendant and newly privy to the intrigues of his superiors, Castro gains a more malleable identity that allows him to observe the official festivities at the viceregal palace as well as slip out into the dangerous streets of Naples after dark.

Like any pícaro, Castro ends up working for a succession of masters, some better than others; when they mistreat him, he leaves, but not without grumbling: "estaba fastidiado de que había tres años que le servía [a Francisco de Cañas] y jamás me había dado cosa que fuese de consideración, ni me trataba como era razón" (I was miffed that in the three years that I had served Francisco de Cañas he had never given me anything worthy of mentioning, nor did he treat me as I deserved) (121). Like Lazarillo de Tormes, Guzmán de Alfarache, and Pablos of *El Buscón*, Castro not only suffers at the hands of his masters, they also sometimes suffer because of him. The lowest point of his picaresque career comes when, having left the service of Captain Francisco de Cañas and acquired a post as an attendant of the viceroy of Naples, the Count of Benavente, Castro finds himself caught in an erotic obsession with the courtesan Luisa. Unable to be away from her for more than a few hours, Castro constantly plots how to escape the viceroy's palace, shirking his duties with increasingly disastrous consequences. The tales of his ingenuity in escaping the count's ever more elaborate precautions are told with comic flair and serve to emphasize the author's cleverness. But when he is finally caught in a lie regarding his whereabouts the previous night, the count punishes Castro severely:

> Haceme desnudar en carnes, como mi madre me parió, y con una cuerda dio detrás de mi a azotazos. Y en medio de la recámara estaba un bufete grande de vestidos, y los dos andábamos alrededor de él: él tras mi con el cordel, y yo huyendo dél, hasta que me vino a coger, y me dio muy bien. Y mas hizo, que con la rabia y colera que tenía me tomó con ambas manos del miembro, y tiró tan recio, que yo pensé que de aquella vez me dejaba sin aparejo, y tiraba tan recio, que me dolió por muy gran rato, y me causó tal desesperación, que de muchas espadas que en la dicha recamara había, casi estuvo movido a tomar una para contra él; pero al fin me acobardé y reporté la ira y enojo.
>
> (He stripped me down until I was as naked as the day I was born, and came after me with a whip. In the middle of the room there was a large trunk of clothes, and we moved around it: he with the whip, and I fleeing, until he caught me, and gave it to me good. And then he did even worse. With rage and fury he took my member in both hands and he tugged it so hard that I thought I might be left without one. It hurt for a very long time and made me so desperate that, of the many swords that were in that room, I was almost moved to take one up against him. But at the end I lost my courage and I repressed my ire and anger.) (104–5)

This scene, which begins with the farcical image of a naked Castro just barely dodging the whip of his master, quickly turns horrifying with the appearance of the twin spectres of castration and murder. Castro only concedes to allow the Count to discipline his body in this way because he reasons that taking up one of his own swords against his master would effectively amount to patricide. Here we see the subversive potential of the pícaro – the rogue who consistently eludes the vigilance of his master – thwarted, as Castro finally submits to painful punishment without defiance. Even still, he is marked by his previous rebellion, isolated from his closest friend, Antonio, who is also punished for his role in covering for Castro's absences, and held for nine days in a windowless closet. This penalty, in addition to its obvious aim of keeping Castro away from his mistress, evokes the pícaro's alienation and leads to only a very short-term, pragmatic submission to authority: not long afterwards, Castro gleefully describes returning to his old habits, and lavishes more detail on the ways in which he outwitted the Count than on the amorous encounters his ruses were meant to ensure. The culmination of these picaresque escapades, in which the author's cunning seems to be the protagonist, occurs when Castro spends an entire night away from the palace and sleeps late into the morning beside his mistress. As Castro has the keys to his master's clothes trunk, when the Count awakens and finds his servant nowhere in sight, he is forced to break into his own furniture and dress himself – a humiliating episode, because it indicates the Count's own difficulties in controlling his servants, which results in Castro's immediate dismissal.[9]

The inclusion of such picaresque episodes in his autobiography does not respond to the discourse of confession – since Castro barely indicates repentance – nor to the self-aggrandizing discourse of the *memorial* or *relación* – since the self-portrayal achieved is emphatically subversive. While the picaresque elements of Castro's autobiography reflect his subordinate status and itinerant way of life, these same elements work within the text to show that the power that Castro's masters hold over him is also paradoxically a form of weakness that Castro the pícaro exploits every time he resists their authority. By overlaying his soldier's tale with references to the picaresque, Castro highlights his youth and incorporates into the text a popular literary sensibility that is both humorous and subversive in that it shows the protagonist getting the better of his superiors time and again, eluding their vigils, and evading their fruitless attempts to control him. By combining the scripts of soldier and pícaro,[10] Castro points to the fluidity of his identity as a soldier capable of maintaining homosocial solidarity at the same time as he is a pícaro whose adventures capture the reader's interest, tickle his prurience, and perhaps even activate an uncomfortable pleasure at the contemplation of a master's misfortune.

The picaresque thus provides a unifying thread through a text where other cultural scripts and borrowed discourses help to illuminate other episodes. At the most extreme, Castro at times lingers over the details of minute incidents and recounts with mathematical precision everything from how much and what type of food he and his companions unloaded from a supply ship on a given day, to the labyrinthine structure of the military pay scale. Later, when describing his new position at the viceregal court, Castro interrupts the narrative to intercalate a document that details the names and occupations of the 263 people comprising the Count of Benavente's household – from the *mayordomo* to two unnamed female dwarves (197–200). Like Jerónimo de Pasamonte's list of prayers, such precise accounting serves to communicate qualities the author must have believed to be important, in this case his exceptional memory and managerial skills.

Given the relative absence of expressions of humility or repentance for wrongs committed in the past, Castro's autobiography does very little to evince any of the typical markers of the confessional – itself an important intertext of the picaresque, where it is often, although not always, parodic. Although Castro expresses a certain amount of regret for the moral lapses that contributed to his economic woes, and at times even refers to his story as a "tragedia" (200), on the whole, as Margarita Levisi notes, the tone of the *Vida* is one of apology rather than confession (195). This seems to indicate that Castro's intended audience is human rather than divine, which would account for the secular nature of the fictional generic conventions employed in the text and the modes of masculinity that they entail. Thus, the impression the reader has is that the author was not primarily a religious man, despite his profession in a religious order. In fact, the forms of masculinity he espouses are distinct from the kind of early modern Catholic clerical masculinity characterized by "humility, silence, and submission to clerical authority" (Bilinkoff 167). Likewise, nowhere in the text is there a description of Castro taking part in any devotional activities that would mark him as a man of God. In fact, Castro's first significant act in the narrative is his escape from home – an escape that signifies his initial disavowal of the clerical life led by his uncles and a rejection of their ecclesiastical mode of masculinity. If Castro's entrance into a religious order towards the end of his autobiography brings the narrative back full circle with the prodigal son returning to the arms of the Church, this is certainly not emphasized in the text. Even if the rest of the manuscript were to be recovered, it is doubtful that the narrative arc would shift substantially, given that the moment of Castro's entrance into religious life is mentioned with a minimum of detail:

> En Malta a quince de abril de mil seiscientes y doce entré en la Congregación de los Congregados de Nª Señora de la Asunción de los Padres de la Compañía de Jesús. Hice la proposición que hacen los Congregados después de algunos días de Noviciado a diez de Junio del dicho año, día de Pascua de Espíritu Santo.
>
> (In Malta on 15 April 1612 I entered the Congregation of the Congregants of Our Lady of the Assumption of the Fathers of the Society of Jesus. I made the proposition that the Congregants make after a few days as a novitiate, on 10 June of the same year, on the feast day of Pentecost.) (222)

Despite the confessional motive that Castro's entrance into a religious order may have provided, the narrative portrays this moment as if it were primarily a business transaction, as indeed it may have been for many in the period, when religious life represented one of a few viable career options.

The military identity that Castro inhabits within the *Vida* has certain parallels with the novelization of honour seen in the *Breve suma* of Diego García de Paredes, particularly in the focus on intense homosocial bonds with other men and in the choice to highlight idiosyncratic episodes rather than historically momentous occasions. In contrast with Paredes, however, the most relevant intertext for Castro's narrative is not the novel of chivalry, but its parodic inversion in the picaresque. After rejecting the austere but relatively privileged ecclesiastical existence represented by the men in his family, Castro revels in the rowdy camaraderie of military life and clearly enjoys new opportunities for travel as well as sexual exploits. During his tours of duty in Italy and the Mediterranean, Castro depicts himself as a brave and able combatant, but the bulk of the narrative describes his amorous adventures and street skirmishes occasioned by late-night carousing. This resonates with observations made by Harry Vélez Quiñones and others that Spanish military forces of the sixteenth and seventeenth centuries were highly visible all over Western Europe, with a reputation for bravery only matched (or perhaps enhanced) by the perception that many of them were also involved in criminal activities, such as theft, prostitution, and even murder (27). The misdeeds Castro recounts as a young soldier recall critiques of the Spanish military articulated in contemporary treatises and autobiographical documents like those of Diego Suárez Corvín and Domingo de Toral y Valdés. In contrast with these, however, Castro frames each episode as swashbuckling entertainment rather than critically portraying his actions as symptomatic of underlying social ills.

One of Castro's first adventures takes place not long after coming to Italy as part of Captain de la Haya's company. Making his way through the countryside and villages ravaged by the Italian tercios, he remarks that, even given the deservedly poor reputation of some Spanish soldiers, the Italians are far worse. Echoing Pasamonte's withering description of Naples and its inhabitants, Castro condemns the depredations of the Italian tercios: "son de tal suerte perjudiciales, que en Sodoma, o en tierra donde no hubiese ley, razón ni justicia, no sé qué más se podía hacer" (they are so harmful that in Sodom, or in whatever lawless land, without reason or justice, I don't know if they could do worse) (6). In a curious preamble to an admission of his own bad behaviour, Castro maintains that "los naturales [de estas tierras], con ser algunos españoles tan malos, quieren más dos compañías de españoles, y aun un tercio, que una de italianos, que tan sin conciencia ni escrúpulo los maltratan" (even though the Spanish are bad, the natives of this land prefer two companies of Spaniards, and even a whole tercio, over a single company of Italians, because they mistreat them without the slightest pang of conscience or scruple) (6).

While the destruction caused by the Italian soldiers is shown to be motivated primarily by greed, Castro's signature sin – as well as that of his commanding officers – is lust. En route to Naples and billeted in the house of a public notary, Castro becomes infatuated with Virgilia, the notary's daughter and a widow of questionable virtue. Admitting that Virgilia is not beautiful (so much so that later she is able to pass for a soldier: "que en la voz casi no se le conoscia ser muger" [from her voice you almost wouldn't know she was a woman] [17]), Castro explains his attraction as a matter of appetite: "y como yo venía hambriento desde Cartagena, tres meses había o más, me contenté por apagar aquella furia" (and as I was hungry ever since Cartagena, three months or more, I was content to put out the fire of lust) (11). As we will see, Castro's materialist designation of passion as hunger is in stark contrast to Catalina de Erauso's more chivalrous admission of preferring "buenas caras" (pretty faces) (122). Here and at numerous times in the autobiography, Castro demonstrates the adverse effects of yielding to appetite; when Virgilia begs to come away with him to Naples, Castro consents, dresses her in uniform, and hides her. The ensuing events would seem to be worthy of a confession, yet Castro's lack of contrition is conspicuous. After successfully fending off an armed attack by

Virgilia's brothers, and with their secret guarded by Castro's fellow soldiers, the two continue the affair until Virgilia is arrested three months later. When she is questioned about the identity of her "kidnapper," who by now is also wanted in the deaths of her brother and brother-in-law, she refuses to denounce Castro. When Virgilia sends a message to Castro detailing her ordeal, Castro becomes frightened that his erstwhile mistress will disclose his name under torture. He then describes how he responded to her urgent appeal:

> No hallé otro remedio que buscalle para que no sintiese más cosa ninguna ... Hecho el compuesto mortífero, enviésele diciendo que era bueno para no sentir el tormento, y que estuviese de buen ánimo ... [El compuesto] por ella recibido, lo que pensó había de ser remedio de su vida, fue causa de su muerte. Tomó el encubierto veneno, el cual hizo su operación, sin que se echase de ver; antes de diez y ocho horas halláronla muerta sin ningún mal color, ni indicios de que veneno hubiese sido, sino lo atribuían al áspero tormento que había recibido, y ansi me dixieron que pues no había testigo ninguno, que bien podía pasearme.
>
> (I found no other solution than to take her pain entirely away ... Once the deadly compound had been made, I sent it to her saying that it would help her not to feel the torture, and that she should be in good spirits ... Once she received the medicine, what she thought would be the remedy of her life was the cause of her death. She took the disguised poison, which did its work, without anybody noticing; before eighteen hours had passed, they found her dead without any discoloration, nor any signs that she had been poisoned, rather they attributed her death to the terrible torture she had received, and they said that since there were no witnesses, I could come out of hiding.) (21)

Far from pausing to indicate remorse for poisoning his former lover, Castro continues on to relate how, even though there was no evidence against him, he was promptly arrested once he came out of hiding following Virgilia's death. He, too, stoically endured torture; without a confession, and with his alibi corroborated by the false testimonies he had managed to buy, Castro was released, sentenced to six years of exile, and then promptly pardoned.

This episode is followed by a shift in emphasis from Castro's own activities to those of his superior officers. Towards the beginning of the text, Castro mentions that at the time he joined Antonio de la Haya's company, the captain was imprisoned in Valladolid for his part in spiriting away a merchant's daughter; whether he did so reluctantly and at the woman's behest – as Castro claims was the case with Virgilia – is not stated (3). Immediately following Castro's negotiation out of charges of adultery and murder, he reports that the officers of his company were all set free after a few months in prison under similar charges (21–2). From the very beginning, then, the Virgilia affair is framed not as an example of the author's corrupt youth, but rather as an illustration of Castro's integration into the military milieu, which is characterized by a subordinate's clever rebelliousness, one that brings soldiers at even the highest echelons into continual conflict with the law, even as that conflict strengthens their own cohesiveness as a group. In this, Castro further echoes the parodically apologetic strategy employed in *Lazarillo*, in which the pseudo-autobiographer states that he is no worse than those at the apex of society.

The stereotypical soldier's propensity for violence, lawlessness, and sexual incontinence, then, places Castro squarely in the domain of the picaresque, though the possibility of intense homosocial bonding is an important additional characteristic of his depiction of the military, bonding that was the object of both praise and obscene ridicule in the period.[11] Castro's *Vida* makes it clear that it is both the unencumbered freedom and the companionship of other soldiers that attracted him to military service. Indeed, it is only through the cooperation of his fellow soldiers that Castro is able to hide Virgilia from her outraged father and brothers. Later, Castro shows how much of his misconduct is abetted by his friends, while his superiors most often work to save him from the worst consequences of his actions.

The hierarchical yet close-knit organization of the military, the enforced physical proximity of the soldiers, and the constant threat of danger all create the conditions for intimate homosocial relationships, as seen in the fervent declarations of love Castro dedicates to his friend and fellow soldier Antonio. The following is one among several effusive passages describing the passionate friendship between the two soldiers:

> [Antonio y yo] éramos los mayores amigos que se puede imaginar, la cual amistad dura hasta hoy en día siempre más firme y verdadera, y es de suerte que excede a la de dos hermanos más amados y conformes que se pueda imaginar. Yo le quiero de suerte que en mí no hay cosa separada para con él, sino que lo que es mío es él más dueño dello que yo, ansí dineros, ropa, como la vida, salud y persona y aun alma, sinceramente, sin haber otro motivo para ello que la pura voluntad y afición de amigo fiel.
>
> (Antonio and I were the greatest friends imaginable. Our friendship continues to this day, always more steadfast and true, and it is such that it

> exceeds that of even the most loving and happy brothers you can imagine. I love him so much that there is nothing of mine that is not also his and even more so: from money and clothing to life, health, body, and even spirit, sincerely, without any other motive than the pure goodwill and fondness of a loyal friend.) (66–7)

Having declared that he and Antonio are more than brothers, later in the passage he compares their relationship to that of a father and son, master and servant, with the difference being that their roles are equal, with each man showing respect and deference to the other. In this way, Castro shows how the conditions of military life – even as it gave rise to otherwise violent and criminal behaviour – could cement the supposedly pure bonds of masculine friendship. As Castro goes on to note, between himself and Antonio there is no need for idle chatter; like brothers or lovers the hallmark of their intimacy is their ability to be silent with one another: "y con estar juntos y en una casa, y tan grandes amigos, se solían pasar los cinco y seis días que no nos hablábamos sino es en el servicio del amo" (and being together in the same house, as such great friends, five or six days would pass that we didn't speak unless it was in the course of our master's business) (67). This masculine silence contrasts with Castro's poetic effusions to and about his various mistresses; interestingly, these heterosexual relationships seem to incite anxiety and compulsive behaviours in the author, whereas his homosocial relations are a source of calm and stability. Yet as the cultural script of the soldier as a loyal friend is overlaid by the scripts of the scheming pícaro and, as we shall see, the passionate courtier, Castro's masculine solidarity with his fellow soldiers and superiors evaporates with each duty shirked, each act of petty thievery, and each risky satisfaction of illicit erotic urges.

While some amorous encounters, like the episode with Virgilia, are succinctly, if sensationally, described as the fulfilment of a fleshly appetite, other encounters point to a more complicated dialectic of desire, one that works to undermine the homosocial bonds of military life and would seem to have no place among Castro's tales of picaresque trickery.[12] In the course of his autobiography, Miguel de Castro does at times describe the thoughts and feelings prompted by various events, yet critics have most often characterized these descriptions as superficial; here, as in other autobiographies from the period, it is difficult to discern the kind of soul-searching self-reflection associated with the autobiographical act since Rousseau. For example, in describing what might have been a profoundly emotional occasion – the author's conversion and entrance into a religious community – Castro the individual slips from sight and in two brief sentences manages to convey only the particulars of time and place. At the linguistic level, however, Levisi has argued that Castro's Petrarchan lexicon and self-consciously lyrical prose is a strategy of self-revelation; according to Levisi, by using the clichés of love poetry to describe some of his mistresses, Castro is able to indicate a depth of feeling that is conspicuously absent in other moments (210–12). While this may at least partially account for his use of an otherwise unexpected literary paradigm, what I find most compelling about Castro's courtly performance is that it indicates his awareness that language can be used to dissimulate, occluding the baseness of his desires, while simultaneously allowing him to try on the persona of his noble superiors – however outmoded this persona may have been.[13] An example of the first effect of this Petrarchan discourse appears in an episode describing a mutually disingenuous conversation Castro has with a woman to whom he is not attracted:

> Si lo creía yo, mala Pascua me venga, pero fingí crello, y que todo aquello era un átomo en comparación de lo que me causaba su amor, y que era menester mucha mayor suma para remunerar una pequeña parte de las lágrimas que me era causa, y que Vulcano, Etna, Cuma y Astrongalo no echaban, ni todo el Infierno junto, las llamas que mi pecho cada día … Tras esto, alabé infinito la belleza de su rostro … prosiguiendo con larga arenga y limada prosa, todo sacado del archivo de la mentira, porque hasta entonces, aun mi memoria no sabía si ella era nacida.
>
> (If I believed her, may I be punished, but I feigned belief, saying that all that was an atom in comparison with what her love did to me, and that a much greater sum was necessary to pay back a small part of the tears that she had caused me, and that Mount Vulcano, Etna, Cuma, and Astrongalo, and even all the fires of hell together, were nothing compared to my inflamed heart … After this, I praised to infinity the beauty of her face … proceeding with a lengthy discourse and refined prose, all lies, of course, because until then I was unaware of her very existence.) (75)

The parodic excess of language purportedly communicating Castro's pain marks his awareness of language's artificiality while showing his appreciation of its usefulness. In this way, the professional recognition that he later reports receiving for his ability to write well has an amorous corollary that recalls Castiglione's pronouncement, in *Il Cortegiano*, that the ideal courtier should be adept at the employment of both arms and letters, able to wield the rhetoric of persuasion verbally and violently. This awareness informs Castro's integration of the three distinct forms of masculine discourse according to which he structures the story of his life. While the soldier script emphasizes masculine solidarity and conformity, which is then undermined by the subversive model of the pícaro, Castro's uneven performance as a courtly lover is heavily influenced by his inferior social and economic class. As a soldier-servant stationed in his master's private chambers, Castro is aware of the most intimate details of his superior's personal life, yet he is also highly conscious of the vast differences between himself and his masters. As a servant of rich men, Castro is subject to a certain feminized status, a marginalized position that he explicitly escapes when in pícaro mode. On the other hand, by adopting the language of his betters – even in an excessive mode verging on burlesque – he forges a connection with a potential, elite readership, even as he performs for the reader the cynical unmasking of the veiled aggressiveness of Petrarchan discourse.

In what follows, we see the same artful manipulation of the figures of the literary pícaro, the swashbuckling soldier, and the nimble courtier as they form an integral part of the autobiography attributed to one of the period's most celebrated avatars of successful self-fashioning: Catalina de Erauso, or *la Monja Alférez.*

~

In 1625, after nineteen years of military service in Chile and Peru, a celebrated Basque soldier submitted an autobiographical manuscript to the publisher Bernardino de Guzmán in Madrid. Like many soldiers' autobiographies, this remarkable text narrates the author's adventures in far-flung corners of Spain's burgeoning empire, with an emphasis on episodes of deception, violence, and erotic intrigue.[14] Unlike many soldiers' autobiographies, which were written with a private readership in mind, this text both reflected and helped to consolidate the author's growing notoriety. The Basque soldier's story reportedly would be published twice in the same year, first by Guzmán in Madrid and then by Simón Fajardo in Seville, before being staged in 1626 under the hybrid epithet that had come to define the eponymous hero: *la Monja Alférez* or the Lieutenant Nun.[15]

Baptized Catalina de Erauso in San Sebastián in 1592, the Lieutenant Nun spent most of her childhood within the confines of a Dominican convent, where two of her sisters also boarded. The autobiography recounts how, shortly before she was to take her vows, at the age of fifteen, Erauso escaped the convent that had been her home for more than ten years, fashioned her nun's habit into men's clothing, and eventually travelled to the New World under the name Alonso Díaz Ramírez de Guzmán. Following a short stint as a trader in present-day Panama and Peru, Erauso joined up with the armies being raised to fight in Chile. There she served in the wars against the indigenous Mapuche and was promoted to *alférez* (ensign or second lieutenant) for her bravery in battle. Erauso's boldness on the battlefield was accompanied by a quick temper, a propensity for gambling, and a taste for violence that on several occasions culminated in murder. After a string of such incidents and on the verge of being arrested, Erauso confessed the entirety of her story, including her birth gender, to Bishop Agustín de Carvajal. The 1784 copy of Erauso's *Vida* contains this almost parodically succinct confession: "me embarqué, aporté, trajiné, maté, herí, maleé; correteé; hasta venir a parar en lo presente, y a los pies de su señoría ilustrísima" (I set sail, I arrived at port, I moved merchandise, I killed, maimed, wreaked havoc, and roamed about, until coming to stop in this very instant, at the feet of Your Eminence) (160).

Once her sex was validated and her virginity proven, Erauso was spared from sentencing and was allowed to join a community of nuns. When word arrived from San Sebastián confirming that she had never finalized her vows and was therefore not obliged to remain in the convent, Erauso set sail for Spain, where she successfully lobbied King Philip IV for a military pension. In Italy, Erauso was granted an audience with Pope Urban VIII, who, much like the king of Spain, was so impressed with the Lieutenant Nun's bravery that he awarded her a dispensation to continue dressing and living as a man. His only admonishment was that she continue her chaste conduct and refrain from violence. Although the autobiography concludes shortly after this episode, the historical record suggests that Catalina, now using the name Antonio de Erauso, returned to the New World and there made a respectable living as a mule-driver until her death around 1650. The deft control that the narrator demonstrates is perhaps due to the fact that, as Kathleen Ann Myers has noted, Erauso's formal petition – which emphasizes her military accomplishments while remaining silent on her banditry – had already been submitted to the Crown by the time the autobiography was composed (Myers 187; Velasco, *Lieutenant* 46–7). As in Castro's case, the extant manuscript of Erauso's *Vida* contains no paratext to indicate the author's intentions or ideal interlocutors, yet clearly Erauso expected that her *Vida* would be read, not by a tightly circumscribed group of superiors, but by a wider public whose interest in her story had already been demonstrated.

Due to its striking subject matter, Erauso's *Vida* has enjoyed the relatively sustained attention of historians and literary scholars alike, from its first publication to the present day. Following the biographical and bibliographical work of Rima de Valbona, Pedro Rubio Merino, and Ángel Esteban, scholars such as Stephanie Merrim, Mary Elizabeth Perry, Encarnación Juárez Almendros, Sherry Velasco, Eva Mendieta, and others have produced compelling interpretations of the text in light of the presumed author's life, by applying a variety of critical frameworks. The plurality of subject positions that Erauso inhabits in the text encourages disparate readings: the Lieutenant Nun has been claimed as a colonial subject, a Basque subject, and a Spanish subject, as well as a woman usurping patriarchal prerogative by transvestism or, alternatively, as a transgendered subject whose self-portrayal aligns with that of the masculine elite. Among the most recent work on Erauso's *Vida* is Marcia Ochoa's thought-provoking article "Becoming a Man in Yndias," which reads the autobiography primarily through the lens of media studies to consider how the Lieutenant Nun's story was mediated during her lifetime, analysing the ways in which "the man became a message that circulated and still circulates" (56). My emphasis, however, is on the ways in which Erauso's *Vida* intersects with and diverges from some of the gendered literary patterns established within soldiers' life writing, particularly the picaresque. Much like Miguel de Castro's *Vida*, the greater part of Erauso's self-presentation is structured according to a roguish mode of masculinity. From her daring convent escape to the final chapter, Erauso is shown stealing from her masters, provoking her enemies, and eluding the law's constraints. As Myers has observed, Erauso's *Vida* "echoes the [picaresque] genre's lexicon … ideology … and emplotment" (187), especially with regard to the "discourse of poverty and the discourse of sexuality" (188), two important features of the literary picaresque. Yet, unlike Miguel de Castro's picaresque self-presentation, Erauso's narrative only flirts with erotic deviance, portraying suggestive episodes in a double register that always emanates from the safety of the Lieutenant Nun's proven virginity.

The curiosity attached to Erauso's case is understandable, especially in light of the prevailing baroque fascination with the monstrous, the marvellous, and the deceptive nature of reality. As Stephanie Merrim has argued, the *Vida* represents a canny negotiation of the promises and pitfalls associated with anomaly (192–5). As many scholars have noted, Erauso is unique among early modern autobiographers in that she was, in some sense, a self-made celebrity; regardless of whether she penned the *Vida* or dictated it to a scribe, her participation in the elaboration and dissemination of her life story – in the autobiography, the official petitions that describe her service to the Crown, her tours of Spain and Italy, and the portraits that she sat for – reflects her investment in the invention of "the Lieutenant Nun" as a public and literary persona. The autobiography registers Erauso's awareness of this split shortly before the end, when the narrator refers to herself by the title inextricably linked to her newly public status: "Entramos en Lima ya de noche, y sin embargo ya no podíamos valernos de tanta gente curiosa que venía a ver a *la Monja Alférez* [emphasis added]" (We arrived in Lima after dark, and nevertheless we could barely make our way for all the curious people who came out to see the Lieutenant Nun) (163). The *Vida* portrays Erauso's fame as being born at the moment of her confession; according to the autobiography, the church where Erauso had claimed sanctuary was filled within hours with crowds eager to catch a glimpse of the virginal soldier and former outlaw (161). Almost immediately, the intrinsic value of her hybridity is established, as the awed crowds christen Erauso as the "Lieutenant Nun," the perfect, if unlikely, combination of two vocations indicating submission to the Catholic Church and the Spanish state. That identity, as I discuss in what follows, is largely a product of the unlikely combination of two component discourses and their complex gender politics: the picaresque, embracing some aspects of the pícaro while avoiding the pitfalls of the pícara, on the one hand; and the religious ideal of the *mujer varonil*, on the other.

The *Vida* begins with the customary catalogue of birthplace and year, as well as with the names of Erauso's parents, but it quickly transitions from exposition to action, and provides a justification for the protagonist's metamorphosis: "Estando en el año de noviciado, ya cerca del fin, se me ofreció una reyerta con una monja profesa … la cual era robusta y yo muchacha; me maltrató de manos y yo lo sentí" (Towards the end of the year of my novitiate, I had a quarrel with a nun … She was a robust, strong woman, and I was still a girl; when she beat me, I felt it) (94). This characteristically picaresque incident provides the motive for Erauso's escape and gender transformation, which takes place over three days in a stand of chestnut trees near the convent walls:

> Corté e híceme de una basquiña de paño azul con que me hallaba, unos calzones; de un faldellín verde de perpetuán que traía debajo, una ropilla y polaínas: el hábito me lo dejé por allí, por no ver qué hacer de él. Cortéme el cabello y echélo por allí, y partí la tercera noche y eché no sé por dónde.
>
> (From my blue woollen bodice I cut and sewed a pair of breeches; and with the green petticoat I wore underneath, I made a doublet and hose: I left my habit there, not knowing what else to do with it. I cut my hair

> and threw it there, and I left the third night, setting out I didn't know where.) (95)

While, years later, Erauso would return to the habit (significantly, the only garment left behind and intact), she would never again fully occupy the female subject position signified by the skirts repurposed into doublet and breeches. Following this act of rebellion, which is framed as a reaction against the mistreatment she received at the hands of an older woman, Erauso becomes a perpetrator of misdeeds rather than a victim, beginning with the first theft of eight doubloons and ending with the murder that precipitates a full confession.

A brief overview of female to male cross-dressing in the period provides the historical background necessary to understand the dangers and possibilities inherent in Erauso's transformation. While transvestism was officially condemned by civil and Church law, examples of gender bending abound in the period, ranging from the cross-dressed actresses of the *comedia* to the spiritual ideal of the *mujer varonil*. In his study on transvestite drama in Golden Age Spain, Sidney Donnell traces the early sixteenth-century polemic on how to cast feminine roles back to the brief moment at mid-century when all roles were played by men (as in the English playhouses), to the integrated casts typical of the end of the century. Curiously, as Donnell notes, "after the ban on transvestite performers was in effect, the *comedia nueva* … adopted the practice of requiring *characters* to cross-dress within a given play's *plot*. Hence, we find hundreds of plays in the seventeenth century in which male and female characters cross-dress" (143). Thus, at the moment when cross-dressing on the stage was no longer motivated by a concern for modesty and required by law, dramatists invented scenarios that would put women into men's clothes, and vice versa, a development that suggests the public's fascination with transvestism. And yet, as scholars have argued, such sensational plot twists were most often excused by honourable necessity and were always resolved with the character's return to the gendered status quo.

Even within this conservative framework, cross-dressing on the stage carried the possibility for subversive laughter and non-normative arousal, and so met with Church disapproval (Merrim 186). At the same time, the ascetic ideal of the *mujer varonil* – in this context, the saintly woman invigorated by masculine virtue – was embraced by the Church. The long tradition of the *mujer varonil* was preserved and disseminated in compilations of saints' lives that included, for instance, the legend of Saint Thecla, who left her family and fiancé and donned men's clothing in order to accompany Saint Paul on his mission to convert the pagans

(Rocha n.p.). In a similar story, the third-century Saint Perpetua was blessed with a vision on the eve of her martyrdom; in the vision, she was transformed into a man capable of defeating a vicious Egyptian, whom she interpreted as a symbol of the devil (Rowe 581). As one scholar states, "Estas dos historias fueron recordadas constantemente como modelos a imitar por las autoridades de la Iglesia y utilizadas por las propias mujeres con la finalidad de legitimar la elección de una vida casta y dedicada a la vida espiritual" (These two stories were constantly brought up as models to imitate by Church authorities and were used by women themseves to legitimate the selection of a chaste life dedicated to spiritual things) (Rocha n.p.). Certainly, both legends demonstrate that a symbolic transformation from feminine frailty to masculine fortitude, when stimulated by supernatural means and with spiritual ends, was regarded positively. Although Erauso could not claim an explicitly evangelistic purpose for her cross-dressing, like Thecla her virginity was taken as evidence of her superior nature; and like Perpetua, Erauso's exceptional strength and courage were taken to be appropriately represented by her masculine attire.

The Lieutenant Nun's synthesis of the discourses of female chastity, virile spirituality, and Spanish imperial expansion is crystallized in the events surrounding the canonization of Teresa de Ávila in 1622, two years before Erauso's return to Spain. Teresa, a Carmelite nun, had established a reform movement that included fourteen priories and sixteen convents at the time of her death in 1582 (Elliott 243). The movement, which emphasized austerity and the practice of mental prayer, flourished as Teresa's writings first circulated in manuscript and then were published posthumously in 1588 (Weber, "Religious" 156). As Alison Weber has demonstrated, Teresa's influential works are shaped by "a rhetoric of 'feminine' ignorance and uncertainty," a precautionary approach that succeeded in creating a space for the author's robust theological, mystical, and administrative activities, even during a time of significant opposition to women's active religious participation (155–6).[16] Although no one would mistake Catalina de Erauso for a saint, her *Vida* nevertheless reflects the theological topos of the *mujer varonil*, woven in and around a rhetoric incorporating the literary form of the picaresque and an alternately proud and critical stance stimulated by Spain's military machine.

The remarkable success of Erauso's self-portrayal as a virginal pícaro and courageous soldier can perhaps best be measured against the well-known case of Elena (or Eleno) de Céspedes, another cross-dressed soldier of whom Erauso may have been aware. Israel Burshatin has compellingly analysed the story of the young surgeon Eleno de

Céspedes, who in 1568 was one of many men who joined Philip II's campaign to crush the Morisco rebellion centred in the mountainous terrain of the Alpujarras (420–3). As a freed slave of African descent, Céspedes had on occasion been mistaken for a Morisco himself, and accusations of treason had briefly landed him in prison. Once his identity had been verified and his name cleared, Céspedes was understandably eager to further prove his loyalty to the "old Christian" regime by joining the forces intent on stamping out the Morisco insurrection. But at least some of Céspedes' fellow soldiers were aware that their comrade was not quite like them. In 1587, seventeen years after the conclusion of the war, the licentiate Ortega Velázquez denounced Céspedes to the authorities for having recently married María del Caño. According to the allegations, it was well known that Eleno was neither a man nor a woman, but had two sexes; as such, the marriage was illegal (423).

Eleno, as it turned out, had been raised as a woman named Elena. Freed from slavery at the age of ten, Elena entered into a series of apprenticeships, rapidly rising through the ranks of weavers and seamstresses until a startling biological shift in her late teens allowed her to dress as a man, to serve in the War of the Alpujarras, to study medicine, and finally to marry. By the time Ortega Velázquez revealed Céspedes's "true" identity to the civil authorities, Eleno had been living as a man for over twenty years (Burshatin 423).

Because Eleno's chief crime was against the sacrament of marriage, jurisdiction over the case shifted from the royal court to the Inquisitional Tribunal of Toledo. As was the norm for Inquisitional trials, Eleno was required to produce an autobiographical document – the *discurso de la vida* – that would serve to explain to the incredulous Inquisitors how Elena had transformed herself into Eleno. As Burshatin has argued, despite the mastery of contemporary medical knowledge and the canny subject positioning displayed in this document, as well as in the transcripts of the trial, Eleno's bid to explain his sexual identity as hermaphroditic was doomed to failure. The court found Elena de Céspedes guilty and sentenced her to two hundred lashes in an auto-da-fé (424).

Ten years after the trial, Gerónimo de Huerta included Eleno/Elena's unusual case among the "anotaciones curiosas" embellishing his translation of Pliny's *Natural History* (Burshatin 421). Whether or not Erauso had read Huerta's translation, the discourses surrounding such transformations were widely known. As Burshatin has demonstrated, in the *discurso de su vida* Elena brought all her medical training to bear in arguing that she had been transformed into a man in a process that was fully explainable and not unprecedented. By citing popular understandings of gender as an unstable, caloric category, Elena attempted to naturalize her desired gender role as a husband before Church authorities. In contrast, Catalina de Erauso's self-presentation is marked by an absence of overtly biological rhetoric and a retreat from an explicitly active sexual identity. Regarding the somatic changes that may have accompanied Erauso's transformation, Perry has noted, "none of the accounts of [Erauso's] life indicate how she disguised or stopped her menstrual periods" ("Convent" 401). In fact, aside from the scene where Erauso, recently escaped from the convent, cuts her hair and turns her dress into men's attire, the *Vida* contains no descriptions of the Lieutenant Nun's appearance. Only the portrayal penned by the cleric Pedro del Valle Peregrino hints at the physical modifications that contributed to Erauso's successful performance of masculinity:

> Ella es de estatura grande i abultada para muger ... No tiene pechos: que desde mui muchacha me dixo haver hecho no sé qué remedio para secarlos i quedar llanos, como le quedaron: el qual fue un emplasto que le dio un Ytaliano, que quando se lo puso le causó gran dolor; pero después, sin hacerle otro mal, ni mal tratamiento, surtió el efecto.
>
> (She is tall and thickset for a woman ... She has no breasts; she told me that as a young girl she had taken I don't know what kind of medicine to dry them up and flatten them out; it was a poultice given to her by an Italian, and when she put it on it caused great pain; but then, without any other bad symptoms it took effect.) (quoted in Valbona 128)

Significantly, within the *Vida* the state of Erauso's physical body is only referred to in a moment that definitively establishes her femaleness, when she is submitted to the inspection of two midwives who find her to be "virgen intacta" (160).

Rather than focusing on the biological underpinnings of the Lieutenant Nun's hybrid gendered identity, the *Vida* shows Erauso to be invested with valuable cultural and spiritual capital. As the descendant of slaves, Elena de Céspedes discovered that the circumstances of her birth would always supersede her actions; although she had fought in the War of the Alpujarras, her dark skin and infamous background cast a shadow over her attempts to perform even a normative masculine role as a husband (Burshatin 420). In contrast, Catalina de Erauso's high birth and virginity – a doubly esteemed status captured in del Valle Peregrino's characterization of her as "una doncella ... bien nacida" (well born young woman) – permitted her to pursue the profession of arms with the blessing of both the king and the pope. The convent education that taught her to read and write was ultimately more useful to Erauso than Elena's medical training, as Erauso's skills provided entry first into the houses of several highly placed family members and then into the mercantile ventures of the New World. By the same token, Erauso's elevated class origins were complemented by her appeal to the discourse of virginity, which, as seen in the various manifestations of the *mujer varonil*, was a paradoxically potent way to affirm female power.

In a testament to the soldier's lived reality and the interest aroused by tales of bloodshed and picaresque scheming, the bulk of Erauso's life narrative does not focus on her virtues; instead, the *Vida* concentrates on descriptions of trickery and violence. The episodes immediately following Erauso's convent escape establish the protagonist within a picaresque trajectory characterized by insubordination and a preference for self-determined change over servitude and stability. Following her initial transformation, one of Erauso's first destinations is Vitoria, where she finds a place in the household of her uncle, Francisco de Cerralta. Cerralta, like many family members to follow, does not recognize in his niece anything other than a promising intellect and an ability to read Latin. In an attempt to refine his young servant, Cerralta insists that Erauso continue in her studies, only to be met with stubborn refusal: "y viéndome rehusarlo me porfió, y me instaba hasta ponerme las manos. Yo con esto determiné dejarle" (and seeing me refuse he insisted, and he pressured me to the point of beating me. And with this I decided to leave him) (95). Far from the feminine humility and passivity strategically deployed by Saint Teresa, Erauso paints herself as a wilful child whose obstinate nature is not a product of appetite – as is Miguel de Castro's – but rather of a strong, undisciplined nature.

Uninterested in the sedentary practice of grammar and rhetoric, Erauso continues her peregrinations, but not before relieving her uncle of a few coins. Now in Valladolid, the young page again comes into contact with an unsuspecting family member. After seven months serving the King's secretary, Erauso is startled to see her father in conversation with her master and decides to slip away before she can be detected. From Valladolid, Erauso sets off "sin saberme yo qué hacer ni adónde ir, sino dejarme llevar del viento como una pluma" (without knowing what to do nor where to go, letting the wind carry me like a feather) (97). Eventually, following stints as a personal servant to several gentlemen, Erauso finds work as a cabin boy in the service of another uncle, Estevan Eguiño, whose ship is bound for the New World. Like Cerralta and Erauso's own father, Eguiño is unaware of his kinship with the young sailor. Nevertheless, in a pattern that will continue throughout the *Vida*, Eguiño is shown to be partial to Erauso as he recognizes their shared Basque heritage. Despite Eguiño's regard for Erauso, when the ship, now laden with silver, is ready to return to Spain, Erauso opts to stay behind. In describing this episode, the *Vida* takes on a characteristically boastful tone: "yo le hice un tiro cuantioso a mi tío, cogiéndole quinientos pesos ... Salté en tierra, y nunca me vieron más" (I took quite a sum from my uncle, stealing 500 of his pesos ... I leapt ashore and they never saw me again) (99–100). This unceremonious leave-taking, occasioned by whim and financed by theft, continues in the New World, where Erauso finds work first as a merchant and then as a soldier.

Viewed against the backdrop of the bustling movement of goods and gold between the Americas and Spain, Erauso's small acts of thievery – always of money, never of merchandise – begin to look like entrepreneurship. Unlike Lazarillo de Tormes, the young Erauso does not steal in an explicit attempt to stave off immediate starvation, and her theft carries no stinging social critique. More than anything, Erauso's portrayal as a self-financing adventurer resonates with the comical rather than the critical aims of the picaresque, as the protagonist astounds with her unconventional resourcefulness. That Erauso – a literate, well-educated member of the lower nobility – steals small sums out of foresight indicates the distance between the Lieutenant Nun's charmingly picaresque youth and the grinding poverty suffered by the protagonists of the literary picaresque. And, by a similar token, her perpetual escape from the households and protection afforded by her respectable family and their associates appears to enact in reverse Lazarillo's intended journey towards the "buen puerto" (safe harbour) of honour and financial solvency. In this way, Erauso's *Vida* begins to reshape the picaresque model from within, as the reader – aware of the protagonist's celebrated stature – sees the rogue's youth written from a perspective of privilege.

Erauso's *Vida* further appropriates the entertaining aspects of the picaresque in a self-aggrandizing fashion by disavowing the sexual dishonour attached to the typical destitute pícaro. A key episode of the autobiography recounts how Erauso avoided replicating the ignominious erotic scenario that structures *Lazarillo de Tormes*. In this episode, one of Erauso's many masters, Juan de Urquiza, attempts to orchestrate a marriage between Erauso and Beatriz de Cárdenas, his mistress. Erauso notes: "Es de saber que esta Doña Beatriz de Cárdenas era dama de mi amo, y él miraba a tenernos seguros, a mí para servicio y a ella para gusto" (I should note that Doña Beatriz de Cárdenas was my master's mistress, and he wanted to keep us both close, me for business and her for pleasure) (104). This triangulation, which recalls Lazarillo's position as the husband of a kept woman, is roundly refused by Erauso, even as Urquiza attempts to convince her with "montes de oro" (mountains of gold) and assurances of "la hermosura y prendas de la dama" (the beauty and talents of the lady) (105). Unswayed by promises of wealth, Erauso also reports to be uninterested in Beatriz's charms: "iba a la casa de aquella señora, y ella me acariciaba mucho ... y una noche me encerró y se declaró en que a pesar del diancho había de dormir con ella, y me apretó en esto tanto, que hube de alargar la mano y salirme; y dije luego a mi amo, que de tal casamiento no había que tratar, porque por todo el mundo yo no lo haría" (I often went to that lady's house, and she would caress me ... and one night she locked me in and declared that come hell or high water I was going to sleep with her, and she pressed me on this so much, that I had to resort to force to leave; and I told my master never to speak of that marriage again, because I wouldn't agree to it for anything in the world) (104–5). Whether out of self-preservation or distaste, Erauso rebuffs monetary and sexual advances, and in so doing eludes an alliance that would have brought her perilously close to the kind of debasement that is the culmination of Lazarillo's abjection.

Just as Miguel de Castro's integration into the military milieu is at times represented in his interactions with women, Erauso's entry into the soldier's life and the masculine solidarity it entails is precipitated by an incident involving Juan de Urquiza's sister-in-law:

> "[Había] en casa dos doncellas hermanas ... con las cuales, y sobre todo con una que más me inclinó, solía yo más jugar y triscar. Y un día, estando en el estrado peinándome acostado en sus faldas, y andándole en las piernas, Diego de Solarte llegó acaso a una reja por donde nos vio y oyó a ella que me decía que fuese al Potosí y buscase dineros, y nos casaríamos."
>
> (There were two sisters in the house ... and with both of them, but especially one who was most inclined to me, I would often frolic and tease. And one day, when she and I were in the front parlour, she combing my hair as I lay on her lap, across her legs, Diego de Solarte passed by a grate and saw us and he heard her urging me to go seek my fortune in Potosí so that we could marry.) (109)

Whether this behaviour was motivated by desire or was part of Erauso's performance of masculinity, the Lieutenant Nun's attractiveness to other women is a recurring motif in the *Vida*. While Beatriz de Cárdenas had lavished her attention on him for questionable ends, Urquiza's sister-in-law is the first of several women apparently won over by Erauso's charm. The *Vida* is unclear as to whether or not Erauso returned her affections, as Erauso is immediately dismissed by Urquiza. Here and in other amorous interludes, the possibility of lesbian desire is not foreclosed; in fact, Urquiza's own suspicions – which are not explicitly contradicted – suppose a sensual frisson between his employee and his wife's sister. Nevertheless, the register of sexual impropriety is undercut by the contemporary reader's knowledge of the Lieutenant Nun as a virgin and as a woman.[17]

Despondent at finding herself unemployed and with few other prospects, Erauso joins up with the forces gathering to fight in Chile. Here, as the *Vida* follows Erauso into maturity, the protagonist's picaresque boyishness hardens into a soldierly identity characterized by financial and physical risk. While Erauso had previously taken her chances with each theft from her masters, as a soldier with a fixed wage, stationed in sparsely populated Chile, she turns to gambling and brawling to pass the time. As Mar Martínez Góngora has shown, gambling in the period was associated with an abject masculinity characterized by a lack of self-control (11). According to Enrique García Santo-Tomás, sixteenth- and seventeenth-century conduct manuals and sermons railed against the waste of money and the dissipation of vital energy that occurred in the gambling halls. One author, taking as his subject "the use of time," wrote:

> Nació el hombre de gastar el tiempo en la contemplación de las cosas de este mundo, y por ellas conocer a su criador es medio para otro fin, que es ganar el cielo, por medio de hacer en el tiempo de nuestra vida buenas obras … el tahúr no halla, ni tiene de todos estos tiempos más que tiempo para jugar.
>
> (Man was born to spend time in the contemplation of the things of this world, and in this contemplation to come to know his creator, and to gain heaven by spending his time doing good works … the gambler doesn't have time to do anything but gamble.) (qtd. in García Santo-Tomás, "Outside" 160–1)

Although gambling, under most circumstances, was prohibited by law, the Spanish Crown collected significant sums by taxing the gambling establishments it licensed to widows and war veterans (151). This vice, both popularly and legally associated with some of society's most unfortunate members, was tolerated in soldiers who were otherwise expected to submit to military discipline, perhaps out of a recognition that both battlefield bravery and monetary risk taking were born out of the same impulse.

Erauso's most conventionally successful military exploits recounted in the *Vida* take place in Chile, where the invading Spanish soldiers were under constant threat of attack. In Chile, as Erauso puts it, "estábamos siempre con las armas en la mano" (we always had our arms in hand) (113). Two of the most important incidents of Erauso's career occur here as part of hotly contested battles. The first battle sees the Araucanians sweep over Erauso's company, killing several captains and taking their flag. Witnessing this, Erauso and two companions determine to recapture the symbol of their company's honour:

> Viéndola llevar, partimos tras [la bandera] yo y dos soldados de a caballo por medio de gran multitud, atropellando y matando, y recibiendo daño: en breve cayó muerto uno de los tres. Proseguimos los dos. Llegamos a la bandera, cayó de un bote de lanza mi compañero. Yo recibí un mal golpe en una pierna, maté al cacique que la llevaba y quitésela, y apreté con mi caballo, atropellando, matando e hiriendo a infinidad, pero malherido y pasado de tres flechas y de una lanza en el hombro izquierdo, que sentía mucho.
>
> (Seeing them take away our banner, we road after it, two horseman and I, through the midst of a great multitude, trampling and killing, and receiving our own wounds: soon one of the three of us fell, dead. The two of us continued on. We overcame the flag and my comrade was felled by a lance. I took a heavy blow to my leg. I killed the cacique who was carrying the flag and I took it from him and I spurred my horse, trampling, killing, and maiming innumerable men, but I was badly wounded and pierced by three arrows and a lance in my left shoulder, which was very painful.) (114)

Falling wounded from her horse, Erauso is greeted with excitement and later promoted to *alférez,* a position entrusted with the same flag she had recovered. In this case, as the *Vida* implicitly recognizes, fortune favours Erauso even as her companions are cut down. After six years as *alférez,* another impulsive act conversely results in Erauso being passed over for promotion. Having defeated an Indian captain in battle, Erauso orders the man to be hanged rather than taking him captive. Just as Diego García de Paredes in his *Breve suma* describes his refusal to spare a surrendered opponent, thereby incurring the wrath of the pope with this rash act Erauso too faces retaliation from her superiors.

The fact that Erauso's virginity is at the heart of her eventual recuperation as the Lieutenant Nun demonstrates the careful negotiation of literary intertexts and gendered scripts required by the autobiographical project. As is hinted in the brawling and clever retorts, Erauso's narrative rests most comfortably in the picaresque mode, although the narrative does not, of course, apply the term to Erauso herself directly. *Guzmán de Alfarache* is often seen as the first picaresque novel because it is the first in which the self-narrating subject explicitly embraces the moniker of pícaro. While the narrative structure might seem to identify Castro and Erauso, the wily speaking subjects, as the pícaro-protagonist within their respective stories, a curious and seemingly minor detail reveals the subtlety of their self-presentation. Unlike the eponymous prostitute of *La Pícara Justina,* neither Castro nor Erauso uses the term to describe him- or herself. In both texts, the word *pícaro* surfaces exactly once, each time in an adversarial context. Miguel de Castro, who describes his own participation in schemes of robbery, violence, kidnapping, and even murder, reserves the term for a cunning and sexually promiscuous woman who entices him to crime. This Celestinesque figure, the sister-in-law of a young and lascivious noblewoman, is described as "astuta y ladina y gran pícara taimada" (cunning, crafty, and a wily scoundrel) (75). As in the female picaresque (including texts like *Justina, La Lozana andaluza* [1527], and *La hija de Celestina* [1614]), the episode is resolved with the containment and control of the two rebellious women.[18] Whereas Castro's autobiography discloses here and elsewhere a surprising affinity for the problematic of desire broached by picaresque works protagonized by female characters, Catalina de Erauso's *Vida* hews more closely to the pattern set by the masculine narrators of *Lazarillo* and *Guzmán de Alfarache*. At a pivotal moment, Erauso reports being attacked and insulted as a "pícaro cornudo":

> De allí á tres noches: viniéndome para casa, como a las once, en una esquina divisé a un hombre parado; tercié la capa, saqué la espada, y proseguí mi camino hacia él. Llegando cerca, se me arrojó tirándome, y diciendo – Pícaro cornudo –. Conocido en la voz, fuímonos tirando, y entréle una punta y cayó muerto.
>
> (Three nights later, on the way home at around eleven, I saw a man standing at the corner. I flung my cape over my shoulder, drew my sword, and continued on my way toward him. As soon as I drew closer, he jumped out in attack, saying "Swindler and cuckold!" I knew him by his voice, and so we fought, I stabbed him with my sword, and he died.) (136)

The picaresque association with dishonour, a familial plight that is overtly sexualized in the female picaresque and alluded to here in the added insult of "cornudo," is in striking juxtaposition with Erauso's later protestations of sexual purity.

Erauso's *Vida* crystallizes the dialectic between individual desires and conformity to expectations that is typical of both soldiers' autobiographies in the period and in the picaresque novel. Like the military life writing studied in previous chapters, Erauso's and Castro's autobiographies draw upon a variety of literary precedents and gendered scripts in order to render their life stories legible and entertaining to their readership. For a soldier, Castro's experiences of Mediterranean travel, noble servitude, thuggish fighting, and scabrous affairs are relatively common; perhaps for this reason, the narrative's picaresque trajectory is sometimes drawn in contradictory directions, oscillating between homosocial harmony and unrestrained desires that bring the narrator into conflict with his superiors. Just as the bizarre details of Castro's *Vida* create a distinctive effect of individuality for the narrator and author, Catalina de Erauso's story domesticates the strange elements of her life by communicating them according to accepted norms. Like Castro's, Erauso's self-presentation is marked by resonances with the literary picaresque. Yet, even though neither soldier can truly claim the pícaro's powerlessness that comes from his birth into poverty and dishonour, Castro seems to embrace the sexual degradation associated with the picaresque underworld, while Erauso always portrays such episodes in ways that show her eluding erotic traps. In the final analysis, both soldiers' nuanced renditions of the picaresque demonstrate how textual lives idiosyncratically adapted the literary and gendered models of the day, creating space for a variety of sometimes mutually exclusive masculine identities.

Over a century after Diego García de Paredes's *Breve suma* adopted a strategy of novelization as self-fashioning, selectively appropriating models from chivalric literature, Miguel de Castro and Catalina de Erauso incorporate certain aspects of the picaresque – itself an inversion of chivalric romance – into their self-presentation. Both exploit, from a position of relative social and economic security, a picaresque undercurrent in their past (dishonour in the instances of sexual excess, insubordination, theft, defrauding, or the inherited impediment of having been born a woman and thus barred from the practice of arms). Just as the literary pícaro's identity is unstable, subject always to the constraints of his surroundings, these soldiers' autobiographies reflect a textual fluidity related to the dislocations of military life. Against the precariousness inherent in the soldier's labour, these texts play with the concept of (dis)honour articulated within the picaresque, fashioning textual selves that explicitly lay claim, not to material or spiritual reward, but to the reader's sustained attention.

Conclusion

The preceding chapters shed light on some of the ways in which the idea of honour operates in the life writing of Spanish soldiers of the sixteenth and seventeenth centuries. As we have seen, honour was a capacious concept with a variety of concrete manifestations, encompassing everything from an individual's sense of personal dignity to professional competence and sexual reputation. A means of mediating the incipient divide between the public and private realms, honour is inevitably gendered, relational, intersubjective, and performative. The discourses surrounding the professionalization of the early modern army frequently point to honour as both the impetus for praiseworthy performance on the battlefield and the highest reward for valour. Honour's status as a surplus value, a kind of capital supposedly superior to money, stands in sharp contrast to the material scarcity and moral precarity that defines the experience of the common soldier, whether mobilized or retired. Each autobiographical work might be understood as the soldier's attempt to make sense of this contradictory dynamic in his or her own experience, and on his or her own terms.

Stephen Greenblatt has defined self-fashioning as a process in which the self is always defined against an Other (9). In soldiers' autobiographical texts, the Other manifests in sometimes surprising forms, not always reducible to different ethnic or incipiently national identities; for Diego García de Paredes, the Other is the civilian – as seen in the gruesome encounter at Coria – or indeed anyone who refuses to recognize his violent imposition of authority. For Jerónimo de Pasamonte, the Other is the superstitious, magic-practising Spanish women of Naples, in whom he sees avatars of an evil even worse than that of his former Muslim slave masters. For Diego Suárez Corvín, the Other is the unproductive, gambling, sexually promiscuous soldier – precisely the kind of figure unapologetically embodied by Miguel de Castro and

Catalina de Erauso, both of whom had the relatively good fortune to find themselves respectively in the Spanish Italian court and the vast expanses of the Americas, spaces associated in the popular imagination with economic productivity, imperial splendour, and the soldier's licence and freedom. The multiplicity of spectral Others, all of whom embody some aspect of dishonour in these texts, demonstrates how the discourse of honour could generate a variety of individual and collective identities, including for non-elites. It also points to the real violence underpinning these gestures of self-fashioning. To some extent, Paredes, Castro, and Erauso metaphorically sign their names in blood, as their autobiographies mark trajectories of extra-legal violence and abuse. Pasamonte may have been tormented by his neighbours and family, but the imagery he invokes to describe them recalls the brutalities to which those who were perceived to be different were submitted (including the Inquisitional investigation that Pasamonte himself endured). Likewise, the vision that Suárez endorses is of a subjugated and forcibly Christianized North Africa. Without glorifying or glossing over these repellent realities, this project has sought to understand how soldiers adapted existing frameworks of honour to make sense of their simultaneously exceptional and marginalized positions.

In the life writing of Spanish soldiers, the protean nature of honour facilitated at least two modes of textual self-presentation: one that produces the self as a spectacle of idiosyncrasy, through the inclusion of unusual or titillating details, and another that, through the opposite operation, aims to blur the distinctive profile of the author, foregrounding instead the knowledge distilled in the interpretation of individual experience.

The first mode of life writing might be thought of as a kind of self-novelization, as authors like Diego García de Paredes, Miguel de Castro, and Catalina de Erauso draw structural and thematic inspiration from the closely linked contemporary genres of the chivalric novel and the exemplary biography, and their parodic inversions in the picaresque. In contrast to the petitionary mode of life writing, which presents the self as a producer of knowledge and the text as a compendium of useful information, this kind of life writing devises a discursive situation in which author and reader are roughly equal; the author asks nothing of the reader but sustained attention, perhaps admiration, and in the case of Paredes, emulation. In these works the historical person of the author is transformed into an extraordinary literary persona: in the work of Paredes, in the register of a disenchanted chivalric tale, and then, a century later, in the accounts of Castro and Erauso, refracted through the lens of the picaresque. The last scene of

Erauso's *Vida* bears an uncanny resemblance to one of the last scenes in Paredes's *Breve suma*, as the narrators seem to relish recounting an otherwise banal encounter with civilians. Both take place in liminal settings characterized by transience: an inn in Coria, Paredes's home province, where he stops en route to a brief visit home between campaigns; and, in Erauso's case, the Neapolitan docks that were an important hub in the early modern military-commercial network. In both scenes, a ragtag group, including two prostitutes, is portrayed as attempting to goad the soldier, until their impertinence is met with deadly violence or threats of violence. These attempts at ridicule illustrate the ambivalence, if not hatred, with which civilians frequently regarded soldiers. Yet both episodes are recounted with evident pleasure, and both demonstrate the extent to which, at least within the narrative, the writing subject is able to command deference, shaping his or her own social reality and reframing experience in a heroic light.

All three works partake of the escapism and fantasy function associated with the novelistic form since its inception. Paredes embodies a legend of almost supernatural strength and dexterity with arms. Meanwhile, Castro's conquests are more amorous than bellicose, and the reader is invited to accompany him in his reminiscences of various affairs with women and his passionate friendship with his close companion Antonio. Despite his relatively humble origins, Castro cultivates a refined sensibility, combined uneasily with the pícaro's cynicism, through his representation of these relationships. As for the Lieutenant Nun, Erauso's self-presentation imagines the dissolution of gendered boundaries, allowing readers to imagine too that a soldier's merit could allow him or her to transcend any inherited limitations. In the case of Paredes and Erauso, the outsized persona in the text parallels the quasi-celebrity status achieved during the life of each soldier. Within the framework of self-novelization, all three authors craft unique and distinctive personae that allow them to project and amplify their memory beyond the present – even, as in the case of Paredes's hastily written deathbed account, beyond the end of life itself.

In contrast to the first mode of self-novelization, the second mode of life writing produces the self as a ground for knowledge and the provider of an intellectual service that unfolds in a discursive situation of inequality. A dynamic of suppliance conditions the relationship between the author and the reader, as the text contains an implicit appeal for recompense or reward. In the autobiographical writing of Diego Suárez Corvín and Domingo de Toral y Valdés, the "I" inhabits a professional habitus bleached of extremes and idiosyncrasies in an effort to render the resulting text more authoritative. For Suárez and

Toral y Valdés, honour consists in trustworthiness, truthfulness, experience, and study; it is a quality acquired actively, by exercise of the will. Jerónimo de Pasamonte accomplishes something similar by recurring to the tropes of hagiography to produce a reading of the text of his life in which each detail has a broader significance. Honour for Pasamonte is integrity, both physical and spiritual, and is defined in terms of the extremes that he has weathered, from sickness and physical privation, to entreaties to conversion, sexual sin, and the slander and abuse of his wife's family. Although Pasamonte's *Vida* is the product of many years of emendations and additions, there is a clear connection among the three narrative threads: captivity, threats to masculine sexual honour, and imperilled spiritual integrity. In response to a situation of penury and against accusations of heresy, Pasamonte interprets his life as one of steadfast suffering; this suffering is claimed to beget knowledge, which in turn begets authority – the authority to call for the punishment of his co-religionist tormenters on earth. In this way, Pasamonte discursively merges the wounds of soldier and saint, and invests his suffering with significance. As in Suárez's autobiographical paratexts and Toral y Valdés's *Relación*, the petitionary mode presents both the soldier's lived experience and the text that recounts it as an engine for the production of knowledge. Every facet of the text is shaped to evoke a response in the ideal reader, who will recognize the importance of the information contained therein and thereby recognize the value of the author's life and service.

As the texts studied here demonstrate, the idea of honour could be employed across diverse discursive situations to render a variety of experiences legible. Indeed, recurring to honour in a gesture of self-fashioning might be one of the only commonalities across the archive of military life writing, as its heterogeneity reflects the cross-class composition of armies, the varied social and geographical experiences of soldiers, the evolving discourses around military service, and the fluctuating value of military labour. As a writing practice, soldiers' autobiographies are uniquely well situated to show us how early modern individuals were able to access, appropriate, and thus redefine existing textual discourses and frameworks of value, such as honour, to make meaning out of their lives.

In *Five Words: Critical Semantics in the Age of Shakespeare and Cervantes*, Roland Greene traces the semantic changes undergone by five words, each of which maps onto different conceptual domains, and each of which is an "everyday word" – thus a window into how early modern people conceived and represented their experiences. Greene pays particular attention to "luminous usages that may alter a semantic history all at once" (4) – usages that shed new light on concepts. Although honour is not among the words in his study, its magnitude merits such an investigation. In fact, Greene imagines a scenario in which *honra* presents itself as an ideal candidate for critical semantic reading as it might be practised by early modern intellectuals: "One feels that if five men and women of letters of the middle sixteenth century – in London, Paris, Lisbon, Florence, and Mexico City – were to embark on their own studies of five words, perhaps in the manner of Erasmus's *Adagia* or Jean Bodin's *Colloquium heptaplomeres,* either the words (*honra, sprezzatura, wit*) or the analyses of them (the meaning of *faith*) would be unimaginably more diverse than for modern scholars and readers" (13). As the preceding chapters have illustrated, honour in the context of the early modern Spanish world was an ever-present concept, as ubiquitous and amorphous as air, with a set of meanings that were far from fixed. Throughout each of these chapters, three equally unstable subsidiary keywords have emerged: *merced, sufrir,* and *pícaro.* Although apparently unrelated, each of these dissimilar terms is in fact linked through a shared military context and consequent correlation with the concept of honour as both symbolic and material recognition and recompense.

The mercenary soldier Diego García de Paredes never refers explicitly to material gain in his *Breve suma,* preferring instead to cite the *mercedes* (favours or gifts) he has received, as when he abandons the forces of Pope Alexander VI to offer his services to his erstwhile enemy, the Duke of Urbino, "el cuál mostró conmigo mucho placer y dióme una compañía de arcabuceros de un capitán que fué muerto la noche pasada, y ofrecióme más mercedes" (who was greatly pleased to see me and gave me a company of harquebusiers whose captain had died the previous night, and offered me more favour and gifts besides) (256). Covarrubias's definition of *merced* posits an etymological link between *mercenario* (mercenary or hireling) and *merced,* a word that – he points out – had come to signify its opposite, encompassing both transactional and non-transactional exchanges:

> En su genuina sinificación vale galardón de lo que a uno se le deve por su trabajo; y assí llamamos mercenarios a los jornaleros. […] Mercedes, las gracias. Las dádivas qe los príncipes hazen a sus vasallos, y las que los señores hazen a sus criados y a otras personas. Finalmente qualquiera cosa que se da graciosa, se recibe por merced. Servir a un señor no por salario señalado, se dize aver hecho assiento con él a merced. Darse a merced, es ponerse en manos del enemigo para que él haga su voluntad; esto se entiende en la milicia.

(Its genuine meaning is compensation that is due to someone for their work; and so we call day labourers *mercenarios* or hirelings. [...] Mercies, graces. The gifts that princes make to their vassals, and that lords make to their servants and others. Finally, anything that is given graciously is received as a favour. To serve a master not for a fixed salary is referred to as having an unremunerated post or apprenticeship, *a merced*. To throw oneself upon another's mercy is to place oneself in the hands of the enemy, so that he may do as he wishes; this is understood in the military context.) (800)

As these various meanings indicate, *merced* – in addition to serving as an honorific form of address (Your Grace) – had evolved from signifying a purely economic interaction, such as that between labourer and employer, to signalling a complex relationship of duties and privileges that is associated with the military-aristocratic social order and coded as morally positive. When Paredes challenges a room of gossiping nobles to a duel, he insists upon this latter understanding of the Great Captain's and his own military labour. Likewise, in the brutal episode at Coria he marks the difference between himself and those whose bodies and labour is explicitly commodified.

While Paredes's *Breve suma* emphasizes the injuries the soldier inflicted over those he received, in the petitionary mode of life writing – exemplified by the autobiographies of Suárez, Toral y Valdés, and Pasamonte – the value of each soldier's life and work is predicated on his capacity to suffer. For Suárez, the (re)writing of imperial history from the dusty plazas of Orán is rigorous work, made more difficult by his lack of formal education; yet what he lacks in advanced training is more than made up for, he argues, by the blood he has shed as a soldier over decades of service, "sufriendo trabajos muy extraños / derramando oscuro sangre de sus venas" (suffering foreign travails / spilling dark blood from his veins) (*Historia* 54). Likewise, the experiential epistemology elaborated in the life writing of both Toral y Valdés and Pasamonte hinges upon suffering as the surest pathway to knowledge, from the disfiguring weight of arms permanently etched into Toral y Valdés's shoulders (*Relación* 508–9) to the superior spiritual insights incised into Pasamonte's beleaguered body and soul (*Vida* 6, 69). The annotation for *sufrir* provided by Benito Remigio Noydens in his 1673 reprint of Covarrubias's *Tesoro* further clarifies the ways in which the term was inscribed within a martial context and linked to the concept of honour through military victory:

A nuestro rey Afonso le sucedió faltarle la comida a sí y a su exército en el assedio contra Candeola, y ofreciéndole un soldado medio pan y un pedaço de queso de Mallorca dixo: "Estando mi exército ayuno ¿será bien que yo coma?" Del emperador Rodulfo se lee que en la guerra contra Ottocaro padecía mucha sed por falta de agua, ofreciéndole una vasija, mandó bolverla a quien la traía, dizendo: "Mi sed era del exército y no mía." Con estas generosas y bizarras acciones, enseñavan al sufrimiento a sus soldados y a sufrir el hambre y la sed, y es cierto que con estas ocasiones consiguieron vitoria de sus enemigos.

(It so happened that our King Alfonso had no food for himself or his army in the siege against Candeola. Upon being offered half a piece of bread and a piece of Mallorcan cheese by a soldier, he responded: "Is it good that I should eat while my army fasts?" And of Emperor Rodulfo we read that in the war against Ottocaro he suffered great thirst because there was no water. When he was offered a glass, he sent it back, saying, "This thirst is not just mine, but my whole army's." With these generous and gallant deeds, these kings taught their soldiers how to suffer hunger and thirst. And it is true that on these occasions they achieved victory against their enemies.) (947)

In the autobiographies of Suárez, Toral y Valdés, and Pasamonte we see the same correspondence between suffering and self-mastery, as the body's weakness and desires are subjugated to a superior intellectual or spiritual principle. And, as in Noydens's two tales of kingly conduct, suffering is figured as a process that creates the conditions for triumph over future adversity. Nevertheless, the open-ended nature of the petitionary mode of life writing – the explicit or implicit request that dictates its narrative trajectory – allows each soldier to ultimately question the productive value of suffering. Citing the many travails and mortal dangers he has endured, and his present state of economic necessity, Toral y Valdés ends his *Relación* with a statement that would seem to deny that suffering has any redemptive capacity: "Que por mi se puede decir, según tantos trabajos he pasado y peligros de la vida, y al presente en más necesidad, que el día siguiente siempre es el peor" (As for me, one could say, in light of so many trials and dangers, and my present state of need, the next day is always the worst) (547).

Unlike life writing in the petitionary mode, the self-novelizing autobiographies of Castro and Erauso make no claim for the transcendence of privation and physical pain. In the course of their narratives, neither soldier appears to learn much from experiences of suffering. Like Lázaro, Pablos, and Estebanillo González, their incorrigibility unifies an otherwise incoherent tale; unlike those literary pícaros, Castro and Erauso playfully adopt picaresque postures from the safety of legitimate social positions – Castro as a member of the Jesuit Company of Malta, and Erauso as a noble virgin and celebrated officer. Perhaps in Castro and Erauso's autobiographies we glimpse the beginning of a transition from the pícaro as a reprehensible being definitionally excluded from agency, and therefore from honour, to a sly swindler whose moral freedom is regarded with a certain amount of admiration and envy. While the etymology that Covarrubias hypothesizes connects the pícaro to slavery and the spoils of war, by 1737 the *Diccionario de Autoridades* records several contradictory meanings, with both positive and negative connotations. According to Covarrubias's 1611 *Tesoro*:

> Se pudo dezir de pica, que es el asta, porque en la guerra, hincándola en el suelo, los vendían *ad hastam* por esclavos. Y aunque los pícaros no lo son en particular de nadie, sonlo de la República, para todos los que los quieren alquilar, ocupándolos en cosas viles.
>
> (This could be said to come from the word pike, which is the lance, because in war, sinking it into the ground, they sold them as slaves *ad hastam*. And although pícaros are not slaves of anybody in particular, they are slaves of the republic, for all who want to hire, giving them vile jobs.) (869)

Likewise, the *Diccionario de Autoridades* includes an adjectival definition of *pícaro* as "baxo, ruin, doloso, falto de honra y vergüenza" (low, contemptible, fraudulent, lacking honour and shame) (257). Yet alternate definitions gesture towards both the usefulness and entertainment value of such features; the pícaro is also "astuto, taimado, y que con arte y disimulación logra lo que desea" (crafty, cunning, by trickery and dissembling he achieves what he desires), as well as "chistoso, alegre, placentero y decidor" (funny, cheerful, pleasant, and well spoken) (257). The central ambiguity of the pícaro is made apparent in a quote from Cosme Gómez de Tejada's *León prodigioso; apología moral, entretenida y provechosa a las buenas costumbres, trato virtuoso y política* (Madrid, 1636), included in the *Diccionario*: "Solo dos suertes de personas halló con entera satisfacción, paz y contentamiento, una la de pícaros, gente que nada tiene y nada desea" (Only two kinds of people did he find who enjoyed full satisfaction, peace, and contentment; the first are pícaros, people who possess nothing and desire nothing) (257). While Castro and Erauso do not depict themselves as unmoored from the dictates of honour that, in turn, are linked to class and gender, their autobiographies portray a certain freedom to improvise. Thus Erauso, for example, challenges a flamboyantly dressed Italian soldier to a duel when he dares to malign Spaniards as shits (*son una merda*) (172), only to gleefully slip away when the duel becomes a melee.

As these examples indicate, and as Greene's work elegantly demonstrates, semantically fluid terms point to ideological and sociological inflection points. The military life writing discussed in the previous chapters is heterogeneous and multifaceted precisely because the material conditions of the soldier's life were extraordinarily unstable. This instability, in turn, made an appeal to the apparently solid and durable concept of honour very compelling, particularly in the larger context of the evolving military institution and in light of the existing generic precedents for narrating a life. Yet honour is a concept perhaps even less stable than any other, as it refers to a system of value that was experienced differently at the intersections of race, class, gender, profession, and religious affiliation. Out of this shifting ground, soldiers fashioned a variety of textual subjectivities whose complexity must necessarily exceed the bounds of a single critical frame. As Greene notes, the promise of tracing the transmutations of key cultural and literary concepts is that "We should see in the words the stages and reactions of the given period ... We should see literary history, refracted" (13). Surveying soldiers' life writing from the optic of honour allows us to see more clearly the abundant variety of literary landscapes and social realities that individual soldiers sought to reflect and shape, while throwing into sharp relief the varied dimensions of their textual self-fashioning.

Notes

Introduction: Arms and Letters

1 All citations are from the 2005 edition by Francisco Rico (*Lazarillo de Tormes*) and appear in the text; all translations are from W.S. Merwin's translation (*The Life of Lazarillo de Tormes: His Fortunes and Adversities*). Unless otherwise noted, all other translations are by the author.

2 The prologue's reflections on literary fame instantiate the split between the anonymous author and Lázaro the fictional autobiographer that the rest of the book bears out. The anonymity of the historical author, in stark contrast to the desire for fame that Lázaro imputes to all authors, is among the first signals of the text's fictionality.

3 For a discussion of the discourse of pacifism in Renaissance humanist thought, see Adams, *The Better Part of Valor*.

4 This book includes a detailed consideration of six of these military-autobiographical works. For a general overview of the corpus, see Cassol, *Vita e scrittura*; Cruz, chapter 5, "From Pícaro to Soldier," in *Discourses of Poverty*; Levisi, *Autobiografías del Siglo de Oro*; Martínez, chapter 5, "Home from War," in *Front Lines*; and Sáez, "Vidas imaginarias." The soldier-autobiographers whose work has been studied most extensively under this rubric include Alonso Enríquez de Guzmán, Alonso de Contreras, and Diego Duque de Estrada. For more on Enríquez de Guzmán, see Gastañaga Ponce de Leon, *Caballero noble desbaratado*. For more on Contreras, see Ettinghausen, "The Laconic and the Baroque" and Calvo, *Espadas y plumas en la Monarquia Hispana*. For more on Duque de Estrada, see García Santo-Tomás, "Ruptured Narratives."

5 Like any metaphorical use of the term "archive," the archive of military life writing is to some extent a critical invention: with the possible exception of the *Breve suma* written by the legendary Diego García de Paredes and later circulated as part of the *Cronicas*, most soldiers may not have read each

other's writing (although it seems that the figure of the autobiography-writing soldier – see Cervantes's "Coloquio de los perros" – was not unknown). The coalescing of a canon began in the nineteenth century with an interest in textual taxonomies, and an interest in autobiography as historical source.

In 1905 Serrano y Sanz published a monumental collection of autobiographical works, organized into idiosyncratic categories – "conquistadores," "adventurers," "travellers," "soldiers," "women" – that described the shape of the lives they tagged. In 1956, Cossío published a selection of these texts in a volume of the Biblioteca de Autores Españoles dedicated to seventeenth-century soldiers' autobiographies.

6 For an overview of subsequent revisions to and refinements of the military revolution thesis, see Rogers, *The Military Revolution Debate.*

7 For more on the representation of soldiers in Golden Age theatre, see Vélez Sainz and Sánchez Jiménez, *El teatro soldadesco y la cultura militar en la España imperial.*

8 While a comparative analysis of European military life writing is beyond the scope of this book, it stands to reason that some of the shared aspects of European military culture would tend to produce similar reflections in military life writing. For a comparative study of military memoirs, written primarily by members of the European nobility, see Harari, *Renaissance Military Memoirs.*

9 For an overview of methods and theoretical approaches to early modern life writing, see Mayer and Woolf, *The Rhetorics of Life-Writing in Early Modern Europe.*

10 Rosa María Gregori Roig notes the difference between *memoriales* and *relaciones*: the latter often refers to the official documents compiled and validated by the bureaucratic apparatus, while *memoriales* were individual reports that would substantiate the account set forth in the *relación* (362). See also Goetz, *Spanish Golden Age Autobiography in Its Context* 59–61.

11 For a detailed consideration of the language and narrative structure of Contreras's *Discurso de mi vida,* see Ettinghausen, "El diálogo en la *Vida* de Alonso de Contreras," 563–70.

12 For a wide-ranging study of the town armies of medieval Iberia, see Powers, *A Society Organized for War.*

13 In regard to the dramatic function of honour on the early modern Spanish stage, Américo Castro notes "Como es sabido, la acción dramática, en los casos en que el honor es tema fundamental, se desenvuelve en estas dos direcciones: o asistimos al crecimiento de una personalidad que lucha y se esfuerza por acrecentar su 'opinión' practicando las 'virtudes' de la época, o en otro caso presenciamos el conflicto interior que suscita la pérdida de la vida espiritual y el planteamiento y ejecución de exquisitas venganzas

con que el héroe pretende instaurarse de nuevo en la estima pública. A este intenso dinamismo de los personajes corresponde una ideología perfectamente encadenada y sistemática, que si fuéramos a estudiarla a fondo habrían de investigarse casi todos los conceptos culturales de nuestra época clásica: la teoría del hombre, de su valer y de su función social" (As is well known, in cases where honour is the fundamental theme, the dramatic action develops in one of two directions: either we witness the growth of a person who struggles and makes an effort to increase his "reputation" by practising the "virtues" of the period, or we witness the internal conflict that brings about the loss of spiritual life and the imagining and execution of exquisite acts of vengeance with which the hero intends to reinstall himself in the public esteem. This intense dynamism corresponds to a perfectly linked and systematic ideology, so much so that if we were to study it in depth we would have to investigate almost all of the cultural concepts of the Golden Age: the theory of man, his worth and social function) (20).

14 As Taylor concludes: "The protection of one's family in general (not solely the sexual reputation of women kin), the maintenance of one's credit and property, the defense of one's office and status, and the competitive nature of early modern male sociability all impinged on male honor. Above all, men needed to be seen performing these roles effectively before their neighbors" (104).

15 For more on the links between the financial crisis in early modern Spain and its social manifestations, see Thompson and Yun Casalilla, *The Castilian Crisis of the Seventeenth Century*. For a thorough and illuminating interrogation of the links between financial and literary discourse, see Vilches, *New World Gold*. For an overview of the historical debate on a generalized global crisis with environmental, financial, political, and cultural resonances, see Parker and Smith, *The General Crisis of the Seventeenth Century*.

16 With habitus I refer to a set of internalized social expectations. Bourdieu defines habitus as "a socialized body, a structured body, a body which has incorporated the immanent structures of a world or of a particular sector of that world – a field – and which structures the perception of that world as well as action in that world" (81).

17 By subjectivation I mean the process by which individuals are formed as subjects. Habermas's account of subject formation strikes me as particularly pertinent to the study of life writing, as it emphasizes the communal and communicative nature of the process: "The self … is dependent upon recognition by addressees because it generates itself as a response to the demands of an other in the first place … The ego, which seems to me to be given in my self-consciousness as what is purely my

own, cannot be maintained by me solely through my own power, as it were for me alone – it does not 'belong' to me. Rather, this ego always retains an intersubjective core because the process of individuation from which it emerges runs through the network of linguistically mediated interactions" (169–70). For a Foucauldian-inflected account of subject formation in the literature of early modern Spain, see Cascardi, *Ideologies of History in the Spanish Golden Age*; and Folger, *Picaresque and Bureaucracy*.

18 My use of the term "textual subjectivity" draws from Anthony Spearing's groundbreaking work of the same name, in which he explores the encoding of subjectivity as a textual feature – an effect of language not necessarily reducible to a singular human consciousness – in medieval literature.

1. Virtue, Honour, and Exemplarity

1 All citations from *Don Quixote* are taken from Andrés Murillo's edition; citations in English are from Ormsby's translation.

2 Diego Clemencín acknowledges the disjunction between the text of the *Breve suma* and the priest's description: "Al final de la crónica del Gran Capitán que se describió arriba, se imprimió una *Breve suma* de la vida y hechos de Diego García de Paredes, escrita por él mismo poco antes de su muerte, y a la verdad no con tanta modestia como adelante dice el Cura" (At the end of the chronicle of the Great Captain, described above, there was printed a *Brief Summary* of the life and deeds of Diego García de Paredes, written by Paredes himself shortly before his death, and without quite as much modesty as the Priest says later) (513). Clemencín also notes, apropos of the phrase "de coronista propio": "Por esta expresión parecería que Diego García de Paredes es el que cuenta las dos noticias anteriores del molino y del puente: pero no es así, porque ni de una ni de otra se hace mención en el *Sumario* de su vida" (This expression would lead one to believe that it is Paredes who tells the stories of the mill wheel and the bridge: but that is not the case, because he mentions neither episode in the *Summary* of his life) (514). Clemencín attributes this imprecision to the fact that Cervantes often quoted texts from memory.

3 Although the text is dedicated to Sancho, there is no mention of his mother, the noblewoman María de Sotomayor. In fact, Paredes's marriage to María ended in divorce; seven months after their marriage and pregnant with Sancho, María took refuge with her mother in a convent, alleging that Paredes's violent outbursts caused her to fear for her life. Unusually for the period, María won the divorce case against her husband and was awarded money and goods. None of this is recounted in the *Breve suma*,

which focuses entirely on Paredes's experiences as a soldier (Muñoz de San Pedro 356–63).

4 The manuscript variants include *Suma de las cosas que acontecieron a Diego García de Paredes y de lo que hizo, escrita por él mismo cuando estaba enfermo del mal [de] que murió* (Biblioteca Nacional de España, Ms. 1752) and *Testamento o sumario de cosas acaecidas a D[iego] García de Paredes, que en gloria sea* (Biblioteca Nacional de España, Ms. 5602). The earliest extant edition of the *Crónica del Gran Capitán* to contain the autobiography was published in 1580 in Seville in the house of the Italian printer Andrea Pescioni (or Pescione) (Sánchez Jiménez 12).

5 These plays include *La contienda famosa de García de Paredes y el capitán Juan de Urbina*, in which Paredes plays a key role, and others where he appears as a minor historical figure (*Las cuentas del Gran Capitán* and *El Blasón de los Chaves de Villalba*). See Sánchez Jiménez, *El Sansón de Extremadura*.

6 The *Breve suma* erroneously gives the date of Paredes's arrival in Italy as 1507.

7 The same episode appears almost verbatim in both the *Suma* and the *Breve suma*, with two key differences: the *Suma* contains the clarifying clause "por la falta de guerra, que no había" (for lack of war) (41–2) and uses the terms *mozas* (young women), which the *Breve suma* renders as *mozos* (young men), indicating that Paredes and his brother supported themselves in part not by pimping, but through the cleverness of their servant boys (255). In either case, Paredes describes making a living in Rome through dishonourable and extra-legal means.

8 Paredes's companions included the Basque Juan de Urbina; Gónzalo Pizarro, the father of the conquistador of Peru and another Extremaduran hidalgo; two other natives of Extremadura, Cristóbal Zamudio and Cristóbal Villalba; and Juan de Vargas, about whom no information is available (Sánchez Jiménez 50).

9 "Yo hice subir mis compañeros por las cuerdas y mataron a la guarda y pelearon con ella. Yo fui a la puerta que estaba con llave y así del cerrojo, y arranqué las armellas y abrí las puertas, por donde metí los nuestros y fuimos a la plaza donde se recogieron los enemigos para pelear con nosotros. Eran por todos ocho banderas de infantería; fueron rompidos y la tierra saqueada, y la otra tierra se nos rindió de miedo" (I had my men scale the walls and they fought and killed the guard. I went to the door, which was locked, and I pulled the bolts off and opened the gates, and I had our men go through them and we went to the main square where the enemy had gathered to fight us. There were eight infantry companies. They were defeated and the land sacked, and the other town surrendered out of fear) (256).

10 Paredes's account supports Rabanal Álvarez's thesis that the battle cry "Santiago y cierra, España" is the conjunction of two previously distinct utterances: one an invocation of the patron saint of Spain and the other a metonymic address to Spanish troops enjoining them to close ranks and charge the enemy (543–5).

11 As Miguel Martínez notes, "The paratextual vocabularies of Renaissance writing cultures help us establish the connection between the classical model and the otherwise utterly different memoir by Paredes. [...] Spanish soldiers such as Paredes and his successors transformed Caesar's detached third-person narrative of war into an engaged and eventually intimate first-person account of soldierly life, a formal transformation of wide-ranging consequences" (193).

12 The 1739 *Diccionario de Autoridades* defines a *suma* as "la recopilación o compendio de alguna facultad, que se pone abreviada, y en resumen en algún libro" (the compilation or compendium of an authority, abbreviated and summarized in a book). Examples of other biographical texts that circulated under the same generic appellation are *Juana de Arco, santa: La poncella de Francia y de sus grandes fechos en armas sacados en suma de la crónica real ...* (Seville, 1520); *Breve relación y suma de la vida y virtudes de la venerable Madre Ana de San Agustín* (manuscript); *Suma de la vida y milagros del venerable Padre Fray Juan de la Cruz* (Amberes, 1625); and the *Suma de la vida, virtudes y milagros de San Francisco de Borja* (Valencia, 1671).

13 "Concebido a partir del caballeresco, el código 'del soldado honrado de infantería' disipaba los rasgos más conspicuamente plebeyos del oficio de armas y depojaba a la militarización popular de gran parte de sus contenidos subversivos. Iba configurándose una imagen del soldado a medio camino entre la hagiografía y la realidad, entre el epos caballeresco y la exaltación de las gestas de los infantes empleados de la conquista y en la defensa del imperio" (Conceived in relation to the chivalric code, the code of the "honourable infantry soldier" dispelled the most conspicuously plebeian characteristics of the office of arms and divested the democratic military of much of its subversive content. There arose an image of the soldier at the intersection of hagiography and reality, between the heroic deeds of chivalry and the exaltation of the infantrymen employed in the conquest and defense of the empire) (10). But see also Rodríguez-Velasco, "Esfuerço."

14 Rolena Adorno clarifies in her introduction to Leonard's *Books of the Brave* the relationship between colonial historiography and chivalric romance: "Bernal Díaz, Castañeda, and Oviedo all suggest that the comparison of their writings with the books of chivalry was inevitable. Their point, however, was the fiction paled by comparison with what they witnessed, that the historical deeds and experiences they described exceeded the only possible model for comparison that existed in their readers' imaginations"

(xxiv). In a similar vein, Miguel Martínez demonstrates how the "gunpowder epics" written by common soldiers "sharply contrasted with the fictional registers of chivalric romance" (70).

15 The privilege conceded to Paredes by King Ferdinand explicitly assigns a gendered value to the legendary soldier's bravery. The pronouncement reads: "Son dignas de memoria, que en el rompimiento del exercito de los Franceses en la Chirinola fue el primero que acometia a los enemigos: i en la toma de la ciudad de Rubo fue de los primeros que subio el muro, i *varonilmente* se metio en la ciudad, i entre los enemigos" (These are worthy of memory, that in breaking the army of the French at the Battle of Cerignola he was the first to throw himself at the enemy; and in the taking of the city of Ruvo he was among the first to climb the wall, and *manfully* entered the city, and among the enemy) (Tamayo de Vargas 110v; emphasis mine).

16 See La Rubia-Prado for more on the symbolic linkage between horses and honour in the medieval imagination.

17 The phrase "las cuentas del Gran Capitán" lives on in contemporary colloquial Spanish and can refer to any ridiculous or overly detailed report, or as shorthand to reject a request for information that one feels is unjustified.

18 The edition of the *Suma* prepared by Antonio Sánchez Jiménez documents the variations among the extant versions of the text.

19 As Luis Avilés notes in his article on the virtue of prudence in Huarte de San Juan, humanists and *letrados* counselled an approach to warfare quite dissimilar from that associated with Diego García de Paredes. For example, Francisco de Vitoria in his relection on the right of war underlined the importance of sparing civilians and avoiding bloodshed whenever possible (44).

20 For more on the historian, bibliographer, poet, and translator Tomás Tamayo de Vargas, see the introductory essay in González Hernández.

2. Professional Honour and the Production of Knowledge

1 Covarrubias's definition for *merced* – as both gift and salary – conveys the destabilizing ambiguity that, I argue, drives much military life writing. (See the conclusion in the present volume for a more detailed reading of this definition.)

2 Suárez was not the only soldier invested in writing the history of the North African frontier. The professional soldier Pedro Gaytán (c. 1518–post-1588) also produced an account praising the defence of Orán in 1563 titled *Historia de Orán y de su cerco*. For more on Gaytán, see Caravaggi, "Avatares italianos."

3 The existence of this manuscript, which prefaced the portion of Suárez's history dedicated to Algiers, is further attested in G. Jacqueton, *Les archives espagnoles du gouvernement géneral de l'Algerie* (1894) and Édouard Cat, *Mission bibliographique en Espagne* (1891). The *Historia del Maestre*, which focuses exclusively on the government of the Borja brothers, is housed in the Biblioteca Nacional de España, Ms. 7.882, and is available in an edition prepared by Miguel Ángel de Bunes Ibarra and Beatriz Alonso Acero.

4 In his "Prólogo al benévolo lector" Suárez tells quite a different story of his recruitment, one that draws a parallel between his ancestors' participation in the battles of the peninsular Reconquest and his own North African service: "siendo desde mi niñez aficionado a la milicia y ejercicio de las armas contra moros y turcos por la tradición que oía de mis pasados que sirvieron, y muchos de ellos murieron, en la restauración de España" (being from my childhood keen on the military and the exercise of arms against Moors and Turks, because I heard that my ancestors served, and many of them died, in the restoration of Spain) (72). According to this version, Suárez left his family home at twenty-two "no por causa de necesidad que tuviese, sí sólo con intención de ir a buscar moros" (not because of any necessity, but only with the intention to look for Moors) (72).

5 See Hess, *The Forgotten Frontier*.

6 See also Neyrey, "The Symbolic Universe of Luke-Acts."

7 For more on the conflation of sexual contagion and religious and cultural Others, see Berco, *From Body to Community*.

8 A relevant example is the humanist Ambrosio de Morales (1513–91), whose historiographical work Suárez may have read. Morales reportedly castrated himself in order to overcome his physical desires. His portraits often contain visual symbols of purity associated with the Virgin such as lilies. Morales's nineteenth-century biographer, Enrique Redel, imagines the scene of self-mutilation: "Éste, siendo nuevo por ordenar, y morando en una celda que está antes de la Celda grande, que solía ser de los Priores, dio en una diabólica tentación y se cortó los miembros viriles totalmente, que quedó tan raso como la palma de la mano" (Newly ordained and dwelling in a cell that is before the great cell, which usually belongs to the Priors, he fell into a diabolical temptation and cut off his testicles entirely, so that he was as flat as the palm of his hand)" (70; quoted in Olga Fernández, "Los 'Ángeles de la tierra.'"

9 Notably absent from Suárez's *Historia del Maestre* is the arrest and subsequent trial for sodomy of don Pedro Luis Garcerán de Borja, the last Grand Master of the military order of Montesa. Arrested by the Inquisition in 1572, after a lengthy trial don Pedro Luis was found guilty of homosexual practices and sentenced to a decade of house arrest and a

fine of 6000 ducats. Upon completing this sentence – and having resigned the mastership of Montesa in favour of King Philip II – don Pedro Luis was fully reintegrated into court society. The ignominious end of his governorship may explain the reluctance of the Borja family to fund the publication of even a mostly laudable history like Suárez's (Monter 136–7).

10 In 1879 the text, based on a mansucript housed at the Biblioteca Nacional de España (H-55/S-31), was published for the first time in the *Colección de documentos inéditos para la historia de España*, in an appendix containing documents relating to the career of Fray Bartolomé de las Casas and a description, from 1603, of the diplomat Juan Fernández de Velasco's peacemaking voyage to London. Although the editors do not articulate the relationship among these texts, it is possible that both their connection to Spanish imperial policy and – at least in the case of much of Las Casas's writing – their critical tone justify their inclusion in one volume.

11 In his 1905 anthology *Autobiografía y memorias*, Serrano y Sanz commends Toral's *Relación* as being one of the few soldiers' autobiographies written with stylistic refinement, with a simplicity that gives greater weight to its historical exposition (LXIII). Randolph Pope, the first scholar to exhaustively analyse the *Relación*, correlates Toral's incisive writing to the concept of Baroque *desengaño*, while connecting the pessimism of the text to Spain's decline under Philip IV (213). More recently, Alessandro Cassol has discovered in the archives of the Biblioteca Nacional de España fragments of Toral's *Relación*, which an anonymous copyist transposed into the third person in order to include them in volumes of historical miscellany. Building upon the work of Pope and Cassol, this chapter highlights the discourses of authority and critique – including the narrative and stylistic markers of history, biography, travel writing, and the military treatise – with which Toral constructs his self-presentation.

12 Although a detailed analysis of these two episodes is outside the scope of this chapter, the hospitality with which Toral describes being received and protected first by a Muslim merchant in the caravan to Baghdad and then by the Jewish community of Aleppo is remarkable. In the first instance, one of the most respected members of the caravan defends Toral from the abuse of his fellow travellers (539–40). In the second instance, the Jewish community of Aleppo rallies around Toral when he is accused of spying and threatened with torture (542–4). Particularly noteworthy is Toral's admiration for both the generosity and intellectual cultivation of an unnamed man he refers to only as "mi judío Rabí" (544). In describing the Rabbi, Toral notes that he had lived in Madrid and was well educated, with a library comprised of histories and poetry, as well as many of the works of Lope de Vega (543). Although his reading preferences are somewhat different, only the Portuguese admiral Ruy Frere da Andrada

is described with a similar level of respect in the *Relación*. In this we might read a tacit critique of the politics of ethnic exclusion practiced within the peninsula.

13 The image of experience as knowledge literally carved onto the body resonates with the epigraph with which Jerónimo de Pasamonte opens his autobiography: "no hay mejor maestro que el bien acuchillado" (there is no better teacher than he who is well experienced) (5). See chapter 3 for more on Pasamonte.

14 In the *Criticón*, Gracián identifies melancholy as a virtue of the wise, as well as a specifically Spanish trait: "¿Quién vio jamás contento a un sabio, cuando fue siempre la melancolía manjar de discretos? Y assí veréis que los españoles, que están en opinión de los más detenidos y cuerdos, son llamados de las otras naciones los tétricos y graves" (Who has ever seen a happy wise man, when melancholy has always been the delicacy of the discreet? And so you will see that Spaniards, who are restrained and sane in their opinions, are called by other nations grim and serious) (9; qtd. in Rodríguez de la Flor 5).

15 Although it is unlikely that Toral would have had direct contact with the writings of Machiavelli, certain tropes were widely disseminated throughout Spain in putatively anti-Machiavellian discourse. For more on Machiavellian political thought in the peninsula, see Howard, *The Reception of Machiavelli in Early Modern Spain*.

3. Spiritual Honour and Religious Authority

1 Despite this affirmation, in Covarrubias's entry on *esperiencia* the reader is cautioned against relying solely on untutored experience: "La esperiencia ... es peligrosa por la variedad de los sujetos y las circunstancias dél; y assí dize el aforismo de Hipócrates, *Vita brevis, ars verò longa, experimentum fallax*" (Experience ... is dangerous because of the variety of its subjects and circumstances; and so Hipocrates's aphorism states, *Life is short, art is long, and experience is deceptive*) (555).

2 In *El Buscón*, Pablos meets a knife seller named Matorral, who flaunts the efficacy of his wares on his face: "traía la muestra de ellas [las cuchilladas] en su cara, y por las que le habían dado concertaba tamaño y hondura de las que había de dar; decía: 'No hay tal maestro como el bien acuchillado'; y tenía razón, porque la cara era una cuera y él un cuero" (he carried the sign of the knife trade on his face, where he had received his share of slashes. Those that he had been given were as long and deep as those he had proffered, and so he often said, "No man is so absolute a master, as he who has been well hacked himself." And he was right, because his face was like leather, and his body all hide) (III.10: 302).

3 In a lively turn of phrase that also presages later scholars' evaluation of Pasamonte's psychological condition, Cossío commends the vitality of Pasamonte's prose even as he censures the author's occult obsession: "saltan en cada renglón, como truchas, términos y frases proverbiales que comunican una vibración viva a la prosa del obsesionado Pasamonte" (proverbs jump out of every line like trout, giving a lively vibration to the prose of the obsessed Pasamonte) (x). Randolph Pope interprets Pasamonte's supernatural explanation for his tribulations as symptomatic of the social and economic upheavals of the period. According to Pope, Pasamonte's invocation of angels and demons is indicative of the author's maladjustment in a rapidly changing world whose workings are otherwise opaque (140). Margarita Levisi reaches a similar conclusion; for Levisi, however, Pasamonte's paranoia and pessimism stem directly from the severe psychic trauma he sustained over more than a decade in captivity. According to Levisi, Pasamonte's use of religious rhetoric responds to his need to explain the inexplicable: the physical and mental disturbances that are the after-effects of trauma (90). Whereas Pope sees a suspicious superficiality in Pasamonte's *Vida* and relates it to the cynicism of the age, Levisi argues for the author's probable sincerity, maintaining that he uses the only means available to him to express and heal the psychic wounds he has suffered.

4 Martín de Ríquer has conjectured that the two men may have coincided in more than just the defiant stance they took towards their masters. Ríquer speculates that Cervantes and Pasamonte met as soldiers in the same division, and that they may even have been reunited in Madrid in the summer of 1594 or the winter of 1595, as they both found themselves in the capital attempting to secure a comfortable bureaucratic position following their redemption (40–1). Due to this meeting, Ríquer believes it is possible that Cervantes modelled the one-eyed galley slave and perpetual autobiographer Ginés de Pasamonte on his old comrade in arms, who, in addition to writing an autobiographical petition describing his service in the galleys, also admits to a gradually worsening visual impairment in his *Vida* (82–3). But the parallel lines of the lives of Cervantes and Pasamonte extend beyond Ginés de Pasamonte's appearance in the first book of the *Quixote*; according to Ríquer and others, Jerónimo de Pasamonte may have been so incensed by his unflattering alter ego that he undertook the writing of a spurious sequel in order to profit from Cervantes's creation and destroy it (140). Under the pseudonym Alonso Fernández de Avellaneda, these critics maintain, Pasamonte published the unauthorized *Quixote*, along with a cruel prologue mocking the original author for his advanced years and crippled hand (120–1).

Supporting Ríquer's claim is the work of Alfonso Martín Jiménez, who has brought to light archival and palaeographic documentation emphasizing the similarities between the historical Jerónimo de Pasamonte and the shadowy figure behind Avellaneda's signature. Others have proposed alternative hypotheses for the authorship of the unauthorized *Quixote*, including Ginés Pérez de Hita, Tirso de Molina, and Cervantes's rival Lope de Vega. For their part, scholars who have studied Pasamonte's *Vida* apart from the Cervantine connection have tended to treat theories of Avellaneda's identity with caution, perhaps because the overwhelming impression left by Pasamonte's text is that of the author's increasing physical and psychological frailty. Although Pasamonte's autobiography evinces the same religious fervour and conservatism that scholars have noted in Avellaneda's *Quixote*, for the purposes of this chapter it seems most productive to view these points of contact as primarily indicative of the authors' shared literary and cultural milieu.

5 In tracing the evolution of the *miles christianus* from chivalric hero to bourgeois paterfamilias R.R. Bolgar describes "the new Christian hero, Galahad's unexpected successor" in the work of Juan Luis Vives: the new Christian paragon of masculine virtue is "humble, practical, studious, devoted to the Bible, soberly wedded, zealous in the performance of good works; except for his learning – which Erasmus thinks necessary – he is a type of man most readily found in the lower middle class, estimable but not spectacular" (136). In many respects this is similar to the portrait that Pasamonte paints of himself in his *Vida*.

6 Among the soldiers taken captive along with Pasamonte was Alonso de Salamanca, author of both an epic poem on the fall of La Goleta and a military treatise. Although Pasamonte makes no reference to a soldier by this name, both men shared a similar trajectory, including captivity, decades away from Spain, and a penurious fate upon their return to Christendom. While Pasamonte responded to these circumstances by penning a defensive autobiographical text replete with religious symbolism, Alonso de Salamanca attempted to transmute his military experience into a remunerative work of military science. Much like Diego Suárez Corvín (discussed in chapter 2), Alonso de Salamanca was unsuccessful in his attempts to secure patronage for his intellectual work. As Martínez notes, "Back in Madrid, after forty years away from Spain, he had no access to the institutional arrangements or to the social networks that facilitated publication and organized authorship in the early modern republic of letters" (121). Seen in this light, Pasamonte's choice to address his autobiography to Church officials, and to frame his self-presentation around honour as the capacity to endure suffering, seems like a strategy to join (or at least to be recognized by) a somewhat different – yet equally

esteemed – social network. For more on Alonso de Salamanca, see González Castrillo and Martínez 105–17.

7 According to Ellen Friedman's research, most Christians languished an average of five years in captivity before being rescued (5).

8 Javier Irigoyen-García argues that the religious significance granted to physical suffering under the circumstances of captivity – widely understood in the period as a kind of martyrdom – explains the nostalgia that marks these reminiscences. Likewise, in the absence of a sanctioned persecutor following his return from captivity, Pasamonte portrays himself as "perdido, confuso y enfermizo" (lost, confused, and sickly) (114).

9 In addition to a commitment to chastity, Jodi Bilinkoff has noted other traits of early modern Catholic clerical masculinity as recorded in the biography of one ideal holy man, including his "docility, his illnesses, his deference to clergymen"(168), all qualities that Pasamonte, too, strives to emulate.

10 Pasamonte does not attempt to explain why the demons in his vision should be wearing Franciscan robes, but he does go on to note: "Y estando mirando el maldito espectáculo, vi otros frailes de diferentes religiones … y de la religión de Santo Domingo no vi ninguno" (And looking upon this cursed spectacle, I saw other friars of different orders … and of the order of Saint Dominic I saw none) (44). Given that one of the text's dedicatees was Master General of the Dominican Order, Pasamonte's inclusion of this detail may speak to the tensions between Dominicans and Franciscans in the period, caused in part by their different missions: Dominicans – much like Pasamonte himself – were concerned with combatting heresy, while Franciscans hoped to lead by example, particularly by pledging themselves to poverty.

11 This gruesome detail resonates with early modern medical thought on the female body's particular propensity for monstruous generation; when favourable conditions of heat and moisture where achieved, in the "fermentation and miasma of [the] womb … worms self-generated even during pregnancy" (Finucci 27). According to Ambrose Paré, Neapolitan women were especially susceptible: "because their diet is based on fruit and herbs, … the resulting mass of putrefying elements in the digestive tract is conducive to the generation of animals" (qtd. in Finucci 56).

12 Pasamonte's experience of a porous subjectivity resonates with the work of various scholars, including John Jeffries Martin and Natalie Zemon Davis, both of whom posit the notion of a permeable or open self coexisting with other modes of being. See Martin's *Myths of Renaissance Individualism* and Davis's "Boundaries and the Sense of Self in Sixteenth-Century France" in Davis's *Reconstructing Individualism*. Within the context of early modern Spanish literature, Hilaire Kallendorf has

demonstrated the existence of a "porous and frangible" (xv) subjectivity in *Exorcism and Its Texts*.

4. Playing the *Pícaro*

1 The work appeared in four editions in the seventeenth century and six in the eighteenth century, indicating it was at least as popular as the bestselling *Guzmán de Alfarache* (Madrid, 1599; Lisbon, 1604).

2 Fernando González de León argues that "the *Estebanillo* can perhaps be said to have created or exposed a third paradigm of command or 'ideal' soldier [in addition to those of the master technician and the grand aristocrat], the officer as amoral and disillusioned pícaro, disengaged from the ideological and dynastic objectives of the war, high standards of professional conduct and the reputation of the army, and concerned mostly with surviving and lining his own pockets with a maximum of comfort and a minimum of risk" (*The Road* 346).

3 Almost fifty years separates the publication of *Lazarillo de Tormes* (1554) and *Guzmán de Alfarache* (1599). As Cruz notes, both texts were often published together, a material disposition that reinforced their resemblances, constituting the kernel of the picaresque canon as scholars would come to define it. Before the appearance of *Guzmán*, however, contemporary readers did not regard *Lazarillo* as a sui generis text; alive to the satiric intent of the work, they connected it to several classical precedents (*Discourses* 5–6).

4 This image is reproduced in Alexander Parker's *Literature and the Delinquent* as well as in David Mañero Lozano's edition of *La Pícara Justina*.

5 Regarding the popularity of the picaresque, many scholars have noted that *Guzmán de Alfarache* was one of the first Spanish bestsellers (Cruz, *Discourses* xv). By 1559, thirty years before the publication of *Guzmán*, *Lazarillo de Tormes* had been placed on the Index of Prohibited Books, indicating both the novel's popularity and the pointedness of its satire. James Amelang and others have attributed the picaresque's "undisputed success with the reading public" to its "realistic representation of specifically lower-class venues," regardless of each individual work's reformist or orthodox tendencies (39).

6 For a discussion of honour as one kind of capital treated in the picaresque novel and conduct manuals, see Ruan, *Pícaro and Cortesano*.

7 Among the various problems presented by the text is its puzzling chronology, starting with Miguel de Castro's supposed 1593 birthdate. In his introduction to the first edition, Paz y Meliá notes that had Castro been born in this year, he would have been remarkably young to have

participated in the military adventures and amorous conquests he describes (vi). Meanwhile, Castro's meticulous accounting of the day, month, and year of other events makes it unlikely that he would err in recording his own birthdate (which is stated down to the hour). On the other hand, scholars have wondered what motive Castro could have had in falsifying his age in order to appear younger. Levisi argues that a second copyist attempted to restore the damaged manuscript of Castro's *Vida* some ten years after it was written. This second copyist, unable to read the birthdate that Castro had originally written, substituted 1593 as his best guess. By reconstructing the chronology of other events in the text and comparing these to historical sources, Levisi deduces that Castro was probably born around 1590. Therefore, although not as dubiously young as once was thought, Castro was still a very young man when he began to write the story of his life – a story that was evidently deemed worthy of recopying a decade later (Levisi 190–1).

8 See chapter 5 in Cruz, *Discourses.*

9 For an intriguing interpretation of the psychoanalytical dynamic in this scene, see Juárez Almendros's chapter on Miguel de Castro's *Vida* in *El cuerpo vestido.*

10 I adopt the term "script" in this context from Mark Breitenberg's study of masculinity in early modern England, in which he elaborates a theatrical model of subjectivity, indebted both to Louis Althusser's concept of ideological interpellation and Judith Butler's concept of gender performativity: "Individuals may be said to be 'interpellated' as subjects by the roles they play and by the scripts they enact, but the improvisations of any given performance ... encourage limited but nonetheless vital versions of agency within its malleable structures ... Furthermore, the process of subjectification in the theater calls attention to the fact that not only is identity performed, but it is performed publicly in front of an audience, always enacted in relation to and dependent upon an Other – a useful reminder of the specifically social basis of subjectivity in the early modern period" (10). The conceptual framework of the script neither forecloses the possibility of agency nor emphasizes it as originary. Instead, it harnesses Butler's notion of identity as performative and highlights the possibility of improvisation in a way that is especially apt in the public and communal context of the early modern period, extending even beyond the boundaries of the theatre proper and into the textual performances executed in autobiography.

11 See Vélez Quiñones's reading of Cervantes' *Numancia* for more on the sodomitical reputation attached to sixteenth- and seventeenth-century Spanish soldiers: "'Templa, pequeño joven, templa el brío'."

12 The way in which Castro narrates episodes such as these may be understood as instances of what Sedgwick describes as "homosexual panic," anxiety over homosocial bonds that betrays "a structural residue of terrorist potential … of Western maleness through the leverage of homophobia" (20). For scholarship that demonstrates the applicability of this concept to the context of early modern Spain, see Weber, "Lope de Vega's *Rimas sacras*."
13 See Middlebrook, "The Poetics of Early Modern Masculinity."
14 In addition to Miguel de Castro's autobiography, the autobiographies of Alonso de Contreras (1582–post 1645) and Diego Duque de Estrada (1589–1649) exploit incidents of violence, deception, and erotic intrigue. For an introduction to both Contreras and Duque de Estrada, see Ettinghausen.
15 The earliest extant manuscript is a copy dating from the latter half of the seventeenth century. For a detailed discussion of the *Vida*'s textual history and manuscript variants, see Valbona 1–30 and Rubio Merino 14–27.
16 Following Teresa's demise, her supporters lobbied for her beatification and canonization, a development that, in addition to recognizing the reformer's exemplary spirituality, would further legitimize the movement she founded. As Erin Rowe has noted, one of the challenges faced by Teresa's champions was how to reconcile her "unfeminine" talent for administration and her ceaseless activity with the fact of her femaleness. Taking a cue from Teresa's own work, her supporters emphasized her hyper-feminine "passivity, obedience, and humility," interpreting it as an effect of a muscular spirituality (Rowe 582). In one of his beatification sermons, Pedro de Herrera affirmed the superior nature of the *mujer varonil*, who, like Teresa, successfully supplemented fleshly feminine frailty with masculine spiritual vigour. Citing the well-known example of Saint Perpetua, Herrera declared that the spiritual manly woman was not without precedent: "no es cosa nueva que una muger se transforme en varon, quedándose en su ser y flaqueza mugeril, la cuenten por varon robuste, y le den atributos masculinos" (it is nothing new for a woman to transform into a man, remaining womanly in her being and weakness, but counted as a robust man and granted masculine attributes) (qtd. in Rowe 596n17). This understanding of the gendered contours of devotion resulted in Teresa's canonization, creating a saint with atypical virtues whose spiritual lineage nevertheless stretches back to the beginnings of the Church. But Saint Teresa was not only a compelling figure within the religious realm; her unique status as an obedient yet reform-minded *mujer varonil* resonated with Castilian imperial aspirations. In 1627 Pope Urban VIII (the same pope who granted a dispensation to Catalina de Erauso) declared Teresa a patron saint of Spain, and for a short time she

joined Saint James as the nation's official spiritual protector and rallying point, adding an element of mystical austerity to the military tradition that he symbolized (586). See also Weber, *Teresa of Ávila and the Rhetoric of Femininity*.

17 For a historical overview, see Velasco, *Lesbians in Early Modern Spain*.

18 In contrast to the multifaceted modes of dishonour displayed by the male protagonists of picaresque fiction, the literary *pícara* is most often characterized by a debased sexuality. As Anne Cruz has stated, the female picaresque "[establishes] an ironic homology between the *pícara* and the prostitute on at least two counts: by pandering to readers' prurient interests and by proposing that women utilize their bodies for their social and economic benefit" (*Discourses* 135). For a detailed analysis of discourses of prostitution in the female picaresque, see Zafra, *Prostituidas por el texto*.

Works Cited

Adams, Robert P. *The Better Part of Valor: More, Erasmus, Colet, and Vives on Humanism, War, and Peace, 1496–1535.* Seattle: U of Washington P, 1962.

Adler, Judith. "Origins of Sightseeing." *Annals of Tourism Research* 16.1 (1989): 7–29.

Alemán, Mateo. *Guzmán de Alfarache.* Ed. Benito Brancaforte. 2 vols. Madrid; Cátedra, 1979.

Alfonso X. *Las siete partidas: El libro del fuero de las leyes.* Ed. Bernal Sánchez-Arcilla. Madrid: Editorial Reus, 2004.

Amelang, James. *The Flight of Icarus: Artisan Autobiography in Early Modern Europe.* Stanford: Stanford UP, 1998.

Appiah, Kwame Anthony. *The Honor Code: How Moral Revolutions Happen.* New York: Norton, 2010.

Avilés, Luis. "La prudencia militar: El capitán y el soldado en el *Examen de ingenios* de Huarte de San Juan." *Rilce* 26.1 (2010): 37–51.

Ayala, Pedro López de. *Corónica del Rey Don Pedro.* Ed. Constance L. Wilkins and Heanon M. Wilkins. Madison: Hispanic Seminary of Medieval Studies, 1985.

Barahona, Renato. *Sex Crimes, Honour, and the Law in Early Modern Spain: Vizcaya, 1528–1735.* Toronto: U of Toronto P, 2003.

Barrio Gozalo, Maximiliano. "El corso y el cautiverio en tiempos de Cervantes." *Investigaciones Históricas* 26 (2006): 81–114.

Bataillon, Marcel. *Pícaros y picaresca: La Pícara Justina.* Trans. Franscisco R. Vadillo. Madrid: Taurus, 1969.

Behrend-Martínez, Edward. "Manhood and the Neutered Body in Early Modern Spain." *Journal of Social History* 38 (2005): 1073–93.

Bentley, Michael. *Companion to Historiography.* New York: Routledge, 1997.

Berco, Christian. *From Body to Community: Venereal Disease and Society in Baroque Spain.* Toronto: U of Toronto P, 2015.

Bilinkoff, Jodi. "Navigating the Waves (of Devotion): Toward a Gendered Analysis of Early Modern Catholicism." *Crossing Boundaries: Attending to*

Early Modern Women. Ed. Jane Donawerth and Adele Seef. Newark: U of Delaware P, 2000. 161–72.

Bolgar, R.R. "Hero or Anti-Hero? The Genesis and Development of the Miles Christianus." *Concepts of the Hero in the Middle Ages and the Renaissance*. Ed. Norman T. Burns and Christopher J. Reagan. Albany: State UP of New York, 1975. 120–46.

Bourdieu, Pierre. *Practical Reason: On the Theory of Action*. Stanford: Stanford UP, 1998.

Breitenberg, Mark. *Anxious Masculinity in Early Modern England*. Cambridge: Cambridge UP, 1996.

Burke, Peter. "Representations of the Self from Petrarch to Descartes." *Rewriting the Self: Histories from the Renaissance to the Present*. Ed. Roy Porter. New York: Routledge, 1997. 17–28.

Burshatin, Israel. "Written on the Body: Slave or Hermaphrodite in Sixteenth-Century Spain." *Queer Iberia: Sexualities, Cultures, and Crossings from the Middle Ages to the Renaissance*. Ed. Josiah Blackmore and Gregory S. Hutcheson. Durham: Duke UP, 1999. 420–56.

Cabo Aseguinolaza, Fernando. "Realidad, ficción y autobiografía: A propósito de Miguel de Castro." *Actas del IV simposio internacional de la Asociación Española de Semiótica: Describir, inventar, transcribir el mundo I & II*. Madrid: Visor, 1992. 587–94.

Calvo, Thomas. *Espadas y plumas en la Monarquia Hispana: Alonso de Contreras y otras "vidas" de soldados: 1600–1650*. Madrid: Casa de Velázquez, 2019

Camamis, George. *Estudios sobre el cautiverio en el Siglo de Oro*. Madrid: Gredos, 1977.

Caravaggi, Giovanni. "Avatares italianos de un soldado español con ambiciones literarias: Pedro Gaytán." *Revista del Departamento de Filología Moderna* 4 (1993): 139–47.

Cascardi, Anthony J. *Ideologies of History in the Spanish Golden Age*. University Park: Pennsylvania State UP, 1997.

Cassol, Alessandro. "Entre historia y literatura: La autobiografía del capitán Domingo de Toral y Valdés (1635)." *Actas del V Congreso Internacional de la Asociación Internacional Siglo de Oro*. Ed. Christoph Strosetzki. 20–4 July 1999, Wilhelms Universität. Frankfurt am Main: Vervuert Verlag, 2001. 308–18.

– *Vita e scrittura. Autobiografie di soldati spagnoli del Siglo de Oro*. Milan: Edizioni Universitarie di Lettere, Economia e Diritto, 2000.

Castiglione, Baldassarre. *The Book of the Courtier*. Ed. and trans. George Bull. London: Penguin, 2011.

Castro, Américo. "Algunas observaciones acerca del concepto del honor en los siglos XVI y XVII." *Revista de filología española* 3.1 (1916): 1–50.

Castro, Miguel de. *Vida del soldado español*. Ed. Antonio Paz y Meliá. Madrid: Biblioteca Hispánica, 1900.

Cat, Édouard. *Mission bibliographique en Espagne: Rapport à monsieur le ministre de l'instruction publique.* Paris: Ernest Leroux, 1891.

Cervantes Saavedra, Miguel de. *El ingenioso hidalgo don Quijote de la Mancha compuesto por Miguel de Cervantes Saavedra; y comentado por don Diego Clemencín.* Ed. Diego Clemencín. Madrid: Aguado, 1833.

– *El ingenioso hidalgo don Quijote de la Mancha.* Ed. Luis Andrés Murillo. Madrid: Castalia, 1978.

– *The Ingenious Gentleman Don Quixote of La Mancha.* Trans. John Ormsby. New York: Crowell, 1906.

Clemencín, Diego, ed. *El ingenioso hidalgo don Quijote de la Mancha compuesto por Miguel de Cervantes Saavedra; y comentado por don Diego Clemencín.* By Miguel de Cervantes Saavedra. Madrid: Aguado, 1833.

Cohn, Henry J. "Götz von Berlichingen and the Art of Military Autobiography." *War, Literature and the Arts in Sixteenth-Century Europe.* Ed. J.R. Mulryne and Margaret Shewring. London: Palgrave Macmillan, 1989. 22–40.

Contreras, Alonso de. *Discurso de mi vida.* Ed. Javier de Navascués. Madrid: Ediciones Internacionales Universitarias, 2004.

Cossío, José María de. "Introducción." *Autobiografías de soldados (Siglo XVII).* Ed. José María de Cossío. Madrid: Biblioteca de Autores Españoles, 1956. v–xxx.

Covarrubias Orozco, Sebastián de. *Tesoro de la lengua castellana o española.* Madrid: Ediciones Turner, 1977.

Cruz, Anne J. "Arms versus Letters: The Poetics of War and the Career of the Poet in Early Modern Spain." *European Literary Careers: The Author from Antiquity to the Renaissance.* Ed. Patrick Cheney and Frederick de Armas. Toronto: U of Toronto P, 2002. 186–205.

– *Discourses of Poverty: Social Reform and the Picaresque Novel in Early Modern Spain.* Toronto: U of Toronto P, 1999.

Davis, Natalie Zemon. "Boundaries and the Sense of Self in Sixteenth-Century France." *Reconstructing Individualism: Autonomy, Individuality, and the Self in Western Thought.* Ed. Thomas C. Heller et al. Stanford: Stanford UP, 1986. 53–63.

Devaney, Thomas. "Loyalty, Autonomy, and Virtue: Redefining Nobility in Late-Medieval Castile." *Prowess, Piety, and Public Order in Medieval Society: Studies in Honor of Richard W. Kaeuper.* Ed. Craig M. Nakashian, Daniel P. Franke, and Richard W. Kaeuper. Leiden: Brill, 2017. 120–39.

– Virtue, Virility, and History in Fifteenth-Century Castile." *Speculum* 88.3 (2013): 721–49.

Diccionario de Autoridades. Vol. 5 (O–R). Madrid: Real Academia Española, Francisco del Hierro, 1737.

Doiron, Normand. *L'art de voyager: Le déplacement à l'époque classique*. Québec: P de l'Université Laval, 1995.

Donnell, Sidney. *Feminizing the Enemy: Imperial Spain, Transvestite Drama, and the Crisis of Masculinity*. Lewisburg: Bucknell UP, 2003.

Douglas, Mary. *Purity and Danger: An Analysis of Concepts of Pollution and Taboo*. Florence: Routledge, 2002.

Eguiluz, Martín de. *Milicia, discurso y reglas militar*. Antwerp: Pedro Bellero, 1595.

Eisenberg, Daniel. "Does the Picaresque Novel Exist?" *Kentucky Romance Quarterly* 26 (1979): 203–19.

– *Romances of Chivalry in the Spanish Golden Age*. Newark: Juan de la Cuesta, 1982.

Elliott, J.H. *Imperial Spain 1469–1716*. London: Penguin, 2002.

El Saffar, Ruth. "The Woman at the Border: Some Thoughts on Cervantes and Autobiography." *Hispanic Issues* 2 (1988): 191–214.

Erasmus, Desiderius. *The Complaint of Peace; To Which Is Added, Antipolemus: Or, the Plea of Reason, Religion, and Humanity, Against War*. Burlington: Charles Williams and D. Allinson, 1813.

Erauso, Catalina de. *Historia de la Monja Alférez, Catalina de Erauso, escrita por ella misma*. Ed. Ángel Estéban. Madrid: Cátedra, 2002.

Ercilla, Alonso de. *La Araucana*. Ed. Isaías Lerner. Madrid: Cátedra, 2011.

Escalante, Bernardino de. *Diálogos del arte militar*. Seville: Andrea Pescioni, 1583.

Ettinghausen, Henry. "El diálogo en la *Vida* de Alonso de Contreras." *Actas del IV Congreso Internacional de la Asociación Internacional Siglo de Oro (AISO)*. Ed. María Cruz García de Enterría and Alicia Cordón Mesa. Alcalá de Henares: Servicio de Publicaciones de la Universidad de Alcalá de Henares, 1996. Vol. I, pp. 563–70.

– "The Laconic and the Baroque: Two Seventeenth-Century Spanish Soldier Autobiographers (Alonso de Contreras and Diego Duque de Estrada)." *Forum for Modern Language Studies* 26.3 (1990): 204–11.

Farr, James. "Honor, Law and Custom in Renaissance Europe." *A Companion to the Worlds of the Renaissance*. Ed. Guido Ruggiero. Oxford: Blackwell, 2007. 124–38.

Fernández, Olga. "Los 'Ángeles de la tierra': El 'argumento angélico' en la 'Defensa de los capones cantores' de Cascales. Mito, arte y literatura en la imagen de los castrados de los siglos XVII–XVIII." *Murgetana* 112 (2005): 95–125.

Finucci, Valeria. *The Manly Masquerade: Masculinity, Paternity, and Castration in the Italian Renaissance*. Durham: Duke UP, 2003.

Folger, Robert. *Picaresque and Bureaucracy: Lazarillo de Tormes*. Newark: Juan de la Cuesta, 2009.

Foyster, Elizabeth. *Honour, Sex, and Marriage*. New York: Longman, 1999. 207–20.

Friedman, Ellen. *Spanish Captives in North Africa in the Early Modern Age*. Madison: U of Wisconsin P, 1983.

Garcés, María Antonia. *Cervantes in Algiers: A Captive's Tale*. Nashville: Vanderbilt UP, 2002.

García Santo-Tomás, Enrique. "Outside Bets: Disciplining Gamblers in Early Modern Spain." *Hispanic Review* 77.1 (2009): 147–64.

– "Ruptured Narratives: Tracing Defeat in Diego Duque de Estrada's *Comentarios del desengañado de sí mismo* (1614–1645)." *eHumanista: Journal of Iberian Studies* 17 (2011): 78–98.

Gastañaga Ponce de León, José Luis. *Caballero noble desbaratado: autobiografía e invención en el siglo XVI*. West Lafayette: Purdue UP, 2012.

Gilmore, David. "Cuenca mediterránea: La excelencia en la actuación." *Masculinidad/es: poder y crisis*. Ed. Teresa Valdés and José Olavarría. Santiago: Isis, 1997. 82–101.

Giovio, Paolo. *La vita del signor don Fernando d'Avalo marchese di Pescara*. Venice: Giovanni de Rossi, 1557.

Goetz, Rainer. *Spanish Golden Age Autobiography in Its Context*. New York: Peter Lang, 1994.

González Castrillo, Ricardo. "La pérdida de la Goleta y Túnez en 1574, y otros sucesos de historia otomana, narrados por un testigo presencial: Alonso de Salamanca." *Anaquel de Estudios Arabes* 3 (1992): 247–86.

González de León, Fernando. "'Doctors of the Military Discipline': Technical Expertise and the Paradigm of the Spanish Soldier in the Early Modern Period." *The Sixteenth Century Journal* 27.1 (1996): 61–85.

– *The Road to Rocroi: Class, Culture and Command in the Spanish Army of Flanders, 1567–1659*. Leiden: Brill, 2009.

– "Soldados Pláticos and Caballeros: The Social Dimensions of Ethics in the Early Modern Spanish Army." *The Chivalric Ethos and the Development of Military Professionalism*. Ed. D.J.B. Trim. Leiden: Brill, 2003. 235–68.

González Hernández, María Cristina. *La "Junta de libros" de Tamayo de Vargas: ensayo de documentación bibliográfica*. PhD diss. Universidad Complutense Madrid, 2012.

Gracián, Baltasar. *El criticón*. Ed. Santos Alonso. Madrid: Cátedra, 1993.

Gravatt, Patricia. "Rereading Theodore de Bry's Black Legend." *Rereading the Black Legend: The Discourses of Religious and Racial Difference in the Renaissance Empires*. Ed. Margaret R. Greer et al. Chicago: U of Chicago P, 2008.

Greenblatt, Stephen. *Renaissance Self-Fashioning: From More to Shakespeare*. Chicago: U of Chicago P, 1980.

Greene, Roland. *Five Words: Critical Semantics in the Age of Shakespeare and Cervantes*. Chicago: U of Chicago P, 2013.

Gregori Roig, Rosa María. "Representación pública del individuo: Relaciones de méritos y servicios en el Archivo General de Indias, siglos XVII–XVIII." *El legado de Mnemosyne: Las escrituras del yo a través del tiempo*. Ed. Antonio Castillo Gómez and Verónica Sierra Blas. Gijón: Ediciones Trea, 2007. 355–79.

Guevara, Antonio de. *Libro de los inventores del arte de marear, y de muchos trabajos que pasan en las galeras*. Pamplona, 1579.

Habermas, Jürgen. "Individuation through Socialization: On George Herbert Mead's Theory of Subjectivity." *Postmetaphysical Thinking: Philosophical Essays*. Trans. William Mark Hohengarten. Cambridge: MIT Press, 1992.

Hale, John R. *War and Society in Renaissance Europe, 1450–1620*. New York: St. Martin's Press, 1985.

Hampton, Timothy. *Writing from History: The Rhetoric of Exemplarity in Renaissance Literature*. Ithaca: Cornell UP, 1990.

Harari, Yuval N. *Renaissance Military Memoirs: War, History, and Identity, 1450–1600*. Woodbridge: Boydell & Brewer Press, 2004.

Harney, Michael. "Ludology, Self-Fashioning, and the Gender Debate in Fifteenth-Century Castile." *Self-Fashioning and Assumptions of Identity in Medieval and Early Modern Iberia*. Ed. Laura Delbrugge. Leiden: Brill, 2015. 144–66.

Hess, Andrew C. *The Forgotten Frontier: A History of the Sixteenth-Century Ibero-African Frontier*. Chicago: U of Chicago P, 1978.

Howard, Keith David. *The Reception of Machiavelli in Early Modern Spain*. Woodbridge; Tamesis; Rochester: Boydell & Brewer Press, 2014.

Hurtado de Mendoza, Diego. *Guerra de Granada*. Ed. Bernardo Blanco-González. Madrid: Castalia, 1970.

Irigoyen-García, Javier. "Topografía del sufrimiento: Narración, identidad y enfermedad en la *Vida y trabajos* de Jerónimo de Pasamonte." *Crítica Hispánica* 34.2 (2012): 101–17.

Israel, Jonathan. *Empires and Entrepôts: The Dutch, the Spanish Monarchy, and the Jews, 1585–1713*. London: Hambledon Press, 1990.

Jacob, Frank, and Gilmar Visoni-Alonzo. *The Military Revolution in Early Modern Europe: A Revision*. New York: Palgrave Macmillan, 2016.

Jacqueton, Gilbert. *Les archives espagnoles du gouvernement géneral de l'Algerie: Histoire du fonds et inventaire*. Algiers: A. Jourdan, 1894.

Jauss, Robert. "Literary History as a Challenge to Literary Theory." *New Literary History* 2 (1970–1): 7–31.

Johnson, Trevor. "Guardian Angels and the Society of Jesus." *Angels in the Early Modern World*. Ed. Peter Marshall and Alexandra Walsham. Cambridge: Cambridge UP, 2006. 191–213.

Juárez Almendros, Encarnación. *El cuerpo vestido y la construcción de la identidad en las narrativas autobiográficas del Siglo de Oro*. Woodbridge: Tamesis, 2006.

Kallendorf, Hilaire. *Exorcism and Its Texts: Subjectivity in Early Modern Literature of England and Spain*. Toronto: U of Toronto P, 2003.

Knecht, Robert J. "Military Autobiographies in Sixteenth-Century France." *War, Literature and the Arts in Sixteenth-Century Europe*. Ed. J.R. Mulryne and Margaret Shewring. London: Palgrave Macmillan, 1989. 3–21.

La Noue, François de. *Discours politiques et militaires du sieur de La Noue. Recueillis & mis en lumière par le sieur De Fresnes*. Lyon: Daniel Bellon, 1595.

La Rubia-Prado, Francisco. "Gift-Giving Diplomacy: The Role of the Horse in the *Cantar de mio Cid*." *La corónica: A Journal of Medieval Hispanic Languages, Literatures, and Cultures* 37.1 (2008): 275–99.

Las Casas, Bartolomé de. *Brevísima relación de la destruición de las Indias*. Ed. André Saint-Lu. Madrid: Cátedra, 2003.

Lazarillo de Tormes. Ed. Francisco Rico. Madrid: Cátedra, 2005.

Lejeune, Philippe. *On Autobiography*. Trans. Katherine Leary. Minneapolis: U of Minnesota P, 1989.

Leonard, Irving A. *Books of the Brave: Being an Account of Books and of Men in the Spanish Conquest and Settlement of the Sixteenth-Century New World*. U of California P, 1992.

Levisi, Margarita. *Autobiografías del Siglo de Oro: Jerónimo Pasamonte, Alonso de Contreras, Miguel de Castro*. Madrid: Sociedad General Española de Librería, 1984.

The Life of Lazarillo de Tormes. His Fortunes and Adversities. Trans. William Stanley Merwin. New York: New York Review Books, 2005.

Linares, Lidwine. "¡Santiago y cierra España! Historia de un grito de guerra desde la Edad media hasta hoy." *Les Cahiers de Framespa: Nouveaux champs de l'histoire sociale* 10 (2012): n.p.

Londoño, Sancho. *Discurso sobre la forma de reducir la disciplina a mejor y antiguo estado*. Madrid: Luis Sánchez, 1593.

López de Ubeda, Francisco. *Libro de entretenimiento de la pícara Justina*. Ed. David Mañero Lozano. Madrid: Cátedra, 2012.

MacCormack, Sabine. "History, Memory and Time in Golden Age Spain." *History and Memory* 4.2 (1992): 38–68.

Machiavelli, Niccolò. *The Art of War. Machiavelli: The Chief Works and Others*. Trans. Allan Gilbert. Durham: Duke UP, 1989. Vol. II, pp. 566–726.

– *The Prince. Machiavelli: The Chief Works and Others*. Trans. Allan Gilbert. Durham: Duke UP, 1989. Vol. I, pp. 10–96.

Mancing, Howard. "The Picaresque Novel: A Protean Form." *College Literature* 6.3 (1979): 182–204.

Martin, John. *Myths of Renaissance Individualism*. New York: Palgrave Macmillan, 2004.

Martínez, Miguel. *Front Lines: Soldiers' Writing in the Early Modern Hispanic World*. Philadelphia: U of Pennsylvania P, 2016.

Martínez Góngora, Mar. *El hombre atemporado: Autocontrol, disciplina y masculinidad en textos españoles de la temprana modernidad*. New York: Peter Lang, 2005.

– *La utilización masculina del espacio doméstico rural en textos españoles del Renacimiento*. Vigo: Academia del Hispanismo, 2010.

Martín Jiménez, Alfonso. "Cervantes sabía que Pasamonte era Avellaneda: La *Vida* de Pasamonte, el *Quijote* apócrifo y 'El coloquio de los perros.'" *Cervantes: Bulletin of the Cervantes Society of America* 25.1 (2006): 105–57.

Mayer, Thomas, and Daniel R. Woolf, eds. *The Rhetorics of Life-Writing in Early Modern Europe. Forms of Biography from Cassandra Fedele to Louis XIV.* Ann Arbor: U of Michigan P, 1995.

Menéndez Pelayo, Marcelino. *Obras de Lope de Vega*. Vol. 11. Sucesores de Ribadeneyra, 1890.

Merrim, Stephanie. "Catalina de Erauso: From Anomaly to Icon." *Coded Encounters: Writing, Gender, and Ethnicity in Colonial Latin America*. Ed. Francisco Cevallos. Amherst: U of Massachusetts P, 1994. 177–205.

Middlebrook, Leah. "The Poetics of Early Modern Masculinity in Sixteenth-Century Spain." *The Poetics of Masculinity in Early Modern Italy and Spain*. Ed. Gerry Milligan and Jane Tylus. Toronto: Centre for Reformation and Renaissance Studies, 2010. 143–67.

Miller, Maureen. "Masculinity, Reform, and Clerical Culture: Narratives of Episcopal Holiness in the Gregorian Era." *Church History* 72 (2003): 25–52.

Miller, Pavla. *Transformations of Patriarchy in the West: 1500–1900*. Bloomington: Indiana UP, 1998.

Monter, E. William. *Frontiers of Heresy: The Spanish Inquisition from the Basque Lands to Sicily*. Cambridge: Cambridge UP, 1990.

Mulryne, J.R., and Margaret Shewring, eds. *War, Literature and the Arts in Sixteenth-Century Europe*. London: Palgrave Macmillan, 1989.

Muñoz de San Pedro, Miguel. *Diego Garcia de Paredes: Hércules y Sansón de España*. Madrid: Espasa-Calpe, 1946.

Murrin, Michael. *History and Warfare in Renaissance Epic*. Chicago: U of Chicago P, 1994.

Myers, Kathleen Ann. "Writing of the Frontier: Blurring Gender and Genre in the Monja Alférez's Account." *Mapping Colonial Spanish America: Places and Commonplaces of Identity, Culture, and Experience*. Ed. Mariselle Meléndez. Lewisburg: Bucknell UP, 2002. 181–201.

Neyrey, Jerome. "The Symbolic Universe of Luke-Acts: 'They Turn the World Upside-Down.'" *The Social World of Luke-Acts: Models for Interpretation*. Ed. Jerome H. Neyrey. Peabody, MA: Hendrickson, 1991. 271–304.

Ochoa, Marcia. "Becoming a Man in Yndias: The Mediations of Catalina de Erauso, the Lieutenant Nun." *Technofuturos: Critical Interventions in Latina/o Studies*. Ed. Nancy Raquel Mirabal and Agustín Laó-Montes. Lanham: Lexington Books, 2007. 53–76.

O'Donnell y Duque de Estrada, Hugo. "El reposo del ejército: Estudio del campamento temporal del tiempo de los Austrias." *Guerra y sociedad en la monarquía hispánica: Política, estrategia y cultura en la Europa moderna (1500–1700)*. Ed. Enrique García Hernán and David Maffi. Consejo Superior de Investigaciones Científicas 1 (2006): 381–400.

Paredes, Diego García de. *Breve suma de la vida y hechos de Diego García de Paredes, la cual el mismó escribió y la dejó firmada de su nombre como al fin de ella aparece. Crónicas del Gran Capitán*. Ed. Antonio Rodríguez Villa. Madrid: Bailly-Bailliére, 1908. 255–9.

– *Suma de las cosas que acontecieron a Diego García de Paredes y de lo que hizo, escrita por él mismo cuando estaba enfermo de mal [de] que murió. El Sansón de Extremadura: Diego García de Paredes en la literatura española del siglo XVI*. Ed. Antonio Sánchez Jiménez. Newark: Juan de la Cuesta, 2006. 41–88.

Parker, Alexander. *Literature and the Delinquent: The Picaresque Novel in Spain and Europe, 1599–1753*. Edinburgh: Edinburgh UP, 1967.

Parker, Geoffrey. *The Army of Flanders and the Spanish Road, 1567–1659*. 2nd ed. Cambridge: Cambridge UP, 2004.

– "Dynastic War." *The Cambridge History of Warfare*. Ed. Geoffrey Parker. Cambridge: Cambridge UP, 2012. 148–66.

– *The Military Revolution: Military Innovation and the Rise of the West 1500–1800*. 2nd ed. Cambridge: Cambridge UP, 2016.

– "The Soldier." *Baroque Personae*. Trans. Lydia Cochrane. Ed. Rosario Villari. Chicago: U of Chicago P, 1991. 32–56.

Parker, Geoffrey, and Lesley M. Smith, eds. *The General Crisis of the Seventeenth Century*. 2nd ed. New York: Routledge, 1997.

Pasamonte, Jerónimo de. *Vida y trabajos de Jerónimo de Pasamonte*. Ed. José María de Cossío. *Autobiografías de soldados (Siglo XVII)*. Madrid: Biblioteca de Autores Españoles, 1956. 5–73.

Paster, Gail Kern. "The Unbearable Coldness of Female Being: Women's Imperfection and the Humoral Economy." *English Literary Renaissance* 28 (2008): 416–40.

Paz y Meliá, Antonio. "Introduction." *Vida del soldado español. Miguel de Castro*. Barcelona: Bibliotheca Hispánica, 1900. v–ix.

Perry, Mary Elizabeth. "From Convent to Battlefield: Cross-Dressing and Gendering the Self in the New World of Imperial Spain." *Queer Iberia: Sexualities, Cultures, and Crossings from the Middle Ages to the Renaissance*. Ed. Josiah Blackmore and Gregory Hutcheson. Durham: Duke UP, 1999. 394–419.

– *Gender and Disorder in Early Modern Seville*. Princeton: Princeton UP, 1990.

Pope, Randolph. *La autobiografía española hasta Torres Villarroel*. Frankfurt: Peter Lang, 1974.

Poska, Allyson. "A Married Man Is a Woman: Negotiating Masculinity in Early Modern Northwestern Spain." *Masculinity in the Reformation Era*. Ed. Scott Hendrix and Susan Karant-Nunn. Kirksville: Truman State UP, 2008. 3–20.

Powers, James F. *A Society Organized for War: The Iberian Municipal Militias in the Central Middle Ages, 1000–1284*. Berkeley: U of California P, 1988.

Pratt, Mary Louise. *Imperial Eyes: Travel Writing and Transculturation*. New York: Routledge, 1992.

– "Scratches on the Face of the Country; or What Mr. Barrow Saw in the Land of the Bushmen." *"Race," Writing, and Difference*. Ed. Henry Louis Gates, Jr. Chicago: U of Chicago P, 1986. 138–62.

Puddu, Raffaele. *El soldado gentilhombre*. Aragón: Argos Vergara, 1984.

Quatrefages, René. "Génesis de la España militar moderna." *Militaria: Revista de Cultura Militar* 7 (1995): 59–68.

Quevedo, Francisco de. *El Buscón*. Ed. Domingo Ynduraín. Madrid: Cátedra, 2005.

Rabanal Álvarez, Manuel. "Notas filológicas sobre 'Santiago y cierra España'." *Compostellanum: Revista de la Archidiocesis de Santiago de Compostela* 2 (1957): 531–47.

Real Academia Española. *Diccionario de Autoridades*. Facsimile ed. Madrid: Editorial Gredos, 1963.

Redel, Enrique. *Ambrosio de Morales: Estudio biográfico*. Córdoba: Real Academia Española (Imprenta del Diario), 1908.

Ríquer, Martín de. *Cervantes, Passamonte y Avellaneda*. Barcelona: Sirmio, 1988.

Roberts, Michael. "The Military Revolution, 1560–1660." *The Military Revolution Debate: Readings on the Military Transformation*. Ed. Clifford Rogers. Boulder: Westview Press, 1995. 13–36.

Rocha, Victor. "El poder del cuerpo y sus gestos: Travestismo e identidad de género en América Colonial: El caso de Catalina de Erauso." *Cyber Humanitatis* 27 (2003): n.p. 5 Sept. 2011. https://cyberhumanitatis.uchile.cl/index.php/RCH/article/view/5687.

Rodríguez de la Flor, Fernando. "On the Notion of a Melancholic Baroque." *Hispanic Baroques: Reading Cultures in Context*. Ed. Nicholas Spadaccini and Luis Martín-Estudillo. Nashville: Vanderbilt UP, 2005. 3–19.

Rodríguez-Velasco, Jesús. "Esfuerço: La caballería de estado a oficio (1524–1615)." *Amadís de Gaula quinientos años después. Estudio en homenaje a Juan Manuel Cacho Blecua*. Eds. José Manuel Lucía Megías and María del Carmen Marín Pina. Alcalá: Centro de Estudios Cervantinos, 2008. 661–89.

Rodríguez Villa, Antonio. "Las cuentas del Gran Capitán." *Boletín de la Real Academia de la Historia* 56 (1910): 281–86.

Rogers, Clifford, ed. *The Military Revolution Debate: Readings on the Military Transformation*. Boulder: Westview Press, 1995.

Rojas, Fernando de. *Tragicomedia de Calisto y Melibea: V centenario (1499–1999)*. Ed. Fernando Cantalapiedra Erostarbe. Kassel: Edition Reichenberger, 2000.

Rowe, Erin. "The Spanish Minerva: Imagining Teresa of Avila as Patron Saint in Seventeenth-Century Spain." *Catholic Historical Review* 92.4 (2006): 574–96.

Ruan, Felipe E. *Pícaro and Cortesano: Identity and the Forms of Capital in Early Modern Spanish Picaresque Narrative and Courtesy Literature*. Lewisburg: Bucknell UP, 2011.

Rubiés, Joan-Pau. "Futility in the New World: Narratives of Travel in Sixteenth-Century America." *Voyages and Visions: Towards a Cultural History of Travel*. Ed. Jas Elsner and Joan-Pau Rubiés. London: Reaktion Books, 1999. 74–100.

Rubio Merino, Pedro. *La Monja Alférez: Doña Catalina de Erauso: Dos manuscritos inéditos de su autobiografía conservados en el Archivo de la Santa Iglesia Catedral de Sevilla*. Seville: Cabildo Metropolitano de la Catedral de Seville, 1995.

Ruff, Julius R. *Violence in Early Modern Europe, 1500–1800*. Cambridge: Cambridge UP, 2001.

Rupp, Stephen. "Cervantes and the Soldier's Tale: Genre and Disorder in 'El casamiento engañoso'." *Modern Language Review* 96.2 (2001): 370–84.

– *Heroic Forms: Cervantes and the Literature of War*. Toronto: U of Toronto P, 2014.

Ruthven, Malise, and Azim Nanji. *Historical Atlas of Islam*. Cambridge: Harvard UP, 2004.

Sáez, Adrián. "Vidas imaginarias: Formas y modelos de las relaciones de soldados del Siglo de Oro." *Studi Ispanici* 43 (2018): 171–82.

Sánchez Jiménez, Antonio. *El Sansón de Extremadura: Diego García de Paredes en la literatura española del siglo XVI*. Newark: Juan de la Cuesta, 2006.

La Santa Biblia: antigua versión de Casiodoro de Reina (1569), revisada por Cipriano de Valera (1602). Madrid: Sociedad Bíblica, 1909.

Sedgwick, Eve Kosofsky. *Epistemology of the Closet*. Berkeley: U of California P, 1990.

Serrano y Sanz, Manuel. *Autobiografías y memorias coleccionadas e ilustradas*. Madrid: Librería Editorial de Bailly, 1905.

Shepard, Alexandra. *Accounting for Oneself: Worth, Status, and the Social Order in Early Modern England*. Oxford: Oxford UP, 2015.

Sherer, Idan. *Warriors for a Living: The Experience of the Spanish Infantry in the Italian Wars, 1494–1559*. Leiden: Brill, 2017.

– "When War Comes They Want to Flee." *Sixteenth Century Journal* 48.2 (2017): 385–411.

Spearing, Anthony. *Textual Subjectivity: The Encoding of Subjectivity in Medieval Narratives and Lyrics*. London: Oxford UP, 2005.

Strasser, Ulrike. "'The First Form and Grace': Ignatius of Loyola and the Reformation of Masculinity." *Masculinity in the Reformation Era*. Ed. Scott Hendrix and Susan Karant-Nunn. Kirksville: Truman State UP, 2008. 45–70.

Suárez Corvín [Montañés], Diego. *Discurso verdadero de la naturaleza, peregrinación, vida y partes del autor de la presente historia.* Ed. Alfred Morel-Fatio. *Bulletin Hispanique* 3.2 (1901): 146–58.

– *Historia del Maestre ultimo que fué de Montesa y de su hermano don Felipe de Borja: La manera como gobernaron las plazas de Orán y Mazalquivir, reinos de Tremecén y Ténez [sic] en Africa.* Ed. Miguel Angel de Bunes Ibarra and Beatriz Alonso Acero. Valencia: Institució Alfons El Magnànim, 2005.

Suranyi, Anna. *The Genius of the English Nation: Travel Writing and National Identity in Early Modern England.* Newark: U of Delaware P, 2008.

Swanson, Robert N. "Angels Incarnate: Clergy and Masculinity from Gregorian Reform to Reformation." *Masculinity in Medieval Europe.* Edited by Dawn Hadley. London: Routledge, 1999.

Tamayo de Vargas, Tomás. *Diego García de Paredes: Relación breve de su tiempo.* Madrid: Luis Sánchez, 1621.

Tausiet, María. "Excluded Souls: The Wayward and the Excommunicated in Counter-Reformation Spain." *History* 88 (2003): 437–50.

Tausiet Maria. "'Patronage of Angels and Combat of Demons': Good versus Evil in Seventeenth-Century Spain." Trans. Adrian J. Pearce. *Angels in the Early Modern World.* Ed. Peter Marshall and Alexandra Walsham. Cambridge: Cambridge UP, 2006. 233–55.

Taylor, Scott. *Honour and Violence in Golden Age Spain.* New Haven: Yale UP, 2008.

Thompson, I.A.A., and Bartolomé Yun Casalilla, eds. *The Castilian Crisis of the Seventeenth Century: New Perspectives on the Economic and Social History of Seventeenth-Century Spain.* Cambridge: Cambridge UP, 1994.

Toral y Valdés, Domingo de. *Relación de la vida del capitán Domingo de Toral y Valdés, escrita por el mismo capitán.* Ed. José Sancho Rayón and Francisco de Zabalburu. *Colección de documentos inéditos para la historia de España.* Volume LXXI. Madrid: Miguel Ginesta, 1879. 495–547.

Urrea, Jerónimo. *Diálogo de la verdadera honra militar, que trata como se ha de conformar la honra con la conciencia.* Zaragoza: Diego Dormer, 1642.

Valbona, Rima de. "Introduction." *Vida i sucesos de la Monja Alférez.* By Catalina de Erauso. Tempe: Arizona State University Center for Latin American Studies, 1992. 1–30.

Vargas, Bernardo de. *Cirongilio de Tracia.* Ed. James Ray Green, Jr. PhD diss. Johns Hopkins University, 1974.

Velasco, Sherry. *Lesbians in Early Modern Spain.* Nashville: Vanderbilt UP, 2011.

– *The Lieutenant Nun: Transgenderism, Lesbian Desire, and Catalina de Erauso.* Austin: U of Texas P, 2000.

Vélez Quiñones, Harry. "Deficient Masculinity: 'Mi puta es el Maestre de Montesa.'" *Journal of Spanish Cultural Studies* 2 (2001): 27–40.

– "'Templa, pequeño joven, templa el brío': Pretty Boys and Queer Soldiers in Miguel de Cervantes's *Numancia.*" *The Poetics of Masculinity in Early Modern Italy and Spain*. Ed. Gerry Milligan and Jane Tylus. Toronto: Centre for Reformation and Renaissance Studies, 2010. 241–65.

Vélez Sainz, Julio, and Antonio Sánchez Jiménez, eds. *El teatro soldadesco y la cultura militar en la España imperial*. Madrid: Ediciones del orto, 2016.

Vida y hechos de Estebanillo González. Ed. Antonio Carreira and Jesús Antonio Cid. 2 vols. Madrid: Cátedra, 1990.

Vilches, Elvira. *New World Gold: Cultural Anxiety and Monetary Disorder in Early Modern Spain*. Chicago: U of Chicago P, 2010.

Walsham, Alexandra. "The Social History of the Archive: Record-Keeping in Early Modern Europe." *Past & Present* 230.11 (2016): 9–48.

Weber, Alison. "Lope de Vega's *Rimas sacras*: Conversion, Clientage, and the Performance of Masculinity." *Publications of the Modern Language Association of America* 120 (2005): 404–21.

– "Religious Literature in Early Modern Spain." *The Cambridge History of Spanish Literature*. Ed. David Gies. Cambridge: Cambridge UP, 2009. 149–58.

– *Teresa of Ávila and the Rhetoric of Femininity*. Princeton: Princeton UP, 1990.

Wicks, Ulrich. *Picaresque Narrative, Picaresque Fictions: A Theory and Research Guide*. New York: Greenwood, 1989.

Zafra, Enriqueta. *Prostituidas por el texto: Discurso prostibulario en la picaresca femenina*. West Lafayette: Purdue UP, 2009.

Index

Toronto Iberic

1 Anthony J. Cascardi, *Cervantes, Literature, and the Discourse of Politics*
2 Jessica A. Boon, *The Mystical Science of the Soul: Medieval Cognition in Bernardino de Laredo's Recollection Method*
3 Susan Byrne, *Law and History in Cervantes'* Don Quixote
4 Mary E. Barnard and Frederick A. de Armas (eds.), *Objects of Culture in the Literature of Imperial Spain*
5 Nil Santiáñez, *Topographies of Fascism: Habitus, Space, and Writing in Twentieth-Century Spain*
6 Nelson Orringer, *Lorca in Tune with Falla: Literary and Musical Interludes*
7 Ana M. Gómez-Bravo, *Textual Agency: Writing Culture and Social Networks in Fifteenth-Century Spain*
8 Javier Irigoyen-García, *The Spanish Arcadia: Sheep Herding, Pastoral Discourse, and Ethnicity in Early Modern Spain*
9 Stephanie Sieburth, *Survival Songs: Conchita Piquer's* Coplas *and Franco's Regime of Terror*
10 Christine Arkinstall, *Spanish Female Writers and the Freethinking Press, 1879–1926*
11 Margaret Boyle, *Unruly Women: Performance, Penitence, and Punishment in Early Modern Spain*

12 Evelina Gužauskytė, *Christopher Columbus's Naming in the* diarios *of the Four Voyages (1492–1504): A Discourse of Negotiation*
13 Mary E. Barnard, *Garcilaso de la Vega and the Material Culture of Renaissance Europe*
14 William Viestenz, *By the Grace of God: Francoist Spain and the Sacred Roots of Political Imagination*
15 Michael Scham, Lector Ludens*: The Representation of Games and Play in Cervantes*
16 Stephen Rupp, *Heroic Forms: Cervantes and the Literature of War*
17 Enrique Fernandez, *Anxieties of Interiority and Dissection in Early Modern Spain*
18 Susan Byrne, *Ficino in Spain*
19 Patricia M. Keller, *Ghostly Landscapes: Film, Photography, and the Aesthetics of Haunting in Contemporary Spanish Culture*
20 Carolyn A. Nadeau, *Food Matters: Alonso Quijano's Diet and the Discourse of Food in Early Modern Spain*
21 Cristian Berco, *From Body to Community: Venereal Disease and Society in Baroque Spain*
22 Elizabeth R. Wright, *The Epic of Juan Latino: Dilemmas of Race and Religion in Renaissance Spain*
23 Ryan D. Giles, *Inscribed Power: Amulets and Magic in Early Spanish Literature*
24 Jorge Pérez, *Confessional Cinema: Religion, Film, and Modernity in Spain's Development Years, 1960–1975*
25 Joan Ramon Resina, *Josep Pla: Seeing the World in the Form of Articles*
26 Javier Irigoyen-García, *"Moors Dressed as Moors": Clothing, Social Distinction, and Ethnicity in Early Modern Iberia*
27 Jean Dangler, *Edging toward Iberia*
28 Ryan D. Giles and Steven Wagschal (eds.), *Beyond Sight: Engaging the Senses in Iberian Literatures and Cultures, 1200–1750*
29 Silvia Bermúdez, *Rocking the Boat: Migration and Race in Contemporary Spanish Music*
30 Hilaire Kallendorf, *Ambiguous Antidotes: Virtue as Vaccine for Vice in Early Modern Spain*
31 Leslie Harkema, *Spanish Modernism and the Poetics of Youth: From Miguel de Unamuno to* La Joven Literatura
32 Benjamin Fraser, *Cognitive Disability Aesthetics: Visual Culture, Disability Representations, and the (In)Visibility of Cognitive Difference*
33 Robert Patrick Newcomb, *Iberianism and Crisis: Spain and Portugal at the Turn of the Twentieth Century*
34 Sara J. Brenneis, *Spaniards in Mauthausen: Representations of a Nazi Concentration Camp, 1940–2015*

35 Silvia Bermúdez and Roberta Johnson (eds.), *A New History of Iberian Feminisms*
36 Steven Wagschal, *Minding Animals in the Old and New Worlds: A Cognitive Historical Analysis*
37 Heather Bamford, *Cultures of the Fragment: Uses of the Iberian Manuscript, 1100–1600*
38 Enrique García Santo-Tomás (ed.), *Science on Stage in Early Modern Spain*
39 Marina Brownlee (ed.), *Cervantes'* Persiles *and the Travails of Romance*
40 Sarah Thomas, *Inhabiting the In-Between: Childhood and Cinema in Spain's Long Transition*
41 David A. Wacks, *Medieval Iberian Crusade Fiction and the Mediterranean World*
42 Rosilie Hernández, *Immaculate Conceptions: The Power of the Religious Imagination in Early Modern Spain*
43 Mary Coffey and Margot Versteeg (eds.), *Imagined Truths: Realism in Modern Spanish Literature and Culture*
44 Diana Aramburu, *Resisting Invisibility: Detecting the Female Body in Spanish Crime Fiction*
45 Samuel Amago and Matthew J. Marr (eds.), *Consequential Art: Comics Culture in Contemporary Spain*
46 Richard P. Kinkade, *Dawn of a Dynasty: The Life and Times of Infante Manuel of Castile*
47 Jill Robbins, *Poetry and Crisis: Cultural Politics and Citizenship in the Wake of the Madrid Bombings*
48 Ana María Laguna and John Beusterien (eds.), *Goodbye Eros: Recasting Forms and Norms of Love in the Age of Cervantes*
49 Sara J. Brenneis and Gina Herrmann (eds.), *Spain, World War II, and the Holocaust: History and Representation*
50 Francisco Fernández de Alba, *Sex, Drugs, and Fashion in 1970s Madrid*
51 Daniel Aguirre-Oteiza, *This Ghostly Poetry: Reading Spanish Republican Exiles between Literary History and Poetic Memory*
52 Lara Anderson, *Control and Resistance: Food Discourse in Franco Spain*
53 Faith S. Harden, *Arms and Letters: Military Life Writing in Early Modern Spain*

www.ingramcontent.com/pod-product-compliance
Lightning Source LLC
LaVergne TN
LVHW040149080826
844660LV00014B/893/J

* 9 7 8 1 4 8 7 5 0 7 0 4 6 *